To David William

in appreciation of his extensive knowledge of antique guns.

With good wishes

Peter McManus.

One Man's Gun Quest

By

Peter McManus

Copyright: Peter A McManus

All rights reserved. No part of this publication may be reproduced, stored in a retrieval system or transmitted in any form, or by any means, electronic, mechanical photocopying, recordings or otherwise, without the prior permission in writing of the copyright holder; nor to be otherwise circulated in any form or binding or cover other than that in which it is published and without similar condition, including this condition, being imposed on the subsequent publisher.

A catalogue record for this book is available from the British Library.

Hardback ISBN 0-9542912-2-0

Published by:
M.E.P. Publishing
Newton Park Farm
Newton Solney
Burton on Trent
DE15 0SS
Tel: 01283 703280

Artwork by Tranters, Markeaton Printing Works, Derby
Printed by Eyetech Graphics, 103-105 Wilmot Street, Derby

To

All collectors and Black Powder shooters who are researching and preserving an important part of our heritage, with special thanks to the gun trade who understand, restore and repair these fascinating guns and rifles.

About This Book

When I decided to write this book recording half a century's quest for fine guns and rifles I realised that the people I met, collectors and dealers of every kind, were every bit as interesting as the firearms! So this book is not merely a gun book but a people book, too.

As Alexander Pope said a couple of centuries or more ago. The proper study of mankind is man. If you are interested in guns and rifles, so much the better, but even if not, it is hoped that you find much to learn and will enjoy reading about the dramatis personae as the book is written for the general reader.

So what exactly is this book about? It is the story of how one man put together a collection of fine antique guns and rifles over a period of about 50 years from the early nineteen fifties onwards. Mantons, predominately, but not exclusively.

So let me start with Joseph and John Manton. They were in the very top echelon of gunmakers of their era, the late eighteenth and early nineteenth centuries and their work has always been of enormous interest to me, but not, by any means, exclusively. It would be difficult, if not impossible, to put together an identical collection today: Certainly impossibly expensive!

Fine English sporting guns and rifles are my interest, both muzzle and breech loading. In addition to that, as an engineer, innovative ignition systems, breech actions and the whole development of guns and cartridges through the nineteenth century have always commanded my attention.

Furthermore, I have always been fascinated by the evolution of the stalking rifle for deerstalking in Scotland.

The rapid development of firearms throughout the nineteenth century is a compulsive study: At the start of the century the soldier's firearm was a smoothbore flintlock musket of about .750 calibre but by the end of the century the breech loading magazine rifle of .300 calibre or less had arrived, together with the machine gun. In addition to that, black powder, which had remained the propellant for centuries, was finally ousted by smokeless powders.

None of them are in my ownership now and should you ask if I have any regrets about that, the answer is No. They are now in the hands of a private museum. I had the enormous pleasure of putting the collection together and thoroughly enjoyed the thrill of the chase, so I have no complaints. Met some marvellous people along the way, too, so that was an tremendous bonus.

A year or two ago I wrote *One Man's Motorcycles 1939-1949*, an account of my schooldays in Rhyl in the nineteen thirties, acquiring my first motorcycle in 1939, going on to serve my engineering apprenticeship in Derby during the War years then starting out in the motorcycle business after the War.

A lighthearted book with short chapters, lots of illustrations, intended for the general reader, not necessarily motorcycle enthusiasts.

It went on to be very successful and the best selling book in its category, autobiography, at the National Motorcycle Museum. Now out of print so it will have to be re-printed.

Soon after, I wrote *One Man's Scotland*, an account of our experiences deerstalking during the last forty years or so, together with the story of the incredible characters who have made stalking history during the last two centuries. A great bonus was fifty or so photographs taken by old friend, Lea MacNally: Five books on Scotland to his credit and an award winning wildlife photographer.

Once again the same formula as before: Short chapters, lots of illustrations, many diversions. The book is proving to be a runaway success boosted by excellent reviews in everything from *The Field* to the *Shooting Times*. The kind of reviews I would never have dared write myself!

The *Scots Magazine* reviewer was a lady who is against shooting but, even so, she liked the book! Orders flowed in from all over the world!

So successful, then, that that the book has already had to be re-printed.

This latest book is inevitably more specialised but it is still hoped that, as before, it will appeal to the general reader though an interest in antique guns obviously helps.

A lighthearted book on motorcycles? Easy! A lighthearted book on Scotland? Not difficult. But a lighthearted book on antique guns? No-one, as far as I know, has done it before, so here goes!

Again the same formula: Short chapters, many illustrations, lots of diversions.

It is not intended to be a "learned tome": Others have written in great detail about Mantons and Purdeys, for example. Even so, I have something new to contribute. Very much a companion volume to *One Man's Scotland*.

My thanks to all who supplied photographs and information. Too many to list at this stage though many feature in the text.

Thanks, too, Anthony Pearson and Andy Macleod of Tranters, Derby, who did all the artwork, designed the dust wrapper and put the whole book on disc.

My wife Edna has always been tremendously supportive in my gun quest so I am most grateful to her.

I must express my thanks, once again, to my talented daughter-in-law Stephanie who has been editor-in-chief of all three books. None of the books would have been possible without her help. She is completely computer literate and has laid the book out and put everything in order. Always competent and helpful, always a joy to work with. Very busy running her own business but somehow finds time to help.

So now, as the newsboys in those nineteen thirties gangster movies used to shout, "Read all about it".

Know then thyself, presume not God to scan;

the proper study of mankind is man.

Alexander Pope (18th Century)

One Man's Gun Quest

Derbyshire photographer Ernest A Drury Smith.

One Man's Gun Quest

The author Peter McManus.

Contents

One	The Nineteenth Century	1
Two	Ernest A. Drury Smith, Derbyshire Photographer	9
Three	MONEY, MONEY, MONEY	13
Four	Time	19
Five	The Collecting Gene	23
Six	In the beginning	27
Seven	Glan Clwyd Farm	31
Eight	The Eccentric Billy Moore	35
Nine	Cockliffe Hill Farm	39
Ten	The War Years and Beyond	43
Eleven	Peter and Wendy Dyson	51
Twelve	Mountains and Mantons	57
Thirteen	Joseph and John Manton	61
Fourteen	Robert Held, Firearms Historian	67
Fifteen	Biggles	79
Sixteen	Hares and Henry Bestwick	85
Seventeen	W. Keith Neal	89
Eighteen	Purdeys	95
Nineteen	The Collectors	101
Twenty	The Ones That Got Away	109
Twenty one	The Art of The Engraver and Colour Hardener	116
Twenty two	Twelve Bore or Twenty	127
Twenty three	Richard Ratner and Kit Ravenshear	131
Twenty four	Sid Bellamy	131
Twenty five	Forsyth	139
Twenty six	Pauly Breech Loaders	147
Twenty seven	Derek Fearn, Master Gunsmith	155
Twenty eight	A visit to the Birmingham Gun Quarter	159
Twenty nine	The Joseph Manton Pelletlock	169
Thirty	Needlefire	175
Thirty one	Pinfire	179
	J.R Ewing's Holland and Holland	182

Thirty two	**Shooting at Bisley**	*187*
Thirty three	**Scott Motorcycles and Gun Trade**	*195*
Thirty four	**Peter Gavuzzi, Wilkinsons and the Classic Rolls-Royce**	*199*
Thirty five	**Some Special Mantons**	*205*
Thirty six	**Manton and Co. London and Calcutta**	*211*
Thirty seven	**Exotica**	*219*
Thirty eight	**Stalking Rifles**	*223*
Thirty nine	**The Search for Black Powder Express Cartridges**	*229*
Forty	**Derek Fearn and the Four Fifty Purdey**	*235*
Forty one	**Deanich Lodge 2003**	*239*
Forty two	**Louie Bierman's Remarkable MacNab**	*245*

One Man's Gun Quest

The height of fashion in 1858, the year before the author's paternal grandmother was born.

Chapter One
The Nineteenth Century

The guns and rifles that interested me most were made in the nineteenth century, the most rapid century of expansion the world had ever seen up until then.

At the beginning of the century life had continued much as it had done for centuries before. The fastest man could travel was the speed of a galloping horse but by the end of the century steam power had transformed the world. Steamships circled the globe and a network of steam powered railways criss-crossed every developed continent. At the time of the Great Exhibition in 1851 Queen Victoria said enthusiastically "We can make anything!" How right she was!

In every field, advance galloped ahead. The internal combustion engine had been established long before 1900. The aeroplane had not quite arrived but experimenters were trying hard and the Wright brothers flew in 1903. The motor car had spluttered into history with the Benz in 1886.

Electricity was making great progress. When Faraday demonstrated electricity to Queen Victoria she said "Very interesting, but what use is it?" The Savoy Theatre opened in 1881, was the first theatre in the world to be lit with electric light.

Many inventions surged forward: The telephone, the typewriter, the cinematograph and much more. Art, literature, architecture, engineering, medicine, all made tremendous strides.

But the greatest change of all was social. If a magical time machine could transport us to, say, London in the 1840's we would be astounded: Most of all by the smell!

It has been calculated that almost half a million tons of horse manure per annum were deposited on the streets of London so despite a continuous process of sweeping up, the smell was always there.

Cleanliness may well be next to godliness but not in London during the early nineteenth century. When Victoria came to the throne in 1837 there was only one bathroom in Buckingham Palace; all the servants had were the kitchen taps so they must have been pretty smelly! Even if the owners of the great houses were clinically clean, which I doubt, their servants were not!

In addition to this, many Londoners lived in abject poverty crowded into stinking tenements with no proper system of sewage disposal. All in all, then, a shocking, stinking environment.

There were also tremendous changes in thought and ideas. Ask your friends which book, written in the nineteenth century, though hardly ever read, has influenced and changed the world we live in today more than any book other than the Bible.

Think about it for a moment.

The book is Das Kapital by Karl Marx which challenged and changed society for all time. Have you read it? I thought not! Apologies, you are the only person I know who *has* read it! The spark of social change ignited a flame that roared into a conflagration in the twentieth century.

Two political giants on opposing sides: Disraeli sans whiskers for a change, on left, and William Ewart Gladstone showing that he was not always a whiskered old-timer!

As technology shot ahead great engineers rose to meet the new challenges: Stephenson, Brunel, Whitworth and many others. Joseph Paxton the gardener and self-taught engineer built the largest conservatory in the country, 300 ft long, for his employer the Duke of Devonshire at Chatsworth. He then went on to design the Crystal Palace erected in Hyde Park, London in 1851 to house the Great Exhibition, the wonder of the age.

The first screw driven iron ship to cross the Atlantic was the *Great Britain* designed by one of the greatest engineers of all time, Isambard Kingdom Brunel. It was for a number of years after 1845 the largest and fastest ship on the Liverpool - New York service. Eventually she ended up damaged in the Falklands but repair costs were considered to be uneconomic so she remained there as a floating storage hulk. She was, however, eventually "discovered" and towed to Bristol for restoration. Thank goodness that this unique maritime milestone has survived.

Before the *Great Britain* Brunel had designed the *Great Western*, the first steam driven ship to conduct regular passages across the Atlantic. He went on to build the Great Eastern, launched, with great difficulty, on the Thames in 1858. Driven by sail, paddles and screw propeller she was the biggest ship of her day whose size was not to be exceeded for almost half a century when the White Star Line launched the *Celtic* in 1901.

Before the *Great Eastern* the largest ship afloat was the American *Adriatic*: 355 ft to The *Great Eastern's* 680; 7,564 tons to 32,160; 4,000 horsepower to 11,000. And she was still underpowered!

Unfortunately she was a "ship too far" for Brunel who had over-reached himself and destroyed his health with this huge leviathan. Never a commercial success she was eventually broken up at Connah's Quay on the River Dee in North Wales, but a gallant effort.

Brunel's talents were not confined to ships as he was also successful in other fields. In the eighteen twenties he was the engineer in charge of the construction of the first Thames tunnel, designed by his father who was also a distinguished engineer. In 1833, aged only 27, he was appointed engineer of the newly proposed Great Western Railway from London to Bristol. He introduced the new 7 foot wide broad gauge line. He designed the Clifton Suspension Bridge and the Royal Albert Bridge over the River Tamar.

He was, without doubt, one of the greatest engineers of all time.

4~One Man's Gun Quest

The Savannah, the first steam driven ship to cross the Atlantic in 1819 though steam was only used for 85 hours during the 27 day voyage. Speed under steam 4 knots. 90hp, length 98.5 ft, 320 tons, 32 passengers. The paddle wheels were collapsible when the ship was under sail.

Nothing demonstrates the incredible technological advance made in the nineteenth century more than shipbuilding. Just compare the 1819 "Savannah", with the 1897 "Kaiser Wilhelm Der Grosse: 627 ft; 14,349 tons; 28,000hp, 1,749 passengers; Southampton to New York in 5 days, 22 hours.

The Great Eastern built by Isambard Kingdom Brunel In 1858. The biggest ship ever built in the nineteenth century at 680 ft long and 7,564 tons.

Idealised picture of Joseph Paxton's crystal palace built in Hyde Park in 1851 to house the Great Exhibition, the wonder of the age.

Ernest A Drury Smith, Derbyshire photographer.

Chapter Two
Ernest A. Drury Smith, Derbyshire Photographer

Ernest, or Ernie to you and I, is a remarkable man blessed with a range of skills. Over the years he has tried his hand at all kinds of jobs: Mining, fish farming, gunshop assistant among others, finally finishing his working life as a building supervisor with Sheffield Borough Council.

He has, however, had a lifelong interest in photography and finally developed his skills to turn his hobby into a business. Architectural photography is a speciality of his, both exterior and interior and he has to his credit some splendid photographs of Derbyshire stately homes.

He is a keen clay pigeon shot who loads his own cartridges and is very knowledgeable about antique guns, having read widely on the subject. He was recommended to me by Derek Fearn, the master gunsmith who works from Catton Hall, South Derbyshire, as the ideal man to undertake the detailed gun photography necessary for this book.

Ernie lives near Bakewell in North Derbyshire, about forty miles from my home, so it is a fair journey for him. Once a week, however, he would come over and we would spend the day photographing the guns required. He is a perfectionist and only the best would do.

So for week after week we would work together on this task and I got to know Ernie quite well. My overwhelming impression was his sense of humour so it was a great pleasure to be in his company; much to learn from him, too.

Ernie was the youngest child in a family of four; three girls had arrived first. His father was sixty years old when Ernie was ten and they were never very close. Victorian standards of strictness were the norm. Ernie's bedtime was 6pm and if his friends arrived at 5pm to ask if Ernie could come out to play his father would glance at the clock and say "No, too late!" So poor Ernie would go to bed at six and peep through the curtains to watch his pals playing football outside.

Although money was never plentiful they were by no means poor, yet Ernie says that his father never bought him anything. What about Christmas and birthdays? Nothing from his father, says Ernie! The only thing he can remember is that his father once gave him five shillings (25p).

When Ernie finally got married his father said gloomily "It won't last five minutes!" but he was wrong and Ernie and Pam are still happily married.

He did, however, have a brother in law, a farmer, married to an elder sister. Ernie was very close to him and was always made welcome at the farm where he would happily bang away with the air rifles. No air rifles were allowed at home!

A lifelong trout fisherman he was once fishing in a river near home with a fishing rod given to him by his brother in law. He was about twelve years old at the time. A man approached him and said: Did you know that you have no right to be fishing here? "I have the fishing rights and they cost me four pounds a year".

Ernie was suitably contrite so the man went on to say: "Look, I'll tell you what I'll do. If you promise to fish only with a fly in future I will allow you to fish here". Ernie, of course, knew nothing whatever about fishing with a fly but that started him off to become a dedicated fly fisherman.

A friend of Ernie's was not so lucky. His strict Victorian father made Ernie's dad look positively profligate! The boy's job every morning before school was to clear out the ashes of the coal fire and lay a new one. Inspired by Ernie's example he dearly wanted a fishing rod. He asked his father but the answer was *no*.

The boy, however, was very helpful to an elderly lady down the street, doing odd jobs for her and running errands. One day, knowing how much he wanted a fishing rod she went out and bought him one. Delighted with his present he ran home to show his parents. His father said nothing.

The next morning when clearing out the ashes he found the blackened brass ferrules of his fishing rod. His father had smashed up the rod and burnt it the night before.

When the tearful boy confronted his father he was told: "I said I wasn't going to buy you a fishing rod and no-one else is!" Let's hope that there is a special corner of Hell reserved for fathers like that!

When he eventually died his son did *not* go to the funeral!

This is the handsome Ernest Drury Smith, Ernie's father, in 1910. A superlative period photograph. What a marvellous device the car is with its external gearchange lever and handbrake and, of course, no front brakes. The straw boater sets the scene so all that is required to complete it is an Edwardian Gaiety Girl gracing the passenger seat in period costume with a huge wide brimmed hat held in place with a silk scarf tied under her chin. The make of the car is believed to be a 1908/9 Métallurgique. And the dog's name? I've forgotten!

The American Express Company is now known all over the world. It was created by the famous Henry Wells and William Fargo in 1850. These first shares were issued in 1857 and their hand-written signatures appear on them. Travellers cheques were an American Express innovation created in 1891.

Economy no more means saving money than it means spending money. It means the administration of a house, it's stewardship; spending or saving, that is, whether money or time, or anything else, to the best possible advantage.

John Ruskin

Chapter Three
MONEY, MONEY, MONEY

Researching this book and looking at the nineteenth century in great detail I have attempted to compare the pound then to the pound today. It is, in many ways, an impossible task because life today bears little comparison to life then. The lifestyle we enjoy today is so far ahead of that of even the most privileged in the nineteenth century that any kind of comparison is incredibly difficult. Remember, too, that wages increased throughout the century.

The period that concerns us most in this book is 1800 to the 1860s so let us make an attempt to look at that. First of all look at the following conversion table converting "old" money to decimal:

Old money	Decimal	Old money	Decimal
1d	½p	1s7d	8p
2d or 3d	1p	1s8d	8½p
4d	1½p	1s9d or 1s10d	9p
5d	2p	1s11d	9½p
6d	2½p	2s	10p
1s	5p	2s6d	12½p
1s1d	5½p	3s	15p
1s2d or 1s3d	6p	5s	25p
1s6d	7½p	20s	100p i.e. £1

In the year 1815 when Napoleon was defeated at last, out of a total U.K. population of about eleven million there were about 250,000 people with an income of over £700 a year: Higher officials, manufacturers, contractors ship-builders etc. There were about 500,000 shopkeepers who were very happy indeed if they could make £150 a year. About a million farmers together with minor clergy and the best paid schoolmasters achieved about £120 a year.

At the lower end of the scale two million artisans and skilled men earned around £55 per year which was the minimum amount for a respectable living but below that the workers were descending into poverty.

Miners working long hours in dirty, dangerous conditions earned about £40 per year and agricultural labourers who also worked appallingly long, back breaking hours earned about £30 a year. But this was by no means the minimum: Unskilled labourers had to manage on less and even below that level there was a vast underclass living in abject poverty.

We have some examples of household income and expenditure for skilled men in 1855. They were not much lower than those just before the First World War though by then working hours and living conditions were greatly improved.

In London a working cutler with four children living in Whitefriars Street had a dreary, damp and sunless house though less unsanitary than most. Water was laid on in the cellar and "latrines". Grandmother helped in the house and his wife carried his work to and from his employer's shop in Oxford Street. Income £1.16.9 per week spent as follows: Rent 7s. 9d., food £1, coal and light 2s.10d., cleaning 1s., school 10d., clothes 3s.2d., sundries 1s.2d.

Note that the only surplus was 1s.2d. per week to pay for all unforeseen items, such as doctor's bills. You will also have noticed the 10d. for school as free education had not yet arrived.

A Sheffield working cutler with five children had an income of £1.5s.6d. per week spent as follows: His small house with parlour, kitchen, two bedrooms and a garden in which he kept pigs and pigeons cost 3s.4d., per week. One child supported herself as a dressmaker and his wife sold ginger pop! In addition to his rent his outlay was: Food 11s.4d., coal and candles 1s.5d., cleaning 6d., school 5d., clothes 3s.7d., sundries 1s.7d.

A foundry-man in Derbyshire with four children did considerably better with a tied house, so no rent to pay, and a garden. He worked twelve hours a day for 355 days a year for a good employer who supported the sick club and the school. Breakfast was at 7am with tea or coffee, milk and sugar, bread and butter and cold meat. The children had bread and milk. Dinner at noon: Meat, bread potatoes, vegetables, fruit or cheese. Tea at 4pm: tea, sugar, bread and butter. Supper at 8pm, remains of dinner.

But these wages only applied to skilled men. Unskilled, casual labourers were in a very much worse situation. In 1851 a "scavenger and night-man" in London earned only fifteen shillings a week. Rent for an unfurnished room cost him 1s.9d. per week. Food cost him 3s.6d. for bread, 2s.4d for boiled salt beef, 1¾d. for pickles or onions, 1d for butter, and a pint of cocoa a day at a coffee shop 10½d. Shaving twice a week 1d, tobacco 7d, beer 2s.4d and gin 1s.2d.

Too much spent on beer and gin? Not for someone spending endless nights in the filth, latrines and sewers of the London of those days. There were countless others in all urban areas doing the worst of work on similar constrained wages.

Much higher up the scale were the clerks, about 50,000 of them in the 1850's. They were expected to be smart, well turned out and very respectable. After many years of reliable service they could aspire to 30.s. per week. A document of 1852 entitled *"Office Staff Practices"* outlined what was expected of them:

1. Godliness, cleanliness and punctuality are the necessities of a good business.
2. The firm has reduced the hours of work and the clerical staff will now only have to be present between the hours of 7am and 6pm.
3. Daily prayers will be held daily in the main office. The clerical staff will be present.
4. Clothing must be of a sober nature. The clerical staff will not disport themselves in raiment of bright colour.
5. Overshoes and top coats may not be worn in the office but neck scarves and headwear may be worn in inclement weather.
6. A stove is provided for the benefit of clerical staff. Coal and wood must be kept in the locker. It is recommended that each member of the clerical staff bring 4lb. of coal each day during cold weather.
7. No member of the clerical staff may leave the room without permission from Mr. Rodgers. The calls of nature are permitted and clerical staff may use the garden beyond the second gate. This area must be kept in good order.
8. No talking is allowed during business hours.
9. The craving for tobacco, wines, or spirits is a human weakness and as such is forbidden to all members of the clerical staff.
10. Now that the hours of business have been drastically reduced the partaking of food is allowed between 11.30am and noon but work will not on any account cease.
11. Members of the clerical staff will provide their own pens.

There is a final note saying that "the owners will expect a great rise in the output of work to compensate for these near Utopian conditions."

In 1851 there were over eight million women of ten years of age and above, about half a million more than males. Almost half a million of them were in domestic service, hard work, long hours, Spartan living conditions and low pay!

A new girl was paid about £6 a year and even an experienced cook was only paid about £18 a year.

Over 100,000 domestic workers in London performed all the tasks to maintain a busy household: The houses to be kept clean, all the coal fires to be laid, cleaned and fed with coal, no bathrooms so hot water would have to be carried upstairs to the tin baths for all the family plus all the other innumerable tasks necessary to run the house.

A very hard life indeed but even harder for their sisters in industry.

It was against this backdrop that the workers in the gun trade of those days practised their trade.

"It's the same the whole world over,
It's the poor wot gets the blame.
It's the rich wot gets the pleasure,
Ain't it all a bleedin' shame?"

Nineteenth Century Music Hall song.

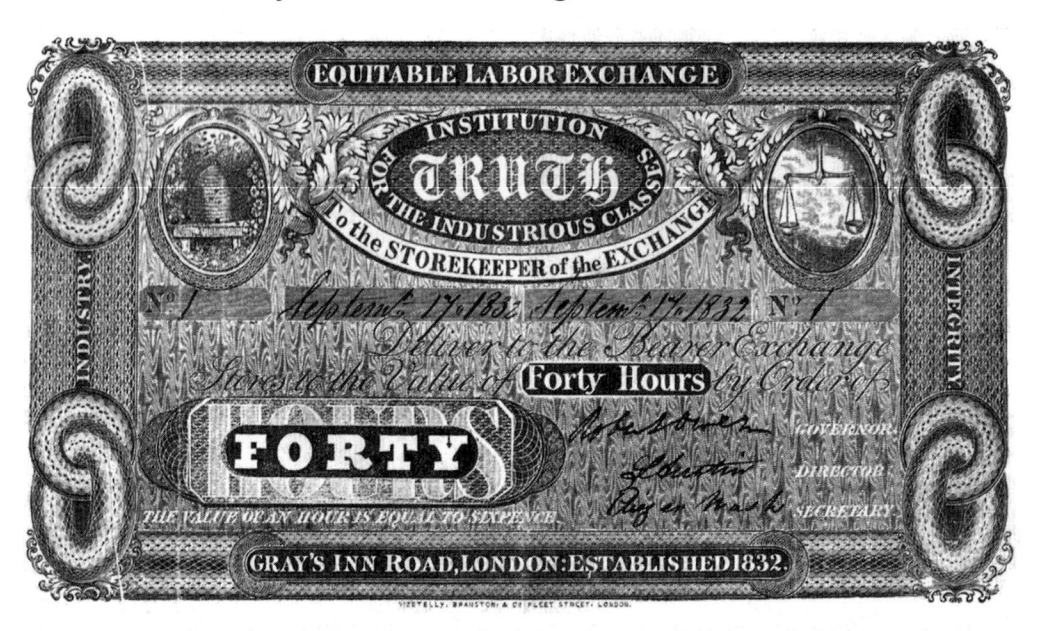

Reformer and visionary, Robert Owen, intended to revolutionise the world of finance. He opened the London Exchange bazaar in 1832 in which notes were issued for hours worked instead of sterling. The venture failed in 1834, but Robert Owen personally paid all the debts.

This "cotton bond", bearing seven percent interest and redeemable over 20 years, was issued by the Confederate States of America, in London and Paris in 1863. The objective was to raise £3 million. The holder had the unusual option of being able to convert the nominal amount of the bond either into cash or cotton at the rate of sixpence sterling per pound of cotton. After the defeat of the Confederacy in 1865, all Confederate bonds and loans were worthless.

18~One Man's Gun Quest

The Monkey Marksman, mid 19th Century. He raises his rifle and aims at the target. His head nods and turns and his jaw and arms move. The pull in the base plays two tunes.
Late 19th century DIY Gothic. You could buy the plans to make this clock. All the woodwork casing cut out with a fret-saw and the clock purchased separately.
Papier-mâché was immensely popular in Victorian times and used for all sorts of purposes, even desks. This clock is an example of the imaginative use of the material.

Chapter Four
Time

To make a fine gun you need skill, money and time. Time is the vital ingredient so let us take a closer look at it.

Time, you will agree, is funny stuff! I should know because I have lived through quite a lot of it!

Napoleon said: "Ask me for anything but time!" He appreciated that it was invaluable, irreplaceable and fleeting!

The physicist, Stephen Hawking, wrote *A Short History of Time* which became a best seller. Everyone has read it, no-one understands it! I exclude you, dear reader, because I'm sure that you have grasped every word! So that leaves you and Stephen Hawking!

No use explaining it to me, however, because I can't even understand Einstein's Theory of Relativity or, come to think of it, my telephone bill.

This brings to mind an anecdote concerning the great advocate F.E. Smith, later Lord Birkenhead.

He had just delivered a long and complicated explanation in a Court of Law and the Judge said, wearily "After all that, I'm none the wiser" to which Smith retorted: "No, my Lord, but at least you're better informed!"

Although I can't match you and Stephen Hawking on the enormous subject of time, I can assure you, without referring to Hawking or Einstein, of one certainty: It's later than you think!

I can also assure you that as you grow older the things you most regret are not the things you *have* done but those you *haven't* done. If you have a long held ambition to learn to fly an aeroplane, walk the Great Wall of China, speak a foreign language or whatever, there's no more time to lose. Get cracking *now*!

Let's take 1939 as a datum year; a momentous date in world history and a vitally important date for me. I was sixteen years old, living in Rhyl, North Wales and bought my first motorcycle, a 1930 175cc Triumph two stroke. If the world was not yet my oyster, the incomparable Vale of Clwyd certainly was. It gave me the freedom and mobility that I found absolutely intoxicating. At that time we did, indeed, live in a modern world undreamed of by earlier generations. So much was new and we considered ourselves incredibly fortunate to be living in the twentieth century with the fusty nineteenth century so far behind in time that we could hardly imagine it.

Aeroplanes had developed to an incredible state of efficiency: We had the Spitfire and the Hurricane and Germany had the equally efficient Messerschmitt 109. Yet the first aeroplane had only flown 36 years before, in 1903 when the Wright Brothers' "Flyer" shakily took to the air for a short flight at Kill Devil Hill, North Carolina.

The comparatively new invention, radio, or wireless as we called it then had developed by leaps and bounds. Practically every home had one, certainly every home that could afford one and newer developments were introduced every year. Even motorised push-button tuning had arrived for those that could afford the latest models.

Television was just around the corner and had already arrived in the London area; clearly it would soon be with us, too. What an amazing prospect to be able to view talking pictures in our own living room….marvellous! I had first seen it demonstrated in Rhyl in 1934 or 35. In winter time trade exhibitions were held in Rhyl Pavilion and they were packed with interest. A local radio dealer and enthusiast named Fowkes, had built a television transmitter and receiver so a television picture was transmitted from one side of the pavilion to the other. I can see it now! A motionless, greenish black and white picture of Mickey Mouse. We watched, entranced. We were witnessing the cutting edge of nineteen thirties technology!

The depression years were behind us, employment was steadily rising and many more people had money to spend.

The cinema was in its hey-day with magnificent picture palaces in every town. A surprising number of the films we saw then are still classics today. Has distance lent enchantment to the view? Not a bit of it! In September 2003 a poll of cinemagoers voted 1939 as Hollywood's greatest year.

Many of the cinema's greatest classics were produced that year including: Gone with the Wind, Goodbye Mr. Chips, Gunga Din, Mr. Smith Goes to Washington, the Wizard of Oz, Wuthering Heights, Stagecoach, (which set John Wayne on the path to stardom), The Hunchback of Notre Dame, Of Mice and Men, Dodge City and Jesse James.

Yes, we were the supreme modernists in 1939!

Amazingly, however, Custer's defeat at the Little Big Horn and Wild Bill Hickock's murder when he was shot in the back during a poker game at Deadwood, Dakota territory, holding his "Dead Man's Hand" of aces and eights, was only 63 years before this, in 1876. Within living memory of older people in 1939.

Even closer in time was the motor car: They were not allowed on British roads until November 1896, only 43 years before, but do not imagine that British roads were crowded with cars in 1897. The first car did not appear in Rhyl, for example, until 1898, owned by Mr. Palethorpe of sausage fame. Come to think of it, whatever happened to Palethorpes sausages? Clearly, then, people in their late forties could remember the time when there were no motor cars on the road and no tarmac roads on which to drive them. Yet by 1939 car design had leapt ahead to provide comfortable, efficient and affordable transport. Just compare the 1939 models with their 1920 predecessors and motorcycles, too, had made equivalent progress.

It all sounds incredible, I know!

Now look back in time from today, 2004, to when I was sixteen years old in 1939. Do you realise that this is two years further away in time, 65 years, than Custer's defeat was in 1939 i.e. 63 years. Makes you think!

"Everything changes, everything remains the same." So say the French, and how true it is.

I remember reading about a German banker in the height of the runaway inflation in the early 1920's. He had lost everything. His world was in ruins.

He looked out of the window to see a young couple with shining faces walking along the street hand in hand and obviously deliriously in love. For them, inflation or not, the world kept rolling along.

So whatever has happened over the ensuing years, the human spirit has survived: People fall in love, get married (most of the time!), and produce children to ensure the survival of the next generation.

Time is the most undefinable yet paradoxical of things: The past has gone, the future is not come, and the present becomes the past, even while we attempt to define it, and like the flash of the lightning, at once exists and expires.

Charles Colton
1780-1832

John Manton Pinfire double about 1860.

Chapter Five
The Collecting Gene

The collecting gene appears to be predominately male. Men collect anything from pictures, objets d'art, cars, motorcycles and everything in between. Is it a survival from hunter/gatherer days? What do you think?

With boys of my generation I suppose it started from collecting cigarette cards, fireworks for Bonfire Night etc. But though the female sex are not normally afflicted, there are exceptions: Think of Imelda Marcus and shoes or Zsa Gabor and husbands: Zsa Zsa claimed that she was a very good housekeeper: She always kept the houses!

An example of how collecting starts is the motorcycle business. Most people who start in the motorcycle business do so because they love motorcycles so collecting them is a natural progression, but it ain't necessarily so, as George Gershwin might have said! Sorry, Ira. It was brother Ira who wrote the lyrics.

Dave and Pete are two incredibly talented motorcycle restorers who run their own motorcycle business near Swadlincote, Derbyshire. They can turn their hand to "as new" restorations of classic Norton and Triumph motorcycles, though such work is not cheap.

Life has not always been a bowl of cherries for Dave but it is always a delight to visit him. He will always have you rocking with laughter with his inimitable one-liners.

So is Dave the perfect example of a motorcycle collector? No!

When asked what bikes he collects he always answers: I collect money, not bikes! I suspect, however, that like many other talented engineers he has never collected anything like as much money as he deserves.

Daughter, Caroline and son, Ross have not inherited my collector gene and Edna never had it in the first place!

Once at Uttoxeter cattle market I was standing next to an old farmer: "Are you in the mood to spend some money today?" I asked. Nodding towards Edna he replied, "It's them that spends money". "Not in our house!" she retorted!

So I did put together a small collection of motorcycles and have always been fascinated by the quality and workmanship of fine English guns and rifles.

I suppose my interest in antique guns started in my early teens when I was given a .577 muzzle-loading Enfield rifle. It was not until 1954, however, that I bought my first quality muzzle loader. This was a D.B. percussion by the great Joseph Manton, one of his later guns. I bought it from Michael Weaving of Ayot St Peter, Welwyn, Herts. This started me on a quest to learn all I could about Joseph Manton and to keep an eye open for other examples.

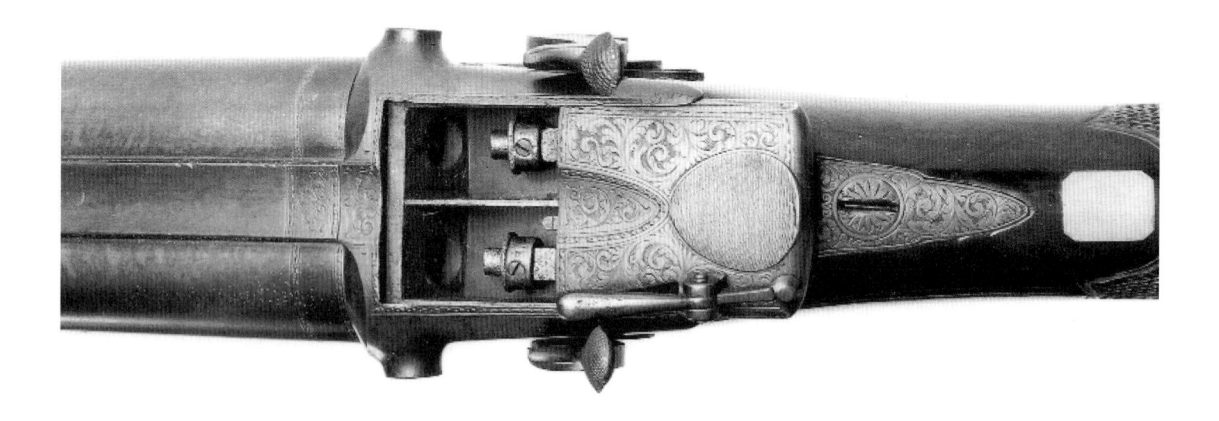

Victorian ingenuity. The Charles Jones patent centre fire percussion gun. The external cocking levers actuate the enclosed hammers which strike "inside out" percussion caps. The cover slides over to keep out the rain.

Joseph Manton tubelock, 1820's.

26 ~ One Man's Gun Quest

No, not a self portrait, this is Rabbity Tam who looks steadily across to us over the years between. Real name John MacKenzie photographed about 1880 by William Smith of Tain, Ross-shire. Described as a poacher but, no doubt, a rabbit catcher. He is holding his long obsolete .577 muzzle loading Enfield rifle exactly the same as the one I used. He, too, would have loaded it with a charge of shot for shooting rabbits unless, of course, taking a shot at a forbidden stag!

Chapter Six
In the Beginning

As a boy in Rhyl, North Wales, in the nineteen thirties, there was no shortage of opportunities to fire guns at a target. Mostly airguns, of course, at the many amusement arcades in the town.

At the Marine Lake amusement park, however, in addition to the airguns that fired darts or corks there was a rifle range with real rifles: .22 trombone action Winchesters, but expensive at sixpence (2½p) for four shots.

But what a delight to fire a real cartridge rifle and from then on it has always been a great pleasure to fire a .22.

My father, however, did *not* share my interest in guns. He had served throughout the Great War in the Royal Welch Fusileers ending up as a Sergeant Major with a war wound that would trouble him for the rest of his life! No, he had seen quite enough of guns!

It was a great occasion when I had finally saved up the necessary five shillings and sixpence (25½p) to buy my first air rifle, a Haenel that you broke open to cock, then loaded into a tube that you extracted from the muzzle. It gave me an enormous amount of pleasure and I must have fired thousands of shots with it.

When I was about thirteen I was given my first firearm: An 1860 .577 Enfield military muzzle loading rifle, though I never used it as a rifle with a solid bullet.

So this was a new dimension!

I made my own gunpowder, using potassium chlorate, not potassium nitrate (don't do it!). A quarter pound cocoa tin served as a powder flask.
The bowl of a clay pipe was an excellent powder and shot measure and another quarter pound cocoa tin was used as a shot flask.

Shot, however, was a problem! Lead shot was used when pocket money would run to it but many other alternatives were tried: I experimented with D.I.Y. lead shot but it was pear shaped and irregular in size: Not satisfactory at all. How to make it? You don't want to know as it could be dangerous!

Tin tacks were good, but expensive! Gravel was tried, but without success: Don't bother with it! Used ball bearings: OK, but difficult to obtain. For wadding I used a wodge of rolled up newspaper: A thick one over the powder charge and a thin one over the shot charge to hold it in position.

Percussion caps? Couldn't afford them! The alternative was a pair of paper caps, as used in toy cap guns, wedged into to the hammer. This was surprisingly effective, most of the time, though you could occasionally get a hang-fire.

Hang-fires were not so good! You would pull the trigger, hear the caps fire, but fail to ignite the charge. As you took the gun from your shoulder it would belatedly go off! Potentially dangerous, of course, but no harm was ever done.

My parents ran a guest house: Stella Maris, 34/35 West Parade opposite Rhyl Pavilion. On one occasion I decided to fire a clay marble at the back gate of Stella Maris. It would, I reasoned, be bound to shatter on impact as the marble was far too small for the bore. Only a light charge of powder was used but, to my horror, the marble went straight through the gate. Fortunately no-one was walking by at the time but it was the kind of experiment that I never repeated.

I had earlier discovered that even a wodge of newspaper without any kind of shot charge could make a very effective projectile and I was reminded of this only a year or two ago.

A Derbyshire farmer had suffered break-ins at his workshop and had decided to put a stop to it once and for all. He extracted the shot from a twelve bore cartridge and replaced it with a tightly rolled wodge of newspaper reasoning that it would only frighten anyone who was struck by it. I could have told him different!

He then rigged it up to fire at any intruder who opened his workshop door. There was, however, one small problem: He forgot about his makeshift intruder deterrent and opened the door himself! The gun fired and the wodge hit his leg like a bullet causing a severe injury that put him into hospital. The Police had to be informed, as with any gunshot wounds, so there were other unpleasant repercussions. Once again, don't do it!

Rhyl Pavilion and children's' paddling pool. The author lived at 34/35 West Parade in the nineteen thirties which is opposite the Pavilion but just out of sight in this picture.

The way it was then. A pair of horses, pulling a single furrow plough.

Chapter Seven
Glan Clwyd Farm

During my schooldays although I lived in Rhyl, a seaside town, I spent my holidays, winter and summer at Glan Clwyd Farm. Beyond St. Asaph and closer to the Clwydian Range lies the Waen where Glan Clwyd Farm is situated with its land extending down to the River Clwyd.

The farm was 105 acres in extent, part of the Llanerch Hall Estate owned by Captain Jones. Good, but heavy land and the rent in the nineteen thirties was £2 an acre which included the farmhouse and buildings. This was the rental for the best agricultural land in the nineteen thirties but although it sounds ridiculously cheap today it must not be forgotten that in those days many good farmers on good land found it difficult, or even impossible, to earn even a modest living.

Captain Jones' son, Master Tony, was in his late teens and greatly envied as the future owner of this magnificent estate, destined to live in lovely Llanerch Hall with its herd of Fallow deer.

Sadly this was never to happen: The estate was broken up and sold and I have no idea what happened to Master Tony.

So did I cut a great swathe through the rabbits at Glan Clwyd Farm with my 1860 Enfield? Sadly, no! I never found it very effective but, no matter, as I quickly graduated to a .410 single barrel shotgun belonging to Bobby Davies.

The farm was run, as tenants, by Bobby Davies and his mother. Bobby's father had died many years before and farming in those days was hard going. A radio, or wireless as it was called then, would have been an enormous benefit but it was a luxury they just couldn't afford. They had a dairy herd of about twenty five Shorthorn cattle so milk sales to Philip Brown, dairyman, of Water Street, Rhyl brought in a welcome monthly cheque which must have been the mainstay of the farm economy. In addition they had a small herd of Welsh Mountain sheep.

The land was all down to grass, other than one field of about eight acres ploughed with a single furrow plough pulled by the two heavy horses, Twm and

Jet. Oats was the usual crop, grown to supplement winter feed and ground into flour by a machine driven by an ancient paraffin engine. Ignition was by hot tube, not sparking plug, and although only started up once a year it ran surprisingly well.

Bobby was a marvellous shot. Today he would have made a clay pigeon shot of the very highest standard, but in those days Bobby shot for the pot: No pennies to spare for busting inedible clay pigeons!

There were two woods on the farm and one or two patches of bracken covered hillside land. Bobby would send his dog onto one of these patches and the dog would flush out a rabbit. The rabbit would race along, bouncing and weaving, with the dog in close pursuit. Bobby would bring the gun to his shoulder and shoot the rabbit in front of the dog's nose. I never remember him missing nor did he ever hit the dog. I have never seen anyone else who could emulate Bobby.

The twelve bore cartridges he used were Eley Kynoch Grand Prix or Bonax, price 3s. 7½d (19p) for twenty five. He always favoured number six shot size. The four/ten was chambered for the short cartridge only. 2s. 1½d. (11p) for twenty five.

My maternal grandfather, who eventually gave me his hammerless 12 bore by the Midland Gun Company, recommended Spartan cartridges at the extremely economical price of 2s. 6d. (12½p) for twenty five. I tried them but might as well have used blanks!

In the Rhyl amusement arcades many of the slot machines were labelled "For amusement only", a slogan that could have been attached, with some accuracy, to my Enfield muzzle loader. The four/ten, however, suited me very well indeed and I would tramp round the fields at Glan Clwyd with it, accompanied by my friend, Howell Jones, who lived across the road.

My first twelve bore, however, was a Webley and Scott semi-hammerless single barrel bought for 7s. 6d (37½p) from Maurice Cotterill of Derby. My mother and Maurice's mother worked together, as girls, in the offices at George Fletcher and Co., Engineers, Litchurch Lane, Derby.

These Webley and Scotts were good enough guns but mine had been in some kind of accident and the barrel was bent to the left so I was never able to make effective use of it at Glan Clwyd.

The way they were. No, this is not Llanerch Hall but Thornham Hall in Derbyshire. The photograph is of a shooting party in 1911 and similar shooting parties would have been held at Llanerch Hall in those golden years (for those who had money!) before World War One. Thornham Hall, I'm delighted to say, is still a private residence.

A horse-drawn canal boat, still a common sight in the 1930's.

Chapter Eight
The Eccentric Billy Moore

In 1937 I decided to spend my summer holidays at Shardlow, Derbyshire, staying with Mr and Mrs Parkin and their two boys at their farm at Wilne Lane. The lane runs down to the River Derwent and then stops, as there is no bridge at that point. I took my dog, Jack, with me.

Mr. and Mrs. Parkin were a kindly couple who made me most welcome and the boys, a year or two older than me, were good companions.

On the other side of the road was a run down farm owned by a well known local character, Billy Moore. He was unmarried, about seventy years of age and lived on his own.

Something of a recluse he lived in confirmed bachelordom! His father had been a very successful cattle dealer and had also bred trotting horses, evolving the Shardlow breed. Very much in demand before the advent of the motor car. Billy Moore had continued to breed them but there must have been very little demand in the nineteen thirties.

The squat, two storey farmhouse reputedly dated back to the seventeenth century and had a strange, menacing air with its windows obscured by decades of grime. The locals were convinced that it was haunted and to quote Mandy Rice Davies' never to be forgotten phrase, "They would say that, wouldn't they!"

A secret passage, they assured me, ran from the cellars under the River Derwent to Sawley church though I never went down to investigate!

After I had known Billy Moore some time I asked him if there was any truth in the opinion that the house was haunted. He told me that, on occasion, an apparition would appear at the top of the stairs "wearing a red coat, like a huntsman" but as he advanced towards it, it disappeared. Must say that I would have raced in the opposite direction!

He did not consider it to be anything remarkable and nothing whatever to be afraid of; after all, it did him no harm!

Billy only lived in two rooms, the comfortless kitchen and a bedroom upstairs. At that time I was learning to play the piano and in one room there was an ancient walnut veneered grand piano, unplayed for decades. He very kindly allowed me to use it.

I would walk through the gloomy, rambling corridors past rooms long unused and filled with ancient dust-enshrouded furniture to reach the music room. The jangling, untuned piano thought it was a barrel organ and as I played, the ivorine key tops would come adrift. A musical experience few could have encountered! If any locals had gone by they would have been convinced that the house was haunted by a phantom barrel organ player!

Billy Moore was completely blasé about his phantom resident but I certainly wasn't! Before I started to play I would open the window so if *THE THING* had attempted to get me I would have been through that window like a shot out of a gun!

Billy Moore and I became great friends and I spent a lot of time on his farm. He loved to harness one of his trotters to a gig (a light two wheeled conveyance for two people) and with me by his side he would whip the horse to maximum speed and we would hurtle across the fields in the wildly bouncing gig. An exhilarating experience. Jack would race along in pursuit! I travelled many miles with him on the roads, too, but always at a more sedate pace!

It was with Billy Moore's gun that I first started to shoot in earnest with a twelve bore. He had an old twelve bore hammer gun of indeterminate make but only the right barrel worked as the left lock had broken and the left barrel was full of cobwebs. A trifling snag was that the top lever spring was also broken: You pushed the top lever to the right with your thumb to open the gun then when you closed it, the top lever spring snapped a tongue back to lock the barrels into position and at the same time returned the top lever.

No problem: Billy demonstrated to me how to keep the barrels closed by wedging a piece of binder twine under the top lever. Not a solution that would gain health and safety approval today!

Very few rabbits on both farms but plenty of wood pigeons that came to feed on the crops so the gun was put to good use.

The Parkin's farm went down to the River Derwent and they also had some land away from the farm with the canal on one side and the River Derwent on the other. Shardlow had been a very important inland port in the canal era and empty canal buildings lined the canal in the nineteen thirties. The post-war boom in pleasure boating was in the future but commercial boats carried their cargoes up and down the canal. Most were powered by heavy oil engines but a fair number of horse drawn boats were still in use. On all these boats husbands and wives lived and, on occasion whole families squeezed into the cramped living quarters. A way of life that is long gone.

Just where the road crosses over the canal at Shardlow was the small shop, post office and house where my mother lived as a girl with her parents. Her father, Harry Arthur Utting, ran the shop and post office. He had been a motoring enthusiast from the very earliest days, starting with a motorcycle and then moving on to cars. I understand that at one time he was the Alvis agent for Derbyshire before changing to oil sales.

In a wooden building next to the shop they kept the two gallon cans of petrol which they sold to motorists and motorcyclists before the advent of petrol pumps. On one occasion her sister, my aunt Dolly, checked whether a petrol can was empty or not. To look inside she unscrewed the cap then held a lighted taper to the open can and you could still see the burn marks on the wall!

Just before you got to the Parkin's farm was a cream painted cottage inhabited by a real old-timer. He told me that he had served in the British Army in China armed with the single shot Snider rifle. The Snider action was used to convert the muzzle loading Enfields, like the one I used, to breech loading about 1860 as an interim measure before the advent of the "modern" design, the .450 single shot Martini Henry in 1872. Some Sniders, then, must have continued in use for some time after the introduction of the Martini Henry.

So a most enjoyable holiday in country that was new to me and very different from the Vale of Clwyd.

The kind of gig driven by Billy Moore.

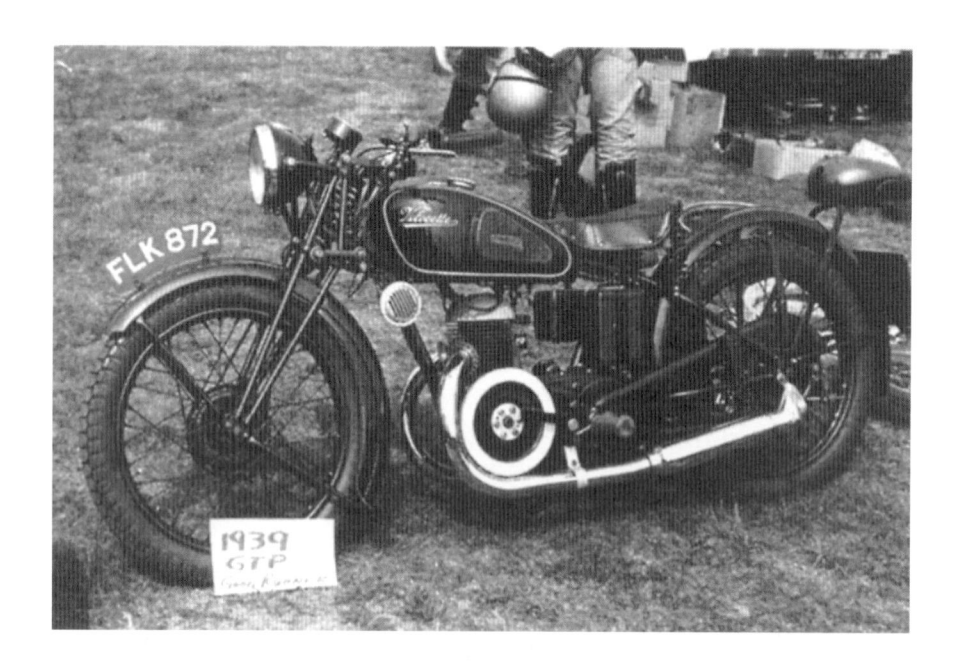

250cc Model G.P.T. Velocette two stroke: An unattainable vision in black and chrome for an impecunious youngster in 1938.

Early 1920's Rolls Royce "twenty" similar to the one that Syd Cotterill bought for a tenner.

Chapter Nine
Cockliffe Hill Farm

For the next summer holiday in 1938 my destination was Cockliffe Hill Farm halfway between Nottingham and Mansfield. The farmer and his wife were a delightful couple with three daughters. Two were married and the other, Freda, was a few years older than me and worked on the farm with her father. A lovely girl and a first class tennis player, so much so that she had created her own tennis court and club where the local young people would come to play.

They were tenant farmers on very light, sandy, stony soil with a rent of ten shillings (50p) an acre. About 100 acres, if I am not mistaken. The rent included a modern farmhouse with the range of traditional farm buildings. The original charming farmhouse was lived in by the MacRaes but whether as owners or tenants, I don't know.

The owner of the estate was Colonel Seeley and there were four keepers who reared huge numbers of pheasants.

There were several woods on the farm and the sandy soil was ideal for rabbits so with a gun borrowed from the farmer unlimited shooting was on hand at both rabbits and pigeons.

The keeper nearest to the farm was named Bob and he very kindly befriended me. He was a marvellous shot with either gun or rifle and I envied him his single shot .22 Martini. Some evenings he would walk round the wood-sides with his Martini and return with about a dozen rabbits, all shot through the head.

At corn harvest time the binder would slowly reduce the standing corn into a smaller and smaller square. The rabbits would retreat into it until, at the very end, they would break cover and race away. The local shots would have been alerted and would gather round the square to shoot the rabbits. Bob, however, would be there without his gun. He would walk round the perimeter of the decreasing square until he could see a rabbit, then he would unerringly despatch it with his catapult. Bob's bag would equal that of any of the guns.

Time, I decided, to buy a twelve bore double of my own so I went to see the head keeper. He offered me the choice of an English hammerless double at £2 or a double hammer gun by Smith and Son of Newark at £1.10s (£1.50p). I tried both but decided on the Charles Smith as, despite its pitted barrels, it shot very well indeed. It gave me years of use and I have it to this day.

When I paid the keeper he gave me back 2s. 6d. (12½p) for luck! So I got a bargain!

Charles Smith and Sons were founded in 1879 and continued until long after World War 2. They were well regarded and made sound guns. Charles Smith died in 1908 and the business was continued by his three sons. They bought the old established business of Peter Knight, Clinton Street, Nottingham in 1951, a firm that had started in the 1880's.

During my stay at Cockliffe Hill Farm I would buy cartridges from Knight's and the girl behind the counter was the chubby, pleasant, well spoken Miss Knight, a grand-daughter of the founder. I once took in a 12 bore hammer gun of the farmer's to have a new striker made and fitted, collecting it a week or so later. The price? 2s. 6d. (12½p)!

At the bottom of the Dutch Barn at Cockliffe Hill Farm was a strange survivor: A World War 1 German Mauser Sniper's rifle. Rusty but all there though without its telescopic sight. Every year a haystack would be built on top of it!

I was very impressed with the extremely efficient telescopic sight mount: A flat base with oblong slots cut into it. The telescopic sight would have had curved lugs that slid into these slots then locked in place with a spring loaded lever, which was still there. A system that would be hard to beat three quarters of a century later.

Freda had a car 'just for fun' for use round the farm. It was an American car, an Overland Whippet two seater coupé of about 1927 vintage. It had been given to her by Eric Lindley, a Long Eaton garage owner who used to come to shoot on the farm.

In a garage on the farm owned, presumably, by Colonel Seeley was a limousine in what appeared to be excellent original condition. Out of date, of course, but I wonder what became of it? It would have made a rewarding find for a collector.

I would often cycle to nearby Arnold on the main road to Nottingham. On the outskirts of the town were the premises of the Nottingham Velocette dealer, Billy Wing, one of the great characters in the motorcycle world and I was to have the privilege of meeting him many years later.

Parked outside the shop there would usually be a brand new 250cc Velocette two stroke, an unattainable vision in gleaming black and chrome.

I would stop and look at this magnificent machine…..and dream! Wouldn't it be marvellous to own such a magical piece of personal transport!

So another rewarding holiday in entirely different country.

I got a lift back to Rhyl in a 1920's Rolls Royce that Derby garage owner, Sid Cotterill, had bought for a tenner! Sid's wife, Kit, had worked with my mother in the offices at George Fletcher and Co. when they were girls. Sid and family were going on holiday to Rhyl, staying at Stella Maris.

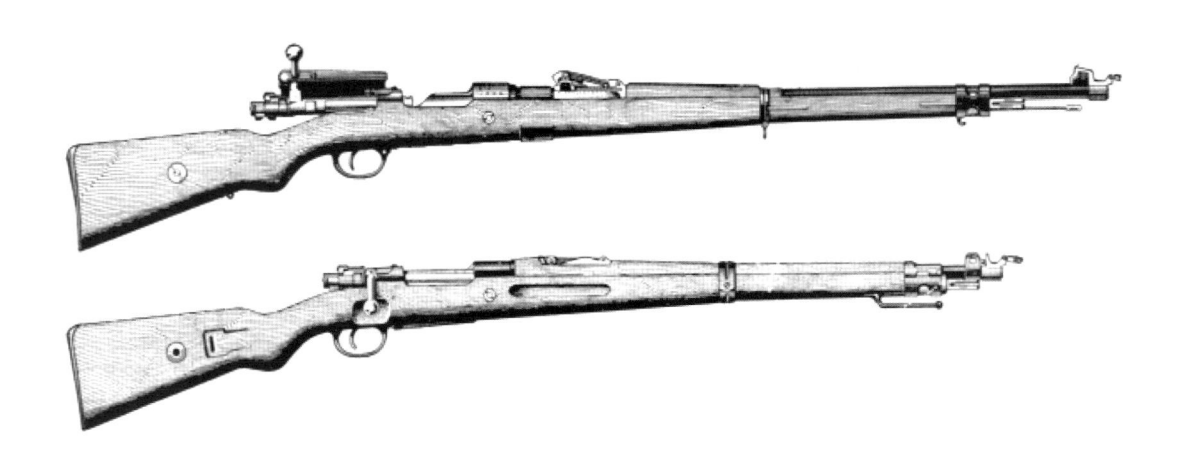

The original 1898 7.92mm military Mauser. Top. Carbine below it. An action still not out of date today. Over sixty variations were made from 1898 to 1945 and they were used in World War One and Two.

In the nineteen seventies Christopher Palmer Tomkinson would climb the Middle Ridge at Deanich Forest with a rope slung over one shoulder and Jim Pilkington's WW1 1898 Mauser Carbine over the other and would always return with a stag.

42 ~ *One Man's Gun Quest*

Stone and railway sleepers in position ready to construct a bridge over the stream to gain access to Ousley Wood.
Mission accomplished! The bridge completed, concrete laid and our Austin A90 Atlantic ready to go.

Chapter Ten
The War Years And Beyond

In 1940 I came to Derby to serve my engineering apprenticeship at George Fletcher and Co., Litchurch Lane. Long hours and hard work in Dickensian conditions producing all kinds of machinery for the War Effort. You can read all about it in my book, *One Man's Motorcycles, 1939-1949.*

Shotguns put away for most of that time though I did occasionally get a shot along the River Trent with Ernie Jackson of Castle Donington, one of the "good guys" of this world. Ernie had married another girlhood friend of my mother's.

A most enjoyable time next at Rolls Royce with a dedicated team of engineers working on aero-engine development until I started in the motorcycle business with my friend, Harry Tunaley after the War.

In the right place at the right time, something that doesn't always happen in life, business flourished.

Married to Edna in 1949 and in 1954 there were three important personal developments for us in the world of guns. The next two are dealt with in the next chapter.

Firstly as we were so busy in business I decided that it would be a good idea to buy a stretch of woodland so that at weekends we could escape for a complete break.

A wealthy dilettante once grumbled, "I hate Wednesday meetings, they ruin two weekends!" Sadly, that didn't apply to us! A weekend meant Sundays as we worked Saturdays.

An advert in the Derby Evening Telegraph brought the offer of several suitable strips of woodland, all around the same price of…..don't laugh….£10 an acre!

We decided on Ousley Wood, Ellastone, about seven miles from Ashbourne on the Derbyshire/ Staffordshire border. The thirty acres cost three hundred pounds. A bargain? You can say that again!

Busting clay pigeons at Ousley Wood, Ellastone.
Caroline and Ross in their replica C type Jaguar by the forester's hut we erected at Ousley Wood.

Ousley Wood was a thirty acre strip of hillside land running for two thirds of a mile along the side of a valley with a stream at the bottom. The woodland followed the Ellastone/Stanton Road for three hundred yards or so then followed the valley as it swung away from the road.

Once part of the estate of the Earls of Shrewsbury but in the nineteen thirties all the trees had been chopped down and the land sold off. We were later to re-plant it but that is going ahead of my story.

For access to the main part of the land we made a bridge of old railway sleepers across the stream where it adjoins the road. We then erected a large wooden shed to house all our tools and tackle. In addition we installed a wood burning stove so that even in winter time we were warm and cosy and could make tea and toast.

Over the years we were to get an enormous amount of enjoyment out of Ousley Wood and we spent almost every weekend there, winter and summer.

The first .22 rifle I bought was a .22 single shot Iver Johnson, an American rifle. This was in 1951. My own .22 at last, a marvellous moment. I bought it from Clement O. Hughes, Ironmonger, of Bodfor Street, Rhyl, North Wales.

This rifle gave me excellent service but when Ousley Wood was purchased in 1954 there were many more opportunities to use a .22 so a better rifle was required.

The choice was a .22 Browning automatic. Strictly speaking, semi-automatic as you just keep pulling the trigger to fire whereas with a true automatic you pull the trigger and the whole magazine is discharged. True automatics are, understandably, not permitted in private hands.

A delightful little rifle to use but somewhat lightweight so I later changed it to a .22 Brno magazine rifle. No complaints about this and there was never any need to change it.

About the same time I joined the Derby Rifle Club so needed a target rifle. At that time quite a few converted Martini's were still in use. They were .450 military Martini Henry rifles converted to .22 for target shooting. I was strongly tempted to buy an excellent example but finally decided on a BSA Model 12 Martini action target rifle, the fore-runner of the BSA 12/15 which was *the* rifle at the time. It, too, was superseded by later designs: Not necessary for me but essential for dedicated target rifle shots.

We laid out an eighty yard range for the modern and muzzle loading rifles and installed a clay pigeon trap. Great fun busting clay pigeons with the muzzle loaders.

When our daughter Caroline was born in 1959 we erected a forester's hut with its integral kitchen and paraffin heating. Electricity was supplied by a

Lucas "Freelight": A propeller driven dynamo at the top of a pole to charge a twelve volt battery.

In 1960 the head forester from the Forestry Commission at nearby Oakamoor came to see us in Derby. "Why don't you start a re-planting scheme?" he asked. "There's money in trees!" He didn't know how true that statement would turn out to be, though it was to be future owners who reaped the real financial benefit, not us!

But, no matter! Over the years we had the enormous benefit of restoring Ousley Wood to its former state, though there were no grants for us in those days.

We commenced by planting a thousand Beech trees in the winter of 1960/61 and through the nineteen sixties we planted over sixty thousand trees. Stopped counting, in fact, at sixty thousand.

We planted a number of species in irregular blocks including Scots Pine, American Red Oak, Lodgepole Pine (which the Indians use to make their wigwams), Thuya Plicata, a lovely tree, Sitka Spruce, European and Japanese Larch, deciduous pine trees with their delightful spring growth, Beech, of course, and others.

We laid out a spectacle shaped scramble course and our friends would come over with their motorcycles to join us in impromptu scrambles…great fun for all. We kept a "resident scrambler" in our shed, a 1954 200cc competition James, which we still have.

In 1964 the old head keeper for the Duncombe Estate died. He lived at Northwood Lodge on the Ellastone/Stanton road. The lodge stood in about an acre and adjoined Ousley Wood at the Ellastone side.

The Duncombe and Shrewsbury Estates had once met at this point but Clive Duncombe had been killed on the Somme in the first World War and the Duncombe Estate had been sold up.

We bought Northwood Lodge for £800 and set about its restoration with great enthusiasm. The facade had been cement rendered over the original stone so our first job was to hack it all off to expose the original stonework. All we would have to do then was to have it all re-pointed……or so we thought!

The reality, however, was very different…. A patchwork quilt of blocked up windows and doors with courses running at all angles, so what to do? We re-faced it in the original stone. The lovely local stone in warm pastel shades that was used to face the new Coventry Cathedral. We succeeded in transforming Northwood Lodge into a delightful modern home with a detached four car garage.

So we had a superb miniature estate and, at a later date, even managed to add the adjoining ten acre Rangemoor Wood to it.

Northwood Lodge, Ellastone after restoration.

48 ~ *One Man's Gun Quest*

Some of the trees we planted at Ousley Wood.
The plaque dedicating the wood to the author's grandmother.

Old friend Lea MacNally, Highland stalker, naturalist, author and wildlife photographer visits us at Ousley Wood.
Lea fires a shot at our eighty yard target.

50~One Man's Gun Quest

Peter and Wendy Dyson in their office and in their showroom with some of the vast collection of antique guns they have for sale.

Chapter Ten
Peter And Wendy Dyson

Peter and his wife Wendy run a highly successful antique gun business at Honley near Huddersfield. Peter was a trained draughtsman but decided to make his hobby his business and started out in the gun trade. He is a highly skilled gunsmith and can tackle any job on antique guns.

They buy and sell antique guns, carry out repairs or restorations of all kinds and, in addition, have developed a whole range of replica accessories for sale from screwdrivers to oil bottles and everything in between. Replica hammers of all kinds are made by the lost wax process. They produce an excellent catalogue showing all their wares, now on the Internet through which much of their business is now done all over the world. In addition they attend many arms shows throughout Europe and America.

Both Peter and Wendy are people of great charm and it is always a pleasure to deal with them: They have done quite a lot of work for me over the years, always to the highest standard. Their son Andrew joined them as an apprentice in the business and under their tutelage I'm sure he will become a worthy successor. Their daughter Carolyn is a partner in a firm of solicitors.

Although their hammers made by the lost wax process are obviously much cheaper than cutting them out from the solid steel blank, Peter is quite capable of doing this work if authenticity demands it.

"A thousand pounds, Peter". That, say Caroline and Ross, is what Peter used to say to me when asked for a quotation to restore an antique gun! And that was twenty years ago! The price for an identical job today would have to be much higher.

One of the first deals I did with Peter in the early days of his business was to sell him a cased S&C Smith single barrel shotgun that had been converted from flintlock. This was a purchase he had to think about for twenty four hours before making a decision. The price? £25! But, remember, this was in the 1960's when prices bore no resemblance to prices today.

Peter and Wendy again with more guns!
Andrew and Wendy with their state-of-the-art computerised lathe.

I have never lost touch with Peter and Wendy and can recommend their work to the most fastidious of antique gun collectors.

We hadn't seen Peter and Wendy for years but in March 2003 we drove over to Honley to renew our acquaintance. Despite being a bit older their appetite for work remains undiminished!

Their shop and premises used to be in Church Street, Honley and they also used to run a gunsmiths business for the public to see at the Royal Armouries, Leeds. Dunblane, however, and the new restrictive legislation it triggered off had a dramatic effect on the gun trade, even the antique gun trade.

For many businesses, trade simply hit the buffers! *Full stop*!

Many were wiped out and even Peter and Wendy were not immune but setbacks, even major ones like this, merely strengthened their determination!

Lateral thinking was called into play: Why not utilise the lower ground floor of their extensive house and run the gun business from there? Not only did this make sense at the time but became even more so as the Internet world wide business developed.

So a major project was started: Workshops, office and showroom all created in the available space and all stock and machinery installed. Their son Andrew, trained by Peter and Wendy, is now a superlative gunsmith in his own right. Not only can he handle every type of work but his speciality is making cased sets of all silver Scottish Flintlock pistols to one third scale. Cost about £4,500 for these unique creations and he has orders for years ahead.

They have installed a computer-operated lathe which Andrew demonstrated to us: He was making flintlock top jaw screws and the computer was handling it all, calling for new tools as required: Amazing!

"But how long does it take to set up a programme on the computer?" we asked. "As little as ten minutes" he replied. He then proceeded to demonstrate and set up a complex shape on the computer screen in a matter of minutes. The lathe could then have been instructed to make it. Space age technology!

The workshop is well equipped with lathes, milling machines etc. to tackle any job.

Pleasant office next, then the showroom with its racks of antique guns: I could have spent days in there examining guns of every type. Time was limited, however, so I had to be content with saying "What's this…and this….and this?" Guns and actions entirely new to me.

In the days of caplock muzzle loaders the hammer rested on the nipple and the gun was perfectly safe until a percussion cap was put on the nipple when the gun was put onto half cock. With the advent of breech loading and before rebounding locks where the hammer bounces back to ensure that the firing pin is safely clear of the cartridge, the only solution was to put the gun onto half cock. Time consuming in the case of a double gun.

Peter reached down a gun that had caught my eye: It had a short lever sticking out from the left hand side of the action. Depress the lever and both hammers shot back clear of the cartridges. An ingenious Needham patent that did the job well enough but was soon obsolete with the advent of the rebounding lock. All new to me and something I had never seen before.

Andrew and his wife Marilyn have a lovely little girl, Lydia, then a year old and Marilyn helps in the business part time. Peter and Wendy are, understandably, excited new grandparents. We were able to explain that had we known grandchildren were such fun we would have had them first! Not much I could tell Peter and Wendy but having had a lovely daughter-in-law much longer than them I was able to offer some advice: "Never get into arguments with your daughter-in-law about religion, money or politics!" This applies equally to sons-in-law!

The hours raced by and we had to leave but very much look forward to our next visit.

Andrew sets up his automatic lathe.

Peter operates his milling machine.
Peter's assistant files up a brand new Damascus barrel, one of a batch that Peter and Wendy commissioned.

Half a century ago, back in 1954, I bought my first Joe Manton. A 14-bore percussion double, with the Holles Street, Cavendish Square address. One of the last Joe Mantons made.

Chapter Eleven
Mountains And Mantons

The second important event for us in 1954 was the purchase of *With a Gun to the Hill* by Stephen Pilkington. This was an account of his stalking days through the Highlands of Scotland with his brother Jim, during the nineteen twenties and thirties.

Little did I know then that I would go on to stalk on many of the forests mentioned in the book and meet many of the *dramatis personae*, but it fired me with the determination to go to Scotland and start stalking.

Edna, however, was far from convinced! Wasn't it cold in Scotland? Surely not a holiday destination?

But she was eventually won over and consented to £16.10s (£16.50p) being expended on the purchase of a new .303 BSA rifle, built on the superb ex-German Army 1898 Mauser action… The same action as used on the incomparable handmade David Lloyd rifles at a later date.

So in 1954 we headed for Scotland at last to start an affinity with the Highlands, and Highlanders, that has never faded. You can read all about it in my previous book *One Man's Scotland*.

The third important development for me in the world of guns in 1954 was the purchase of my first Joseph Manton. This started me on getting together a worth-while collection of Joseph and John Manton guns and rifles over the next forty years or so.

That first Joseph Manton, a 14 bore double caplock muzzle-loader, was purchased from Michael Weaving of Holly Cottage, Ayot St. Peter, Welwyn, Herts., one of the many "remarkable" characters I was to encounter in the world of guns.

So let's devote a few words to Michael Weaving.

Strangely enough, although we corresponded for years, I never met Michael Weaving. Over the years I bought several Mantons from him and he restored a number for me.

Michael was a bachelor who lived with his mother at Holly Cottage and when I first got in touch with him in 1954 he worked for Bowater in London.

He was enormously knowledgeable about antique guns in general and Mantons and Purdeys in particular. In those days no book had been written specifically about Mantons and very little was generally known about them. Piecing together information about them was a very difficult task indeed.

Michael and I would pick up snippets of information from wherever we could and fit them together like the pieces of a jigsaw puzzle. During the nineteen fifties I would have thought that with the exception of the great collector of English guns and rifles, W. Keith Neal, no-one had got together more information on Mantons as Michael and I. Unless, of course, you know different!

Michael, then, was always at hand with advice, information and practical help. He was a very competent amateur gunsmith who, over the years, carried out quite a lot of work for me, always to the very highest standard.

On a part-time basis he bought and sold antique guns, specialising in Mantons and Purdeys. Modern Purdeys, too, were a great interest of his and he also bought and sold them. In the process he got to know the people at Purdeys quite well.

When David Back, assisted by W. Keith Neal, decided in the late 1950's to write a definitive book on Joseph and John Manton he appealed for information and I gladly handed over to him the results of all our research.

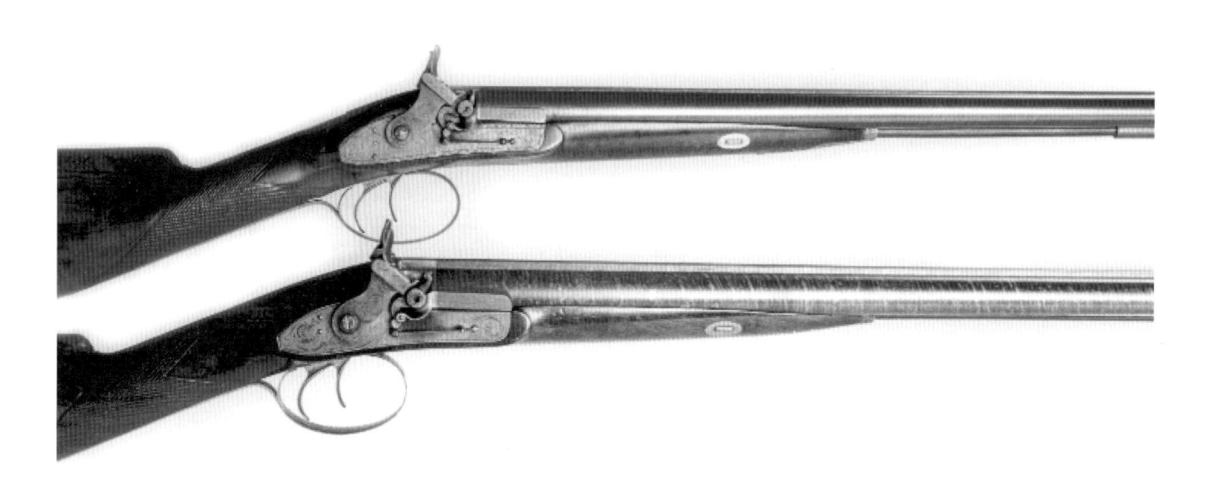

Two tubelock Joe Mantons.

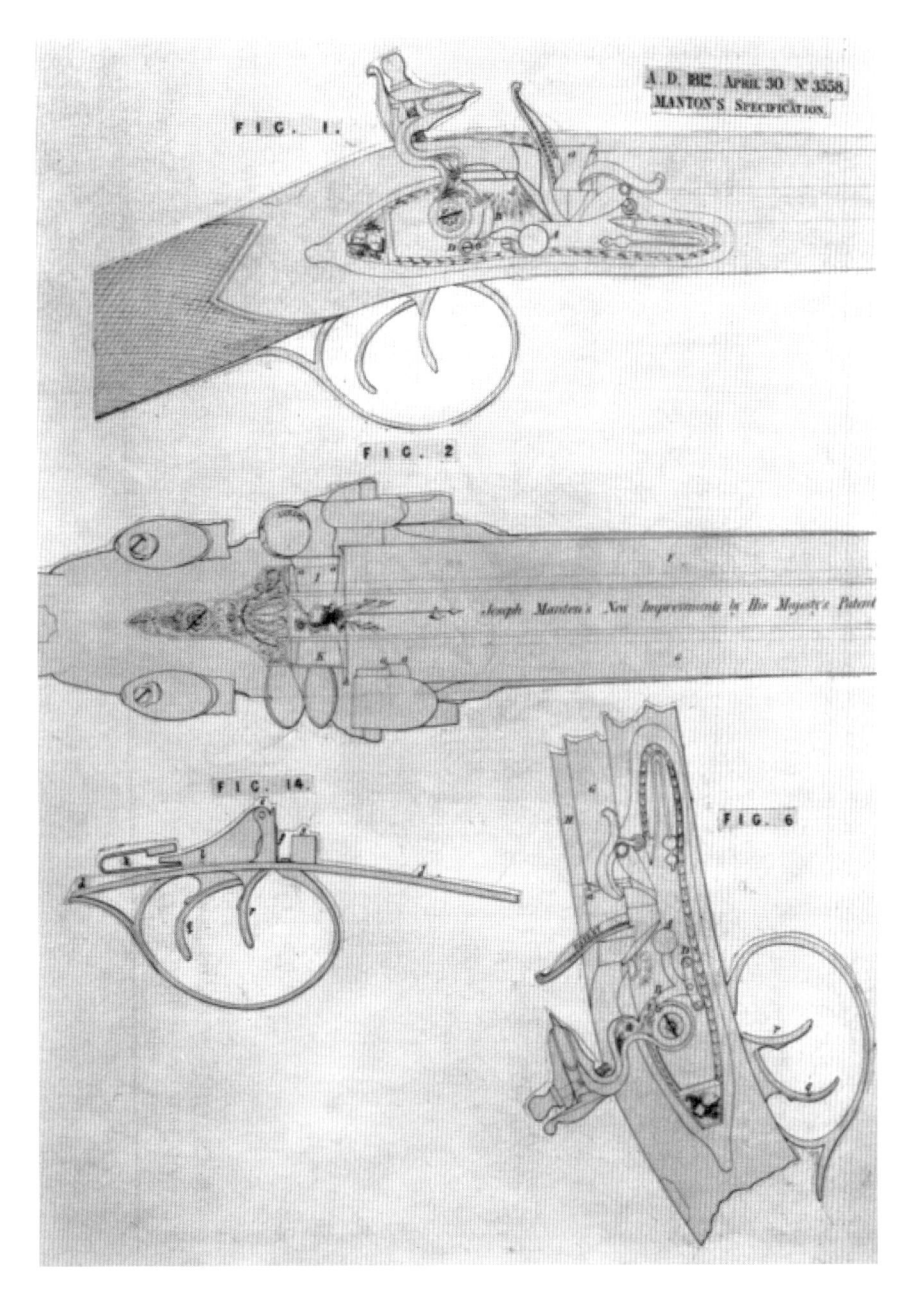

Timeless elegance. The last word in flint-lock design. Details from Joseph Manton's patent specification of 1812 showing the recessed breeches, elevating rib and gravitating stop. When the gun was held vertical for loading, the weight of the "stop" gravitates down to allow the other end to engage the notch in the hammer, so the hammer could not accidentally fall during reloading.

Joseph Manton, firearms genius. By kind permission of the Mitchell Library, Sydney, Australia.

Chapter Thirteen
Joseph and John Manton

When muzzle loading gun collectors talk about Mantons they mean Joseph Manton and his elder brother John.

They were both from a Grantham family and both served their apprenticeships in Grantham.

John Manton was born in 1752 and moved to London in the 1770's to work for the famous gunsmith Twigg of Piccadilly where he eventually became foreman. In 1781 he started his own business at 6, Dover Street and the business continued there until it closed in 1878. About 1815 he took his son, John Henry into partnership and from then on, even after his death in 1834, the business continued to be named John Manton & Son. About 1868, foreman, Charles Coe was taken into partnership and from then on the title changed to John Manton Son & Coe.

So the business continued right through from the days of flintlock ignition to breech loading.

Younger brother Joseph, achieved pre-eminence at a time when London was blessed with some of the world's finest gunsmiths.

Joseph Manton was born in 1766 and after his apprenticeship in Grantham he moved to London about 1784 to join his brother John as an apprentice. About 1790 he started In business on his own, at first experimenting with rifled cannon, hoping to get the government interested, but without success. He was soon, however, making fine sporting guns, rifles and pistols at Davis Street and on his way to becoming the most celebrated gunmaker in London. So how did he do it? And what made his guns superior to those of his contemporaries? There were several reasons, but let's start with the patent breech.

Look at the long barrels of the guns of the 18th Century and before. This was because a long barrel was necessary to enable the powder charge to burn fully.

The patent breech was a narrow anti-chamber ignited via the flintlock touch-hole. This drove a tongue of flame through the main powder charge, creating vastly improved ignition and allowed much shorter barrels to be used. Joe Manton did not invent the patent breech, but developed it to perfection.

In addition to speeding up ignition and reducing the time from pulling the trigger to firing the charge, Joe Manton cut down the width of the breech. Going even further than that he ensured that the flint dipped as deeply as possible into the pan.

But his masterstroke was the "Elevating Rib", the raised rib between the barrels of a side by side double that provided a much more effective sighting plane. Before the "Elevating Rib", the barrels of side by side doubles were simply soldered together but when you look along the raised rib of your modern, side by side double, remember you have Joe Manton to thank.

Most important of all was that the gun was created to the very highest standards of workmanship.

All these improvements meant that the Joe Manton flintlock at the peak of it's development meant that the "lines" and proportions of the gun had reached the ideal. Joe, had, in fact, created the proportions of the double gun we use today even down to similar barrel lengths. With a Joe Manton D.B. flintlock in your hands, you could outshoot all the opposition and his inventive genius has endured for two centuries.

Having achieved the ultimate flintlock design, Joseph Manton did not rest on his laurels. As new ideas came along, percussion ignition, for example, he saw the way in which development would have to proceed and move forward. Sadly his vision leapt ahead more rapidly than that of many of his customers!

Always looking ahead he realised that the proposed new percussion system, pioneered by Forsyth, would make flintlocks obsolete so despite having brought the flintlock system to the peak of perfection he devoted his energies to the development of percussion guns.

The Forsyth system relied on loose percussion powder so he looked at how this could be improved. The answer was his new pelletlock: Which he introduced in 1816. A percussion pellet was put into a striker that was snapped into the hammer nose. After the gun was fired a twist of the thumb and forefinger quickly extracted the striker and a replacement striker was simply snapped into place. Loaded strikers, ready to use, were kept in containers in the shooter's pocket.

The importance of the Joseph Manton pelletlock has been greatly underestimated by firearms historians and has often been condemned as a failure. But it was *not* a failure and worked very well indeed.

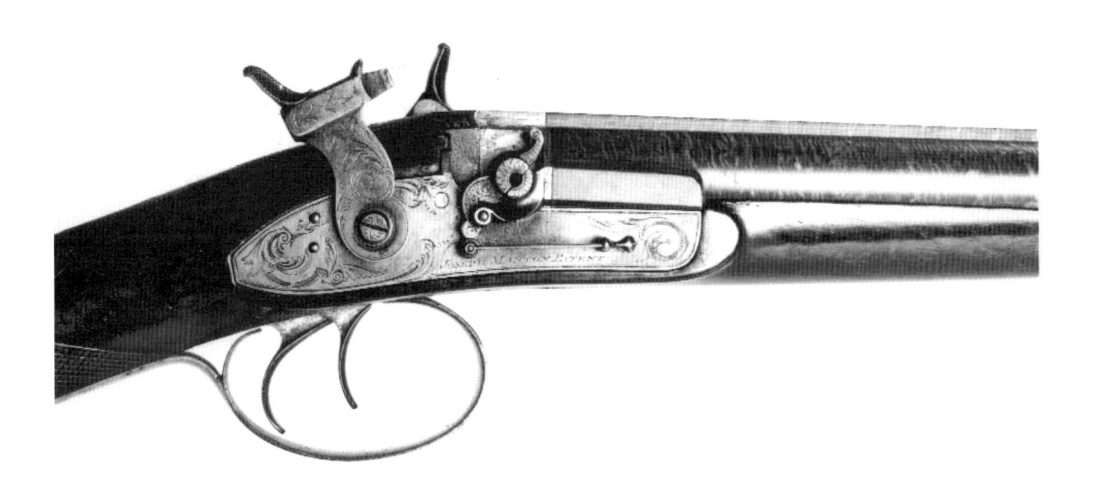

The Joseph Manton tubelock.

The great firearms historian, W. Keith Neal, has fired them without trouble and so have I. The strikers, of course, had to be kept clean and cleaned after use but it was a great step forward after the loose powder detonators.

Two years later, in 1818, Joseph Manton took a step further with the invention of the tubelock which was a great success and continued for many years, even alongside the copper cap. It was the success of the tubelock, so shortly after the pelletlock, that mistakenly branded the pelletlock as a failure.

His thinking was absolutely correct but there were two major snags: Firstly many of his customers were far less forward looking than Joe Manton and secondly he was entering a legal minefield as Forsyth considered that his patent covered any and every type of percussion gun. Putting his faith into the new percussion system, then, was a financial disaster from which he never recovered and led to bankruptcy in 1826.

About 1820 he moved to Hanover Square, in about 1828 to Mary-Le-Bone Park House, New Road, London and in 1834 to 6 Holles Street, Cavendish Square under the new name "Joseph Manton and Son". Joe Manton died in 1835 and the business struggled on under his son, John Augustus Manton until December 1838. The business was then sold to Charles and Henry Egg who then advertised as "Successors to J.Manton and Son". A very confusing title when you consider John Manton and Son!

Both brothers made fine guns, rifles and pistols but you cannot lump the work of Joseph and John Manton together and consider it to be all the same as it certainly was not! Now, however, I am going to set the record straight: Joseph, in his era, was considered to be *the* finest gunmaker of all *and with good reason.* Not only was his workmanship of the very finest, arguably *the* finest, but his flintlocks fired faster than all the others. With a Joe Manton in your hands you could outshoot all the others.

Without doubt, one of the greatest inventive geniuses in the world of guns.

When he made the change to percussion, the tradition of superlative workmanship continued unchanged.

I was once told of a cased pair of John Manton muzzle loading guns in the possession of an antique dealer in the south of England. I rang him up about them only to be told that they were definitely not for sale and, in any case, were beyond restoration.

Years later Peter Smith, of Brailsford Derbyshire, turned up with them for sale! Yes, they were in poor condition as they had obviously been stored in a damp attic or cellar but beyond restoration? Surely not. A first class antique gunsmith could make a good job of them...at a price!

This pair of 14 bore percussion doubles were in their original mahogany double case complete with trade label and the case had survived remarkably well. There was a ducal crest on the case escutcheon and on the silver escutcheons on the small of the stocks. Both guns had grip safeties.

They were numbers 11901 and 11902, made in about 1847 for Lord Cawdor, descendant of MacBeth who was, you will remember, the Thane of Cawdor so the opportunity to buy them could not be missed.

Now forgive me if I divert for a moment. When you next drive north from Perth on the A9, about ten miles on you will see on the right hand side a sign to Birnham where MacBeth fought his fatal battle with MacDuff. The three witches had said to MacBeth:

*"MacBeth shall never vanquished be until
Great Birnham Wood to high Dunsinane hill
Shall come against him."*

MacBeth, then, should have been safe enough but MacDuff had ordered his army to cut branches from the wood to hold over their heads as camouflage on their march so, in effect, Birnham Wood *did* move to Dunsinane.

Too busy racing north to visit Birnham? Don't worry. Because a few miles beforehand you will have stopped at The Macbeth Centre at Bankfoot where you can enjoy the Macbeth Experience, look round their extensive gift shop and enjoy a meal or snack at their excellent coffee shop. We always stop there on our drive north.

Just past the Birnham sign you will see a tiny Highland railway station looking much the same as it did a hundred and fifty years ago. Long may this unique survival endure.

Just past that, on the left, you will see a sign to Grandtully: It was on Grandtully Moor that the legendary Marharajah Duleep Singh made the biggest bag of walked up (not driven) grouse shot in a day. This record still stands.

A bit further on……….I could go on, but you know that Scotland is steeped in history and legend.

Back to the Lord Cawdor Mantons!

The man to tackle such a massive restoration was Peter Dyson of Honley. Nothing daunted he set to work and did a magnificent job making an excellent cased set. Not cheap, of course, but worth every penny.

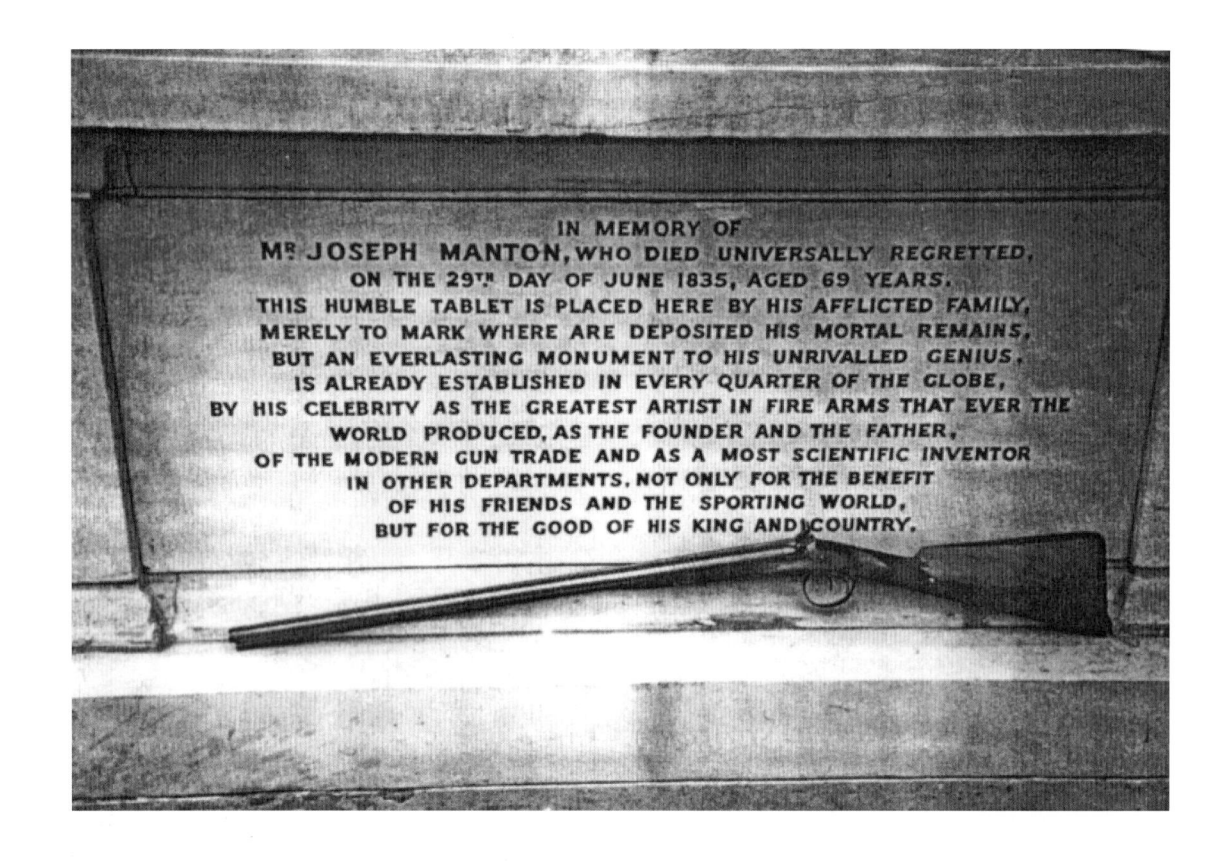

IN MEMORY OF
M**R** JOSEPH MANTON, WHO DIED UNIVERSALLY REGRETTED,
ON THE 29TH DAY OF JUNE 1835, AGED 69 YEARS.
THIS HUMBLE TABLET IS PLACED HERE BY HIS AFFLICTED FAMILY,
MERELY TO MARK WHERE ARE DEPOSITED HIS MORTAL REMAINS,
BUT AN EVERLASTING MONUMENT TO HIS UNRIVALLED GENIUS,
IS ALREADY ESTABLISHED IN EVERY QUARTER OF THE GLOBE,
BY HIS CELEBRITY AS THE GREATEST ARTIST IN FIRE ARMS THAT EVER THE
WORLD PRODUCED, AS THE FOUNDER AND THE FATHER,
OF THE MODERN GUN TRADE AND AS A MOST SCIENTIFIC INVENTOR
IN OTHER DEPARTMENTS, NOT ONLY FOR THE BENEFIT
OF HIS FRIENDS AND THE SPORTING WORLD,
BUT FOR THE GOOD OF HIS KING AND COUNTRY.

The tomb of Joseph Manton in Kensal Green Cemetery, West London. Restored by the staff of Holland and Holland in 1995.

Chapter Fourteen
Robert Held, Firearms Historian

Robert Held in his magnificent book *The Age of Firearms*, 1957, wrote:

"It is generally agreed that Joseph Manton was not only a worker who rose above the standards of his London colleagues, themselves towering above any other in the world, but that he has rarely been equalled and never surpassed in the 122 years since his death in 1835. To this the present author subscribes, with the qualification that Manton was *almost* equalled by a few of his contemporaries - perhaps eight or ten - and by fewer still in the succeeding century and a quarter".

He goes on to record the immensely high regard in which Joe Manton was held by one of the most famous shots of the era, Colonel Peter Hawker, author of *Instructions to Young Sportsmen In All That Pertains To Guns And Shooting*. This famous book was first published in 1814 and went on to many subsequent editions. Republished again by Eric Parker in the nineteen twenties.

Robert Held goes on to write:

"The most objective contemporary view was published by Thomas Johnson in *The Shooter's Guide* of 1816, a man who was not at all a fanatic gun enthusiast and for whom shooting was only one occupation in the busy week of a moderately wealthy squire:

"As to who is the best gunsmith, it is a question, if an individual must be selected, of no easy solution. There are many country gunsmiths who make excellent fowling pieces, but the London guns are certainly turned out in the neatest manner. Manton has obtained the highest celebrity, and justly merits much of the praise bestowed upon him; but to rank him as the very pinnacle of excellence, unattainable by any other person, which has been attempted, is going too far. By this I would not be understood to be decrying the work of Manton; on the contrary, I am willing to give him his due share of praise. Assuredly, he has acquired a name of the importance of which he seems to be fully aware, for it brings him much business and enables him to charge a higher price than his fellow-labourers. However, it is not always to the name merely that merit attaches, nor should I be willing to give an extra ten guineas for that alone. *Mortimer* sounds just as well in my ears as *Manton*; *Knox* as Mortimer;

Gulley as Knox; Parker as Gulley; Stephens successor to Clark as Parker. These are all esteemed manufacturers and have alike sent forth guns of first-rate excellence".

There are important points to reflect upon in this contemporary quotation: First you will note that by "Manton" he means Joseph Manton. Secondly, John Manton fails to be included in the five named competitors.

Remember, too, that if a gun was selected from any of the five competitors named, the Joe Manton flintlock breech would outshoot them all.

Robert Held goes on to say :

"But it must be remembered that in addition to the five competitors named, there have never been more than half a dozen gunsmiths to equal Manton; and in the opinion of the present author no one has ever really *quite* equalled him for precision of parts and elegance of finish……….. Manton seems to have been a slave to the obsession that he must convert raw steel and iron into a degree of precision hitherto unknown, not because it would serve any further practical purpose once the optimum had been passed, but because the goal of absolute precision, like an unclimbed mountain to others, was simply *there*. Long after he had gotten rich, old and famous, he worked molelike through the night to polish away at parts which his employees - all master craftsmen - had put aside as finished".

So there you have it! The opinion of an expert in the field of antique guns and, needless to say, I am in agreement.

I do disagree, however, with Robert Held on one point: He felt that Joe Manton had missed the opportunity to use more imaginative engraving, but that is not the English way: The restrained style has continued on the finest English guns to the present day and Joe got it absolutely right two centuries ago.

In muzzle loading days pistols were usually made in pairs but for game shooting "walking up" was the way pheasants were shot rather than driven so pairs were not necessary. Pairs of muzzle loading shotguns, then, are comparatively rare.

These guns are a pair of 14 bore John Manton muzzle loaders with grip safeties made for Lord Cawdor about 1847. You will remember that the original Thane (lord) of Cawdor was Macbeth.

Badly neglected when purchased by the author but still in their original double case. Beautifully restored and case re-lined by Peter and Wendy Dyson of Honley, Yorkshire.

Joseph Manton invented the tubelock but this is one of the few tubelocks made by brother John.

Three John Manton rifles. The bottom one was made for the Duke of Hamilton.

Early SB flintlock Joseph Manton.
John Manton "Baker" military flintlock rifle made for Lieutenant Alan MacNab of the Queen's American Rangers.
Joseph Manton DB flintlock.

DB Lewis and Tomes loose powder detonator.
DB Forsyth roller primer loose powder detonator.
Joseph Manton DB percussion converted from flintlock.

One Man's Gun Quest ~ 73

1816 Joseph Manton pelletlock.
1818 Joseph Manton tubelock.
1812 Pauly. *The first gun to fire a cartridge with its own percussion system.*

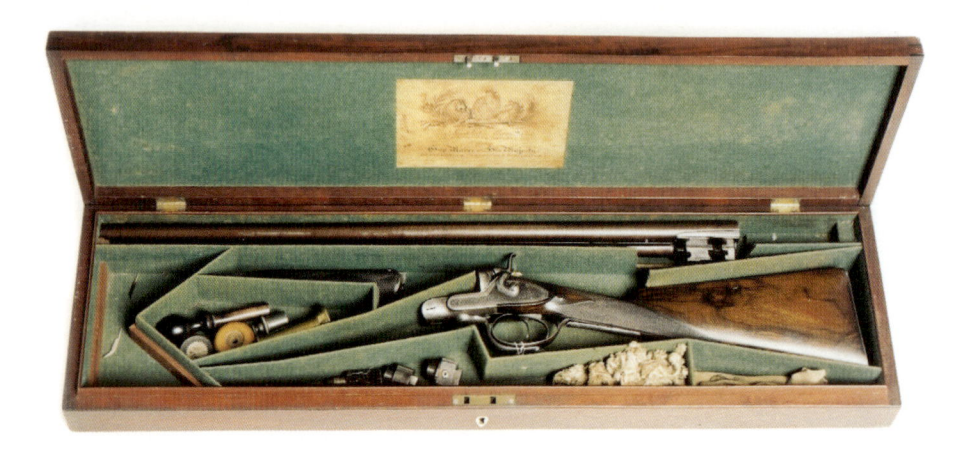

D.B. Joseph Manton made for the great 19th Century Prime Minister Lord Palmerston. Originally flintlock, now underlever centrefire.
Cased DB Joseph Manton. Originally tubelock, now underlever centrefire.

Pair of John Manton D.B. percussion guns made for Lord Cawdor in the 1840's
Pair of Purdey S.B. .400 percussion rifles. Stocks in bottom of case.
Same pair. Barrels in top of case.

S.B. Joseph Manton percussion rifle.
D.B. percussion Joseph Manton with the rare Oxford Street address. Made in 1826 for the Dakins family of Derbyshire.
Joseph Whitworth .451 Target rifle with hexagonal bore.

Austrian D.B. 16 bore made for the Emperor Franz Joseph of Austria.
Purdey D.B. beautifully engraved and gold inlaid. (owner unknown)
Purdey D.B. .450 Black Powder Express restored by Derek Fearn after a 100 year sleep.

For the man who had everything! Cased .500 falling block Black Powder Express with every possible accessory made by the great Alexander Henry for JCL Kay of the 15th Kings Hussars. Shooting the Black Powder Expresses at Deanich Lodge, August 2003. Grandson Adam fires the .400 Holland and Holland, the .450 Purdey is in front of it. Grandson Clive holds his ears, stalker Marcus Munro on left, his assistant spies, daughter Caroline takes photographs.

Chapter Fifteen
Biggles

What the devil has Biggles got to do with a book on antique guns?" I hear you ask. Patience: All will be revealed!

When I was a boy I loved to read about the exploits of Biggles in *The Modern Boy* price twopence, weekly. Biggles flew his Sopwith Camel, armed with its twin Vickers guns, through the war-torn skies of the Western Front in World War One.

This stimulated an interest in World War One aviation that has never waned: The amazing development of the aircraft, stimulated by the urgent necessities of war and the even more amazing pilots who flew them.

The Biggles books were written by Captain W.E. Johns who flew on the Western Front. In his squadron was a Derby man named Wigglesworth, always shortened to Wiggles: Hence the inspiration for the fictional Bigglesworth.

Over the years I have built up a reasonable collection of books on this fascinating subject, including many of the classics printed in the nineteen thirties.

A local man, named Douglas Whetton, had devoted his life to the study of World War One aviation. He had written extensively on the subject, contributing many articles to magazines. He had compiled dossiers on many of the greatest pilots, putting together information gleaned from all possible sources.

The results of his researches were often at variance with accepted wisdom but as he had studied the subject in such great depth, he was probably right! Mick Mannock, the highest scoring British World War One pilot was officially credited with 72 victories. Douglas, however, calculated that the correct score should have been 52½.

How exactly Douglas earned a crust I have no idea as, as far as I could see, all his time was taken up with the study of his chosen subject. I only met him once, when he was about fifty years of age. He lived in a 1930's semi-detached house with his elderly mother at Littleover on the outskirts of Derby.

Chatting to him at his home I found him to be a fascinating character, immensely knowledgeable on all aspects of World War One aviation. He had amassed a huge collection of books on the subject including all the rarities. The small box room in the house was crammed from floor to ceiling with aviation books. Among the rarities he showed me a signed copy of Eddie Rickenbackers book, the highest scoring American pilot, written in the early 1920's.

Now the old journalistic dictum says "Dog bites man, that's not news. Man bites dog, that's news."

The same reasoning must, surely, apply to foxes! Man kills fox, that's not news but Douglas was killed by a fox!

Not long after I met Douglas he was driving home towards Derby northwards on the A38. It was winter time and the road was snow covered. Near the old Burnaston airport where the new Toyota factory is now, a fox darted across the road in front of the car. The car hit the fox which jammed the steering gear….. The car crashed and Douglas was killed.

Shortly afterwards Edna was at the hairdressers and she heard the lady in the next chair discussing Douglas Whetton. She lived next door and she was saying that Douglas' mother was arranging to sell his aviation books. Naturally Edna was very interested and obtained Douglas mother's address and I went to see her.

I have spent a lifetime in business and have always held onto the resolution "Never tell a lie when trying to buy or sell." It is not your brief to tell the customer *all* you know but untruths are quite unacceptable. In any event, tell a lie and it will inevitably come back like a boomerang and slap you in the back of the neck! You can read more about my philosophy in *One Man's Motorcycles.*

A book dealer had offered £3,000 for the collection but, up to then, no final decision had been made so I offered a little more. I explained my long term interest in the subject, pointed out that I had met Douglas and said that Douglas, as a Derbyshire man, would have far preferred to have his books kept together by a fellow enthusiast in Derbyshire.

I pointed out that I wanted the books to keep, not to sell. All compelling reasons, or so I thought!

So did I get the books? No!

The book dealer came again to see Douglas' mum. The books, he said would be housed in a beautiful library in a lovely Cotswolds manor house. Book lovers from all over the world would come into these elegant surroundings to admire and handle Douglas' books.

He got the lot!

But, you will note, no lies were told. It was not up to him to emphasise that the object of the exercise was to sell the books! So, unfortunately, I lost out!

On one occasion, however, I almost acquired a gun that had a compelling connection with World War One aviation history.

One of all the greatest German aces in the early part of World War One was Max Immelmann whose name will always be remembered by the Immelmann turn. He would start his plane into a loop and at the summit of the loop he would put the plane into a roll and fly in the opposite direction.

Before he became a pilot he flew as an observer on the Russian Front and in those early days the observer had no machine gun so he armed himself with a Mauser automatic pistol fitted with a shoulder stock which saw action against Russian machines.

About thirty five years ago this important historic pistol came up for auction engraved with Immellmann's name and it was estimated that a bid of over £1,000 would have to be made to secure it. A lot of money!

But it combined two of my interests.....antique guns and World War One aviation so I thought long and hard. Eventually, however, I felt that I could not justify spending that kind of money so I never did put in a bid.

A year or two later I met the gunsmith Kit Ravenshear who not only knew about the Immelmann Mauser but he had been in the workshop when Immelmann's name was being engraved on it! A lucky escape!

The 1914 Luger automatic pistol with detachable shoulder stock. An additional circular magazine could be attached. Not unlike the Immelmann Mauser.

The Allied answer to the Fokker was a B.S.A. manufactured Lewis Gun mounted on the top plane and firing over the propeller arc.
The Sopwith Camel with its twin Vickers machine guns. The most successful Allied fighter of the War.

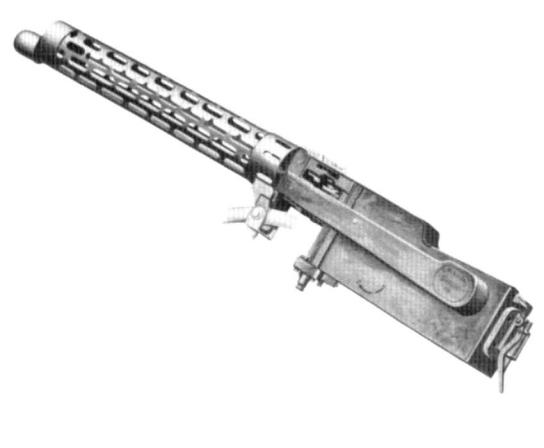

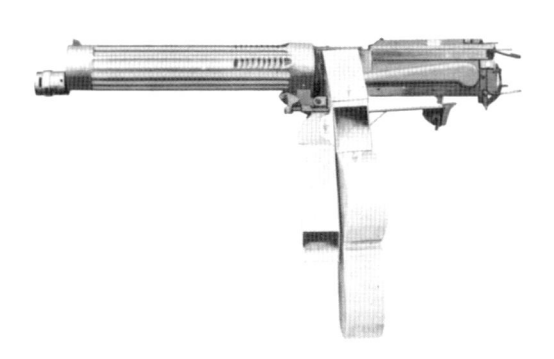

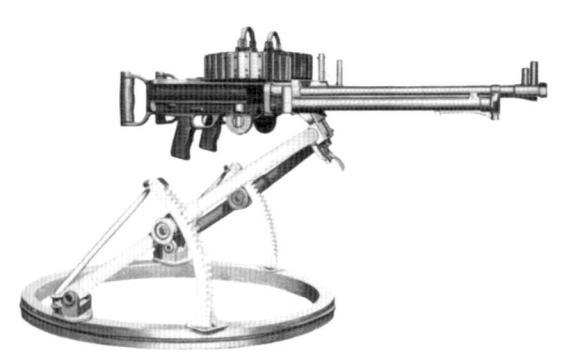

Lieutenant Max Immelmann, whose Fokker "Eindekker" (monoplane) with its synchronised Spandau machine gun firing through the propeller blazed a deadly trail through the skies over the Western front in 1916.
Spandau 7.92 mm machine gun.
Vickers .303 machine gun.
Twin Lewis guns on a Scarf mount.

A hare with her leverets.

Chapter Sixteen
Hares And Henry Bestwick

Fascinating creatures, hares. Lovely animals and over the centuries the subject of folklore and superstition. It was considered unlucky for a hare to cross your path because witches were thought to transform themselves into hares. In *Flamborough Village* and Headland it states that "if a fisherman on his way to the boats happens to meet a woman, parson, or hare, he will turn back, being convinced that he will have no luck that day."

It was once thought that hares changed their sex every year.

"Hold with the hare and run with the hounds" i.e. to support, or pretend to support, both sides. A phrase by no means out of date today!

"Mad as a March hare" due to their habit of standing on their hind legs and "boxing" during their mating season in March.

There is much more on the same lines but I must correct one misconception: Mrs Glasse, the pen name of Doctor John Hill 1716-1775 wrote the *Cookery Book* and it is believed that she gave the instruction "first catch your hare", but this is not correct: The exact words were "take your hare when it is cased, and make a pudding……" "To case" did not mean to catch but "to skin".

Stephen Pilkington in his book, *With a Gun to the Hill* writing about shooting hares claimed that the only satisfactory way to shoot them was with a rifle, not a shotgun and I agree entirely. Though, come to think of it, I never liked shooting them anyway! We have a small resident stock of hares at Newton Park Farm though none are ever shot either with gun or rifle.

This discussion on hares brings me to another remarkable character, Henry Bestwick. Henry is a Derbyshire man who served in the Royal Navy in the Second World War. He is a tall man, fit as the proverbial fiddle and blessed with enormous charm. Henry, like my brother Brian, was at Mulberry Harbour a few days after D. Day facing German bombs and machine gun bullets and, on one occasion, not quite quick enough to get out of the way! Fortunately, however, he survived.

Henry comes from Chapel-en-le-Frith and one of his first jobs was as a signalman on the railway in North Derbyshire. His signal box was in an idyllic situation close to a trout stream. His colleague had a trombone action .22 Winchester rifle similar to those you used to see on every fairground shooting range and during their lunch breaks they used to bag rabbits for their evening meals with a hare as an occasional bonus. Trout, too, were caught in the stream.

Although the situation was idyllic, the wages were not and eventually Henry became a barber working in Derby.

One day Henry told me a strange story: He had been to visit his mother at Chapel-en-le-Frith and was driving back to Derby on the A515 Buxton to Ashbourne road. This is a lovely run with marvellous views over the limestone walled fields whose wide open spaces are ideal for hares. If you are ever in the area on a sunny day, do take the opportunity of driving along that road. Southwards gives the best views with the landscape opening out before you. Don't forget to stop at the quaintly named Bull i' th' Thorn Inn for coffee or lunch.

Swooping down one of the long descents a hare darted out across the road and before Henry could apply the brakes the car struck the hare and killed it. Henry stopped the car, checked the dead hare and, rather than waste it, put it in the car boot.

Just as he was closing the boot a van pulled up behind him and the driver got out. "Was that a hare you were putting in the boot?" he asked. Henry confirmed that it was and explained how the hare had darted in front of his car before he was able to stop.

"I'm from the RSPCA" said the man "would you mind if I had a look at the hare?"

"Of course not." said Henry and opened the boot.

The RSPCA inspector looked carefully at the hare which was obviously as dead as the proverbial doornail then said to Henry "Just a moment!". He returned to his van and came back with a small attaché case. From the case he took a syringe, injected the hare and a few moments later the hare opened its eyes, shook itself, leapt out of the car boot and went bounding away over the fields.

Henry was astounded! "Look" he said, I know that hare was stone dead. whatever was in that syringe?"

The man snapped his attaché case closed, turned to Henry with a smile and replied "Hare restorer!"

Hares boxing.

Guernsey (0481) 64833
La Terre Norgiot,
St. Saviour's,
Guernsey,
Channel Islands.

26th March 79

Dear Mr. McManus,

I was glad to have your letter & take this opportunity of thanking you for the help you have given us in supplying details for our Manton books.

It would be a pleasure to meet you. I come to Derbyshire occasionally — & I would be glad to show you my Mantons if you care to visit Guernsey. I will have a look through & see what I can find & write again.

I can spare you an original 1816 pattern full lock two piece striker — as I have a supply in my set of Joe Manton parts. Whether I can find a hammer to go with it I cannot yet say.

Meanwhile — this is just a hurried acknowledgement of your kind letter.

Yours sincerely,

W Keith Neal

Letter from W. Keith Neal.

Chapter Seventeen
W. Keith Neal

The greatest private collector of fine English guns, rifles and pistols of all time was W. Keith Neal. He had the largest collection of Mantons in the world, about a hundred of them.

The time finally arrived when I had arranged to go over to Guernsey to meet the great man. Driving to his house, La Terre Norgiot, we followed the instructions but eventually lost our way so I stopped and asked a local farmer if he would be kind enough to direct us. He pointed out the correct route and said "When you get there you will find him dozing in his armchair with an antique gun on his knees."

W. Keith Neal was enormously knowledgeable and there was so much to discuss. Naturally I started out by asking him about his unique Manton collection and was amazed to discover that although he was, of course, very interested in Mantons they were not his greatest interest.

I asked him what his greatest interest was in the world of antique guns and he told me that it was Queen Anne flintlock pistols. He showed me one that his wife had given to him on the occasion of their wedding.

But his Manton collection was simply incredible. Not only had he a vast number but he had acquired almost all the rarest and most famous ones.

Peter Hawker's 14 bore Joe Manton Dandy Joe and his huge duck gun Big Joe. The pair of John Manton rifled flintlock pistols with which Horatio Ross had shot 10 brace of flying swallows at his home, Rossie Castle before breakfast and much more.

All the rarities were there, too: Joseph Manton flintlocks, pelletlocks, patchlocks, tubelocks and even a Joe Manton pistol in which the charge was ignited by compressed air!

The barn in the grounds of W. Keith Neal's Guernsey property, had been adapted to house his incredible collection. The interior was wood panelled and around the walls cased guns were piled up about four feet or so high. Above them racks ran right round the room housing unbroken rows of guns.

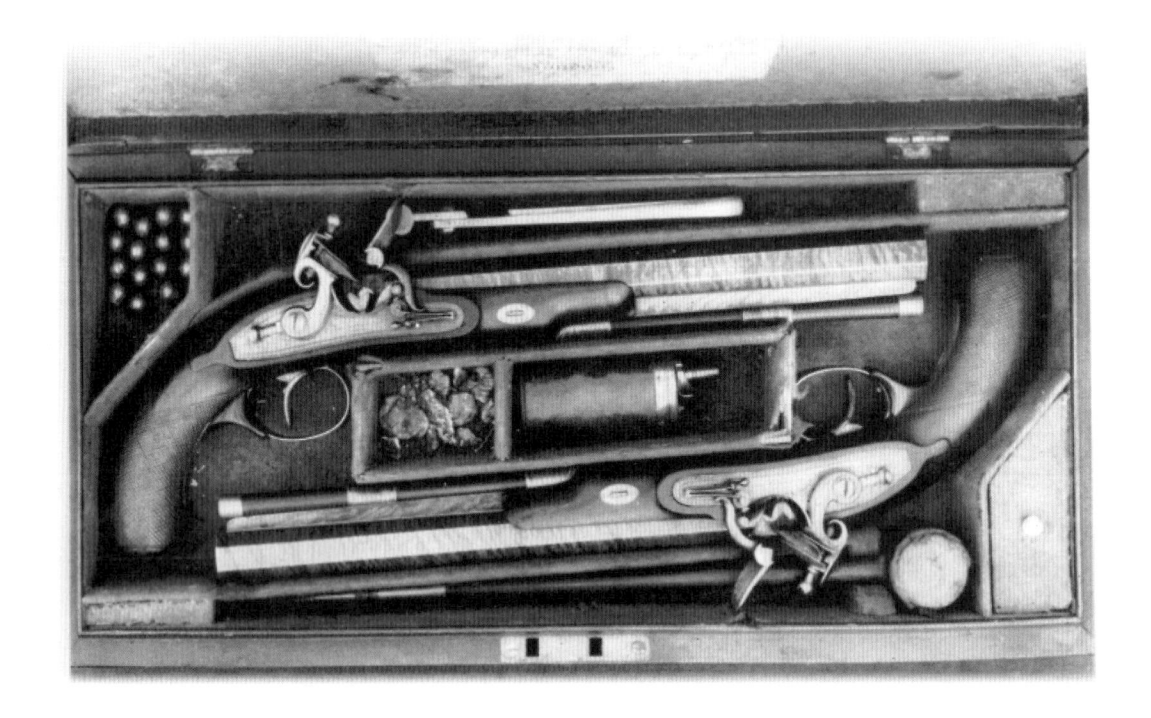

The pair of rifled flintlock target pistols with which Horatio Ross, for a wager of £100, shot ten brace of swallows before breakfast at his home, Rossie Castle on 5 July 1825. It is surprising that he chose flintlocks when percussion had taken over. This would have made it much more difficult to hit a moving target.

James Purdey, as previously explained, worked for Joe Manton then went on to run Forsyth's shop in London to sell the new percussion guns that made flintlocks obsolete, before starting in business on his own. You would have thought, then, that all his customers would have wanted the new, much more efficient, percussion guns but, believe it or not, this was not always the case.

In pride of place today in Purdey's famous "Long Room" there is a double flintlock Purdey, a great rarity, but I had never heard of another. Looking over W. Keith Neal's racks of guns I shouted to Edna "Come and look at this. A flintlock Purdey". "Yes" said Keith Neal "and if you look there, there, there, there and there you will see another five!" Surely no other antique gun collection in the world could claim six flintlock Purdeys.

During correspondence with Keith Neal before I had met him he had noticed that I owned Joseph Manton double percussion no. 9047 that had been converted from tubelock to copper cap percussion. At the time of conversion, probably about 1830, the gunsmith had taken out the original breeches, hammers and tubelock mechanism and put them in a drawer, there to lie forgotten for over a century. Eventually the business was wound up and in the nineteen thirties all the old stock was bought by Keith Neal. Joseph Manton lockplates are numbered so having found them, he was able to identify the numbers. When we met he very kindly let me have all these parts so that the gun could be put back to its original tubelock system. The price? A nominal £25!

At that time I had in my collection a magnificent Joseph Manton tubelock, no. 8474, that retained its original barrel browning. The browning was most distinctive, quite unlike the usual colour. As no. 9047 had been made at virtually the same time, would it be possible to reproduce that unusual original browning?

The re-conversion back to original tubelock and complete restoration of the whole gun had been entrusted to a highly competent gunsmith so I asked him. "Yes, I'm sure I can reproduce that original browning." He said: But he couldn't! The secret was lost. The barrels are, indeed, nicely re-browned but the browning is conventional.

We visited W. Keith Neal several times and were always made most welcome. On his death the bulk of his collection was put up for sale and there were many Mantons that I would have loved to have bought. Sadly, however, it was at a time when every penny was needed for more important matters so I deliberately avoided taking any interest in the auction. Yes, I missed out, but I had already acquired a worthwhile collection of Mantons so I cannot complain.

There were not many Mantons in my possession that were not in Keith Neal's collection but I did have one or two rarities that were the exception.

John Manton did not share the flair for invention and innovation that was the hallmark of his brother Joseph and he continued to make flintlocks far longer than most other London gunmakers. Many of them manufactured modifications of the new Forsyth percussion system then quickly moved onto caplocks.

John Manton missed all this but did make a few tubelocks in the late 1820's when he should have been making caplocks.

Few were made and fewer survive. As far as I know, unless others have turned up since, the only existing tubelocks at the time of the publication of the Manton Supplement were as follows: One in a Manchester museum, one owned by the Duke of Buccleuch, one owned by an American collector and the other by me! The gun is a cased 14 bore double in good condition. Not unlike a Joseph Manton tubelock but the ends of the hammers are hooded to prevent the tube shooting out sideways when detonated.

So how did I acquire such a rarity?

A collector had bought it and realised that it represented an opportunity to make an instant profit if offered to a Manton collector. Fortunately he chose me and we arranged to meet at Buxton one evening. I examined the gun, was very pleased with it and filthy lucre changed hands! It seemed a lot of money at the time but, of course, looks like peanuts today.

Joseph Manton specialised in shotguns rather than rifles and made far less rifles than his brother John. Here, however, is an example of a Joseph Manton rifle.

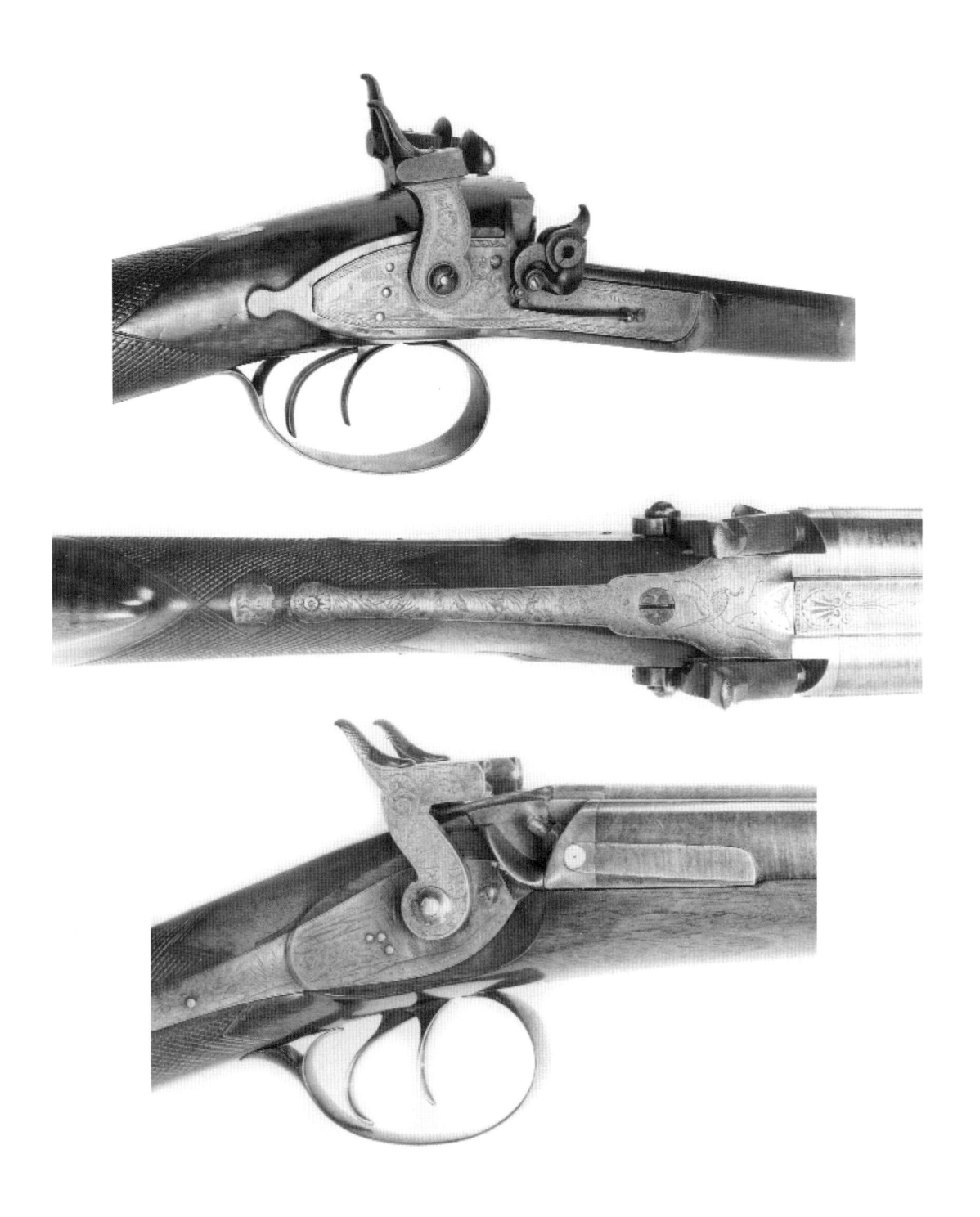

A rare John Manton Tubelock.
Beautifully made double by Samuel Nock but with late barrels by Joseph Manton.

James Purdey the founder. 1784-1863. Portrait attributed to Sir William Beechey.
James Purdey the Younger. 1828-1909. Painted by Stuart Wortley in 1891.

Chapter Eighteen
Purdeys

The two greatest names in sporting guns today are Purdey and Holland and Holland.

James Purdey was born in 1784 and was apprenticed to his brother-in-law Thomas Keck Hutchinson at the age of fourteen. Having completed his apprenticeship in 1805 he went to work as a gun stocker for the greatest gunsmith of the day, Joseph Manton.

When the Forsyth Patent Gun Company was set up to make guns with the new Forsyth percussion locks in 1808, Purdey left Joe Manton to work for them as a stocker and lock filer.

He started his own business in 1814 and in 1826 he took over Joe Manton's old premises in Oxford Street.

James Purdey never lost his admiration for Joe Manton and said later: "But for him we should all have been a parcel of blacksmiths."

James Purdey was equally regarded by Joe Manton. Colonel Peter Hawker, the famous sportsman and brilliant shot with Joe Manton guns wrote in the 1844 edition of his famous book *Hawker on Shooting*, nine years after Joseph Manton's death:

"Mr Purdey has still perhaps the first business in London, and no man better deserves it. I once asked Joe Manton whom he considered the best maker in Town (of course excepting himself), and his answer was "Purdey gets up the best work next to mine!" This was when Purdey occupied a small shop in Princes Street".

James Purdey died in 1863 and his son, also James, carried on until 1909.

Purdeys moved to South Audley Street in 1883 and continue there to this day.

The first Purdey I bought in the nineteen fifties was 9237, a 12 bore double hammer gun with side lever opening. Bought for £30 by a postal bid from the gun auctioneers, Wallis and Wallis of Lewes, Sussex. Sound but shabby. Restored by the Birmingham gun trade for £30. They made a splendid job: Stock re-polished and chequering re-cut, barrels re- browned and all metalwork beautifully polished resulting in a splendid gun.

The next Purdeys were a pair of .400 SB muzzle loading rifles made for shooting park deer on a Leicestershire estate. No 3314 was made in 1839 and the other one to match it, 4194, was made sometime between 1846 and 1848. Although not consecutive numbers, 4194 was clearly ordered to make a pair with 3314.

They had passed to the gunsmiths, Clarkes of Leicester and when they closed down, Harvey Taylor bought them. I bought them from Harvey.

Excellent original condition with barrels retaining their original browning and some original blue on the trigger guards. Both had set triggers. Ribs engraved "J. Purdey, 314½ Oxford St, London". Lock plates engraved "Purdey". Cased with accessories in an original Purdey double mahogany case with trade label.

The next Purdey I bought from J.M. Macdonald Peattie. At the same time he offered me a lovely .500 double rifle by Charles Lancaster which I didn't buy and lived to regret it! Both had been owned by the American millionaire, deerstalker extraordinary, Walter Winans.

The Purdey is a 16 bore centre fire breech loader in excellent condition made in 1867. Complete in its original oak case with trade label and accessories.

Next were the pair of Thumbhole Purdeys bought from Peter Gavuzzi and already described though none of them are in my ownership now.

Peter Griffiths of Brailsford is another one of the remarkable collectors I have been fortunate enough to meet and he could tell a tale or two about his gun collecting experiences but this is one of them: Alexander Henry the great Edinburgh gun and rifle maker made some superlative guns and rifles and a Derbyshire man was an Alexander Henry collector. He commissioned Peter to make a beautiful gun cabinet to house about two dozen guns and rifles but, sadly, his marriage broke up. He emptied the cabinet, loaded all the guns into the boot of his car and drove away!

His wife later sold the cabinet back to Peter and it then went to Scotland, finally coming back to within a few miles of Derby.

Although I briefly knew the Alexander Henry collector I had no idea, at the time, that he was a gun collector so I never did have the opportunity to see this unique collection.

Caroline and Ross were two marvellous children. As youngsters they never asked for anything. True, they were never deprived but they were incredibly undemanding. They had everything they wanted and never demanded anything else though, of course, this was before the age of DVD's, computer games et al.

Shooting pigeons at home on our farm, Ross always chose an S.B. Russian 12 bore that had cost me £13 in part exchange for a motorcycle. He once said to me that he would love to have a quality twelve bore by one of the top makers such as Purdey or Holland and Holland. What he didn't know was that we had already bought him one in readiness for his birthday.

It was a beautiful twelve bore hammerless, self opening Purdey double complete with a spare pair of barrels, both different lengths and different chokes. Complete with all accessories in its original oak and leather Purdey case with trade label.

We will never forget the look on his face when we presented it to him on his birthday. It is now, of course, with the rest of the collection.

In the 1960's I had a D.B. 14 bore percussion Purdey for sale. It was complete in its original mahogany Purdey case with trade label. The gun was sound but well worn. The chequering on the stock spoke of years, if not generations, of handling. I advertised it in The *Shooting Times* for £30.

So was I snowed under with replies? Far from it! Only one reply received from a Birmingham industrialist. I described the gun accurately but, understandably, he wanted to see it. He asked if his traveller could collect it so that it could be taken to his gunsmith for examination. I was none too keen on this arrangement but, as it was my only reply, I accepted on the clear understanding that the price was £30 *and no offers*. This was agreed and the gun was collected.

A week or so later he wrote to me. No criticism of my description. No comments from his gunsmith. Just his offer of £10!

Needless to say this offer was instantly rejected and the gun was returned, to be eventually sold elsewhere for £30: But I wish I had it now!

About the same time I had for sale an S.B. 12 bore percussion by John Manton. Re-finished and in very good condition. Originally a flintlock but beautifully converted to percussion with a new breech. I had originally bought it from the great sportsman, naturalist and writer, J. Wentworth Day.

The price was £16 10s. and it did attract some interest. A potential buyer came to see it, examined it carefully and couldn't fault it. Finally he said with a sigh "That's a lot of money!" What he meant was that it was a lot of money *for him*. Even so, he did steel himself to hand over that £16 10s. and he had every reason to be delighted with his purchase!

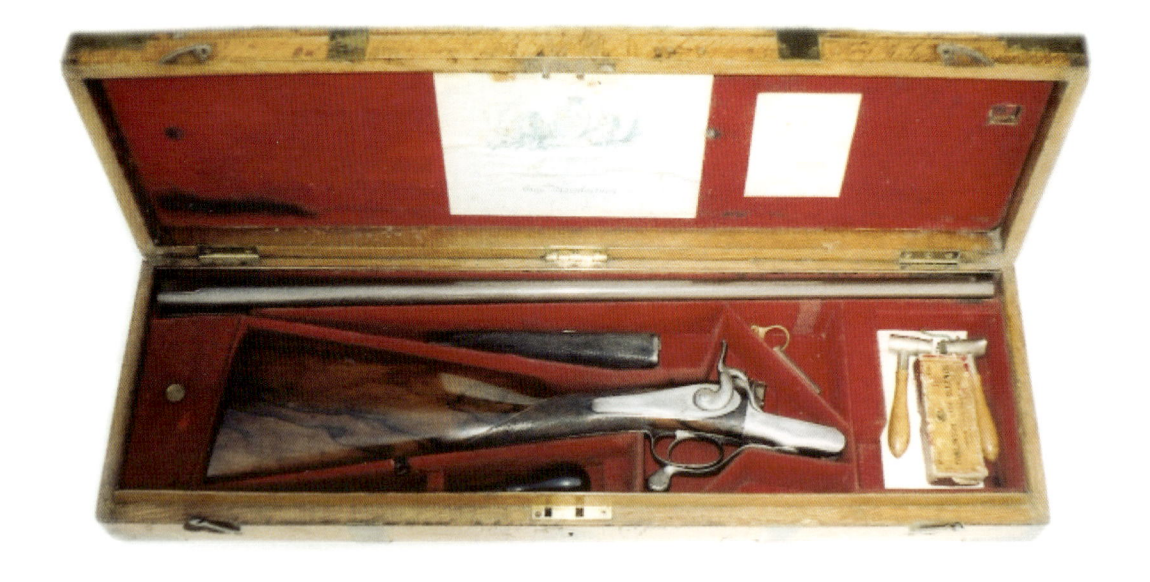

A cased sixteen bore Purdey that belonged to the legendary stalker, Walter Winans. Cased hammerless self opening Purdey with two pairs of barrels. Different lengths and chokes.

A splendid Purdey D.B. twelve bore side opening early breech loader.

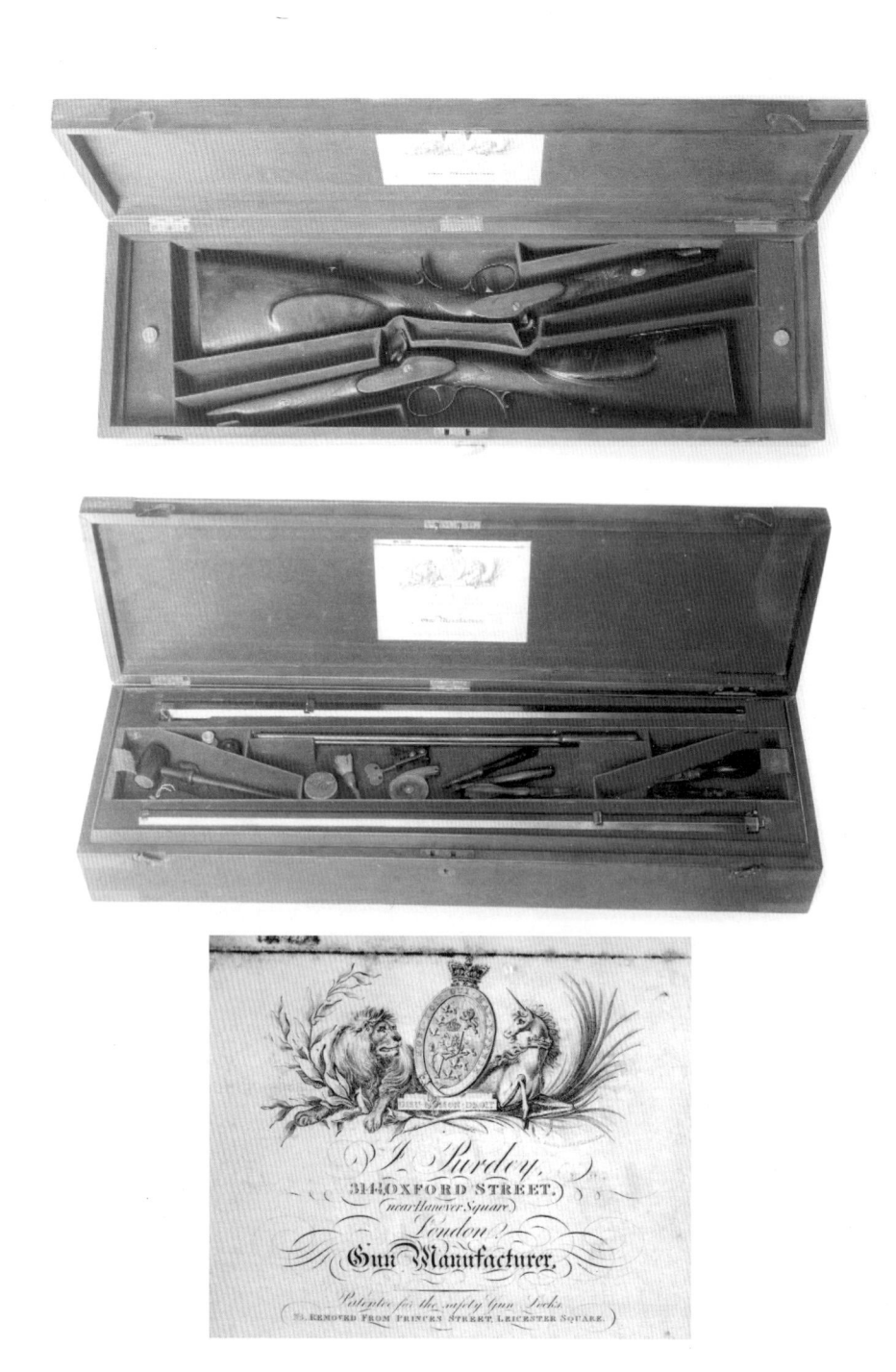

Harvey Taylor's pair of .400 muzzle loading Purdey rifles with set triggers made for shooting park deer on one of Leicestershire's great estates.

Chapter Nineteen
The Collectors

"The collected letters of Harvey Taylor ought to be gathered together and published". So I used to write to Harvey Taylor, only half in jest, in the nineteen sixties.

They would, without doubt, be a most valuable source of reference today as such a range of fine antique guns went through his hands. If Harvey offered you an antique gun it would be precisely described and you would know exactly what you were getting.

There are many different approaches to gun collecting.... As varied as the collectors themselves: The specialist, the bargain hunter, the shooter, the militaria man and all varieties in between!

Harvey's interests were fine English pistols, sporting guns and rifles and he was, above all, a perfectionist. All his guns had to be as perfect as possible and he went to great lengths to research the history of the makers. In addition to that he would, where possible, trace the previous owners to glean any further information.

Harvey and his parents lived in a lovely old house at Oakham, Rutland and he and his father ran a business supplying the yarn trade in Leicester.

He got married later in life than most of us to the lovely Marlene, a talented concert pianist and has lived in Leicester ever since. Harvey eventually decided to buy an old established book business in Leicester, Bacchus Books who at one time had published a number of titles.

As capital was required, the gun collection had to go and he offered it to me at about £10,000. But, of course, as you get older the things you regret are not the things you *did* do but the things you *didn't* do!

Just at the time that Harvey's collection was offered for sale, Harold Wilson came up with one of his habitual squeezes.

In those days British governments had a child-like faith in the effectiveness of credit squeezes: Artificially restrict consumer spending and economic problems would melt away like Judy Garland's lemon drops in

"The Wizard of Oz". The reality, of course, was different: Things were never that simple!

But there it was! We could find the £10,000 but the credit squeeze would undoubtedly restrict our sales. Would the cash be needed in the business?

We thought long and hard but after much soul searching, caution prevailed. Of course, with hindsight, it was very much the wrong decision. Harvey had put together a superlative collection of antique pistols, guns and rifles. Many of them would be virtually impossible to repeat today and the collection would be worth at least a quarter of a million pounds now…. Possibly very much more. But, as you know, we all have 20/20 vision in hindsight!

"We all miss opportunities". I once said this to an old farmer who had never added an acre to the 65 acre farm his father had bought in 1916 yet I know he had turned down the opportunity to buy an additional 10 acres at £100 an acre some years before. At the time when I was speaking to him it had appreciated to at least £1,000 per acre.

"I have never missed an opportunity in my life." he replied.

My case rests!

Missing Harvey's collection was not my only lost opportunity in that direction. Harvey once had a breech loading flintlock from the famous W.W. Greener collection. This famous gunmaker had written "The Gun and its Development" in the mid nineteenth century, a classic that has endured to this day. During his lifetime he had put together a vast collection of antique guns with a particular interest in the rare and unusual. The collection was eventually sold and Harvey had bought this early breech loader by Tatham and Egg.

Harvey had owned the rifle for some time before selling it on to me. These very early breech loaders were never a practical success because the problem of gas sealing at the breech was destined never to be solved until the advent of the metallic cartridge. Even so, however, it was a great rarity and I should have hung onto it.

The snag was that it was such an ugly brute! It was full stocked and at some time in the past it had been very clumsily re-stocked so after a year or two I sold it.

W.W. Greener, despite his undoubted expertise, was a long way wide of the mark when he predicted in the mid nineteenth century that despite breech loading having taken over for small arms, muzzle loading cannon would still be in use in a hundred years time. Unfortunately he had been born too early to hear Sam Goldwyn's famous pronouncement; "Never make predictions. Especially about the future!"

A purchase from Harvey that I did have the sense to hang onto was a pair of S.B. muzzle loading Purdey rifles. Beautifully made .400 calibre with set triggers. They had been made for shooting park deer on a Leicestershire estate and had passed into the hands of Clarkes the Leicester gunsmiths. When they finally gave up business Harvey bought them and eventually he passed them on to me where they remained until I disposed of my collection.

Charles Jones Patient D.B Percussion centre fire with rainproof cover.

I first met Bill Curtis and his charming wife, Mary, in the nineteen sixties. Bill is an avid collector and fanatical rifleman, shooting muzzle loaders competitively at Bisley and elsewhere.

Bisley is, without doubt, Bill's spiritual home and he has a caravan permanently based there. He shoots the Enfield muzzle loading rifles and is particularly interested in the beautifully made specialist target rifles of the era such as the Whitworth and the Gibbs. These lovely rifles are still shot in competition at up to a thousand yards today.

The Whitworths, in particular, are a special interest of his and when Jeremy Clarkson recently produced a programme on the evolution of guns and rifles, Bill was featured on the programme shooting the Whitworths.

Of recent years he has become increasingly interested in the Crimean War and is a member of the Crimean War Association. They make regular visits to the Crimea and carry out digs on the old battlefields.

Digging on these battlefield sites has produced all sorts of interesting artefacts from a range of lead bullets used by all nations in the conflict to a collection of food tin labels! The tinplate has long since rusted away but the brass labels have survived to provide Bill with an unique collage. They include labels from French tins of "Boeuf Boulli" translated to "Bully Beef" by English soldiers, a description that has survived to this day.

Bill is a big, powerfully built man whose son Reg continues his interest in antique guns and rifles.

He was the assistant manager at the Zurich Insurance Company, Nottingham when I first knew him though later his work was to take him to South Wales and elsewhere. This was a pity as the Nottingham base suited him very well indeed.

He lived at The Old Manor House, Radcliffe on Trent which was the perfect residence for Bill and Mary. It was a house of enormous character, ideal for a gun collector with a room that acted as a strong room to house his collection and another as a workshop in which he carried out his gun maintenance and repairs. Plus, of course, its central location making easy access to all parts of England.

In those Nottingham days Bill and Mary would often visit us at Ousley Wood where Bill would join us in shooting muzzle loading guns and rifles. At Christmas time we were always made most welcome when we visited them at Radcliffe on Trent.

Among Bill's interests is books: He is a dedicated bibliophile with a collection of books on guns and shooting that would be hard to match in private hands. This has led him to commission the re-printing of many of the old shooting classics. He is now retired, living in a very attractive house near Prestatyn, North Wales.

Harvey Taylor, as previously explained, was a perfectionist who required his guns to be of the highest standard. It was not always possible to buy guns in that condition so, on occasion, some repair work could not be avoided.

Harvey, however, had found a man who could produce work to measure up to his exacting standards……Oliver Nightall.

Oliver was an engineer who had fought across Europe in tanks during the Second World War. After the war he returned to his old trade then eventually set up his own business making virtually anything in metal. He was, however, very interested in antique guns and turned his hand to antique gun restoration, though only on a part time basis.

Gun barrel browning was an art he had perfected and "striking off", i.e. filing up and polishing prior to browning, was done by his wife Joan…..always called "Dick" by Oliver. Where did the nickname come from? Don't know! They had a son but he did not share his father's interest in antique guns.

Oliver was one of the "good guys" of this world. Always brimming over with vitality and great fun to be with. He lived at Collyweston near Stamford, Lincs. and spoke with that distinctive Lincolnshire burr. Good shot with gun, rifle and pistol, too.

Harvey had introduced us to Oliver and Dick and they were frequent visitors to Ousley Wood where Oliver would join us in shooting the muzzle loading guns and rifles. On these occasions Oliver would return the guns he had taken for restoration and collect another batch.

This was an association that lasted many years and suited both of us very well indeed, but where are all the talented amateur antique gun restorers today? There must be some still around but, unfortunately, I don't know any!

Oliver had a modest antique gun collection of his own but was perfectly happy tackling the variety of work provided by collectors such as Harvey and I.

Among his many talents was a flair for producing beautifully constructed model aeroplanes that he flew successfully.

A better view of the leather covered box containing the range of front and rear sights for the Whitworth Rifle.

Nock's flintlock breech loader in which the powder and ball are loaded into a re-usable tubular metal "cartridge" like the Tatham and Egg.

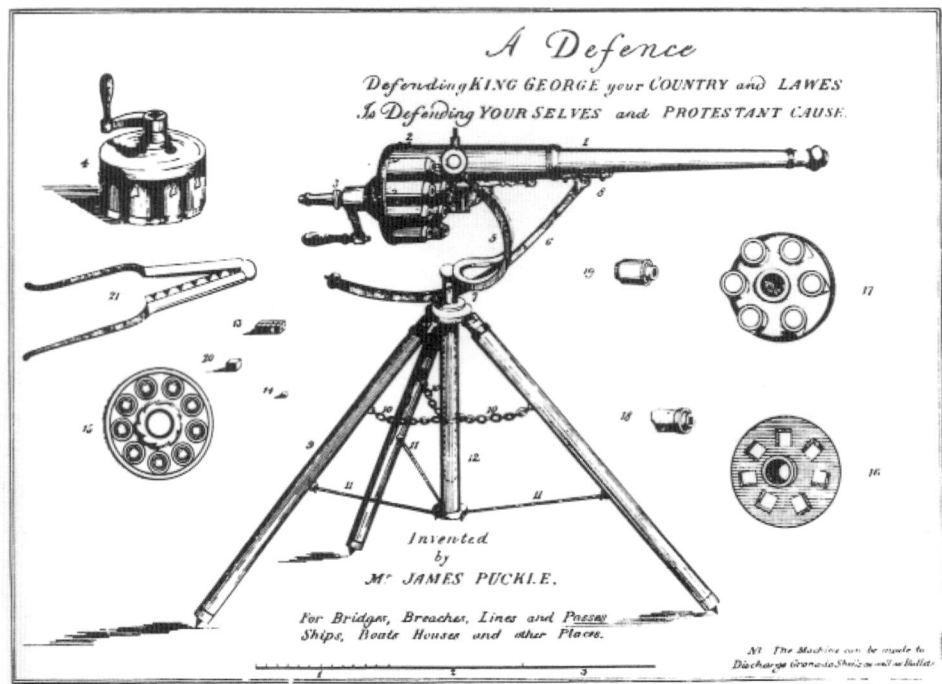

The revolving gun patented by James Puckle in 1718 and the printed patent card for his invention. Both Tower of London.

The Puckle flintlock machine gun that fired round bullets at Christians, square bullets at Turks. An invention far before its time.

Chapter Twenty
The Ones That Got Away

All collectors regret not having bought notable guns when they had the opportunity to do so. They all have such a list and I am no exception!

An outstanding "miss" that springs to mind is a pair of rifles offered to me by Bill Curtis back in the 1960's.

Bill brought over two rifles he wanted to sell: One was a cased .360 double Black Powder Express rifle in excellent condition by the great Edinburgh maker, Alexander Henry. I missed it and was never to acquire another .360 Express.

The other was a .400 pinfire double Black Powder Express by another fine Scottish maker, Paton of Perth. This, too, was in splendid condition.

Now pinfire Expresses are very thin on the ground. Although some of the first breech loading Expresses were pinfire they were very quickly superseded by centrefire. Most rifle makers, however, missed pinfire completely and went straight over to centrefire. This rifle was an absolute gem retaining all its original finish and beautifully browned Damascus barrels. Once again, I never did acquire another pinfire Express: Come to think about I have never even *seen* another pinfire Express!

The price for the two was £120! Not expensive, even at the time. So why didn't I buy them? Don't know! Perhaps the £120 was earmarked for something more important, unconnected with the world of guns but, whatever the reason, I missed them both and the opportunity was never to occur again.

Another gun that I very much regret missing was an early breech loading shotgun made by John Manton and presented to John Brown by Queen Victoria. It was coming up for auction and I knew that a good price would have to be offered to secure it.

I sought expert advice and was told that my proposed offer was far too high….it would never realise that kind of figure. So I pitched my offer halfway between what I thought and what the experts thought………I didn't get it! But my figure would have secured it. What would it be worth today? Twenty or more times than the figure it realised then. The mounted head of a stag shot by John Brown is on display at the superbly run Glenmorangie Lodge Hotel, Tain Ross-shire.

J. M. MacDonald Peattie. How's that for a real Scottish name? He was a collector and part time dealer in antique guns.

I first met him when he turned up with a canvas sack full of pistols which he tipped out onto the floor. Antique pistols of all kinds: Flintlocks, caplocks, duelling pistols, pocket pistols, target pistols, travelling pistols…..the lot!

"Ah," he said "this is what I want to show you." Reaching into the pile he pulled out, like Little Jack Horner, a John Manton duelling percussion pistol which I bought. Many years later, in, I believe, 2000, a dealer rang and asked if I wanted to sell it as he had just sold the other one of the pair to a customer. I said that I didn't want to sell but would be very pleased if he would be kind enough to put the customer in touch with me, but I heard nothing further.

Duelling pistols had to be smooth bore without the advantage of rifling but some were secretly scratch rifled up to about one inch of the muzzle which was absolutely against the rules. This pistol, was, indeed, scratch rifled to within about one inch of the muzzle.

This meant that the owner could practice with his rifled pistols and become an extremely competent shot, yet, in the event of a duel, when his opponent's second would look down the bores, they would appear to be smooth-bored.

As my great interest was longarms this was the only duelling pistol I retained. Yes, with hindsight, a selection of Manton duelling pistols would have been a good idea but, as I keep reminding you, we all have 20/20 vision in that!

Macdonald Peattie also brought with him two most interesting longarms both of which had been owned by Walter Winans. The first was a 16 bore S.B. breech loading Purdey in excellent condition and complete in its original case with trade label. I bought this so I secured a link with the legendary stalker. There is a photograph of it in the chapter on Purdeys.

The next was a breech loading double rifle by Lancaster. Can't be sure about the calibre now but believe it was a .500 Black Powder Express. The firing pins were struck by the breasts of the hammers which had no "tops", a most unusual system. A very desirable rifle in good condition, so why didn't I buy it?

Well, it was not cheap and money for gun purchases was by no means unlimited but the deciding factor was the necessity to get Police permission to put it on my Firearm Certificate. Nowadays such obsolete calibres are free of Certificate if they are not to be fired and no ammunition is required but at that time, as far as the Police were concerned, a breech loading rifle was a rifle regardless how old or obsolete it may have been. Even needlefire rifles had to be on Certificate.

So another one that got away to my later regret!

Macdonald Peattie was a most interesting and knowledgeable man but, regretfully, I only met him once or twice as he died quite young.

I have already described missing Harvey Taylor's collection but the biggest collection I ever missed was that of Arthur Hamon of Guernsey.

I had, at last, arranged to meet W. Keith Neal at his home, La Terre Norgiot in Guernsey and see his unique and extensive collection of antique English guns, rifles and pistols. They were kept in a beautifully converted barn on his property.

During her student days, my daughter Caroline had met Deborah Falla from Guernsey so we called in to see Deborah and her parents. Having told them that we had come over to see a collection of antique guns they said "Oh, you must mean Arthur Hamon's collection."

We had, of course, never heard of Arthur Hamon but were told that he had the most important collection of antique guns on Guernsey. Clearly he was a man we must meet as well as W Keith Neal.

He was an amazing man! A Guernseyman through and through, who before the War, had run his own plumbing business. During the economically difficult 1930's one of his jobs was to supply and fit all the plumbing equipment in the new Guernsey council houses. The price per house was £36. Sounds incredible today.

When the Germans invaded Guernsey, Arthur bundled his wife and family onto a ship bound for England and he himself was fortunate enough to get aboard the very last ship to leave the island. His only luggage was just one suitcase!

When he arrived in England he had no idea what had happened to his family though weeks later he was reunited with them. As a plumber he was skilled in working with his hands so he got a job in Liverpool on war work. But, of course, they had left Guernsey with virtually nothing so it was hard times for them all with very little money.

They survived the War, however, then returned to Guernsey and Arthur was able to re-start his plumbing business.

During the German occupation the Germans had lived in their house but nothing had been taken and Arthur told me that the only damage was a cracked cup!

Over the years Arthur had put together a tremendous collection of about 200 antique guns, rifles and pistols. His great interest was the unusual: breech actions, ignition systems etc., very much reflecting my own interests.

He only had one Manton: A 14 bore Joseph Manton percussion double but included in his collection were about fifty breech loading pistols of all types. Firearms regulations in Guernsey were very much more relaxed than in England at that time. In England they would have to have been held on a Firearm Certificate if, and this is a very big if, Police permission could have been granted to hold them. Virtually impossible for anyone but a Registered Firearms Dealer.

Arthur made us most welcome and there was much to see and discuss.

A year or two later Guernsey decided to introduce a Firearm Certificate system similar to the mainland and this meant that Arthur faced a dilemma: No way would he have been allowed to retain rifles and pistols ruled as modern. In addition to that he would have been obliged to face unwelcome restrictions and paperwork together with the necessity of installing proper security.

Arthur was no longer young so he decided that the whole collection would have to go. The price he had set was £50,000 and a wealthy antique firearms dealer named Jenkinson, who had moved from England to Guernsey, was prepared to pay it.

As soon as we heard about the proposed sale, Edna and I flew over to see Arthur and look over the collection with the objective of assessing its value. We decided that we could match the price and pointed out to Arthur that it would be far better for the collection to go to a fellow collector rather than be disposed of by a firearms dealer.

The "modern" pistols and revolvers were a problem but I had explained the situation to the Derbyshire Firearms Department and they had very kindly agreed that if the purchase went through I could bring them over from Guernsey on the understanding that I disposed of them immediately.

I explained this to Arthur and told him that although I intended to keep the bulk of the collection, the rest would have to be sold.

Arthur made no decision about who would get the collection while we were in Guernsey but said he would get back in touch. About a week later I phoned him only to be told that he was still undecided and had left the final decision to his son.

Arthur, as already explained, was a Guernseyman to the core and he was strongly influenced by Jenkinson's assurance that if he bought the collection he would keep the whole thing intact in Guernsey. I explained to Arthur that Jenkinson was a businessman whose business was buying and selling antique guns: No way would the collection remain intact on Guernsey but, as money talks, I upped the offer to £60,000 i.e. £10,000 more than Arthur's asking price.

Now I told you that money talks and the extra £10,000 would surely impress upon Arthur that it was, as Hughie Green used to say on "Opportunity Knocks", make-your-mind-up-time.

So did I get the collection? No!

But did Jenkinson, whose business was buying and selling antique guns, really buy Arthur Hamon's guns on the assurance that they would all remain on Guernsey? I have thought hard about this but it does seem unlikely. What is certain, however, is that Arthur was absolutely convinced that this was the case.

There was, however, one bright spot: On my last visit to Arthur he had produced a circular lignum vitae box that held about twelve detachable strikers to fit in percussion hammers.

The pellet lock Joseph Manton strikers were very similar and kept in an almost identical lignum vitae box. When the percussion system was introduced nipples were screwed into the breeches and the pellet lock strikers were replaced with solid strikers with their faces recessed to take a paper percussion cap. The copper cap soon took over and the new strikers then had a plain face though they still fitted into the original pellet lock hammers.

Other makers used this system though it was, of course, invented by Joe Manton and these strikers were for a Samuel Nock gun and took paper caps. Virtually identical to Joe Manton strikers but with slightly different dimensions. During my last meeting with Arthur, knowing my interest in Mantons, he said "Whatever happens I want you to have this." And pressed the circular striker box into my hand. A most generous gesture.

And Arthur's solitary Joe Manton? W. Keith Neal nipped in and bought it before the collection was sold!

During my visits to Arthur there was much to discuss as he was immensely knowledgeable about antique guns. A friend of his once said to him "When we were boys we used to play cowboys and indians with an old pistol we have at home. It is no use to us now but as you are so interested in old guns you might as well have it." It was an original and unaltered Roller Primer Forsyth! It turned out that it was one of a pair and the other one belonged to an American collector. I wonder if the pair were ever reunited?

In 1717 Puckle invented a repeating flintlock which fired round bullets at Christians, square bullets at Turks. After all, it was reasoned at the time, why should Turks enjoy the luxury of being killed by the same bullets as Christians?

The Puckle was another invention far ahead of its time so could never be a practical success but, even so, a notable milestone in firearms evolution. Do any Puckles survive? If so there cannot be very many of them.

Arthur, however, being a very skilled worker set to and made a replica which, at that time, he had lent on permanent exhibition at Castle Cornet, St. Peter's Port, Guernsey.

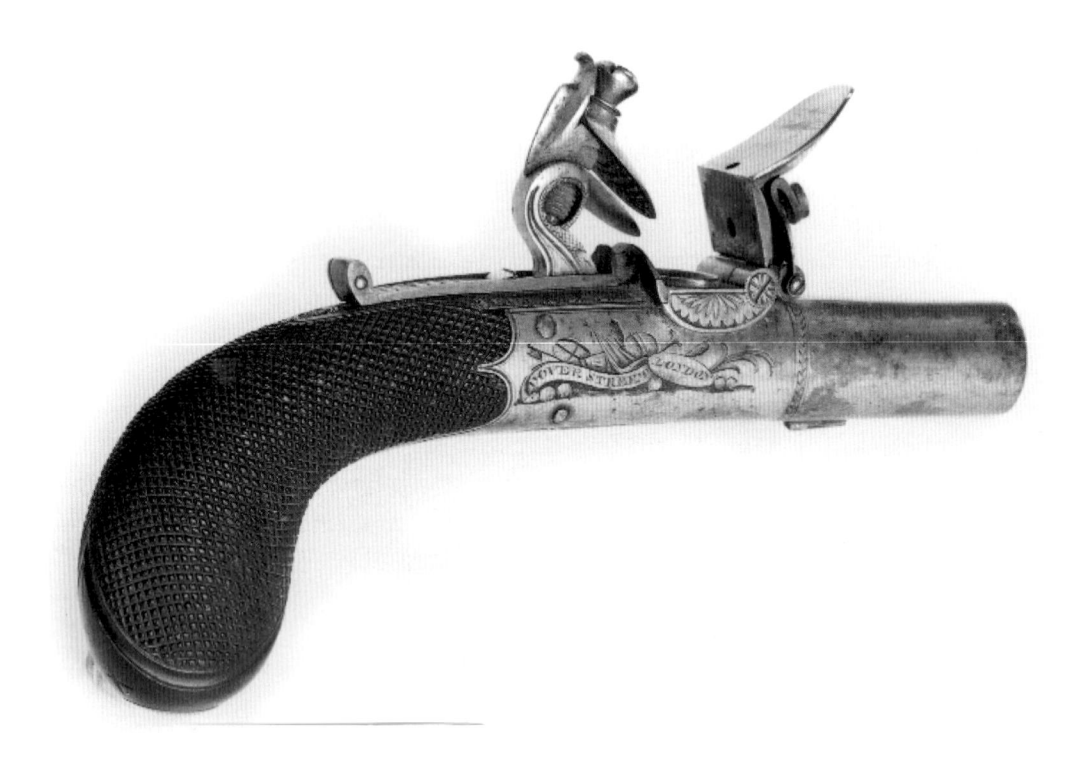

John Manton flintlock ladies' muff pistol. Made as one of a pair. But where is the other one now?

John Manton duelling pistol with secret scratch Rifling no. 9515. The pair to it does exist, but location unknown.

Pistol by Thomas Manton, 144, Long Acre, London. Thomas was a cousin of John and Joseph. He could not have made many guns and very few survive.

Chapter Twenty One
The Art of the Engraver and Colour Hardener

In the next section you will see some superlative examples of the engravers' art. The engravers also execute the gold inlaying. All such work is, of course, commissioned by the buyer and the cost is astronomical, so who is prepared to pay such prices?

There is a tiny minority of extremely wealthy people who demand the very best....the absolute ultimate. These people are prepared to pay the very top price for what they want and, if necessary, wait for years to get it.

The number of engravers capable of creating this kind of artistry is extremely limited but, even so, there are never enough of them to meet the demand.

One of the best known of all, probably for his work on Purdeys, is Ken Hunt though none of his work is shown here. The engraving on English guns in the following pages is by A.M and J.P Brown and Phil Coggan, artists and craftsmen extraordinary.

The gun by Hartmann and Weiss of Hamburg is exquisitely beautiful, built to the Boss over and under design of 1909 and still up to date. The engraving, surely beyond compare, is by a Belgian of staggering talent named Louvenberg.

How much does such work cost? Well, as they used to say about Rolls Royce cars, if you ask how much it costs to run one, you can't afford it!

Such work would not be costed in thousands but in tens of thousands.

Now spare a thought for the colour hardeners like the St. Ledger family whose skill and craftsmanship is essential to achieve the finished product. One wrong move and the gold melts! What a responsibility!

All the following colour photographs were supplied by the St. Ledger family.

Young Ray St. Ledger learns the colour hardening trade from his tutor, Bill Woodward.

118 ~ One Man's Gun Quest

Ray St. Ledger and his merry men. Richard left and Robert right, colour hardeners all, where craftsmanship shades into artistry.
The sparks fly upward as Richard quenches a workpiece.

One Man's Gun Quest~119

120~*One Man's Gun Quest*

One Man's Gun Quest ~121

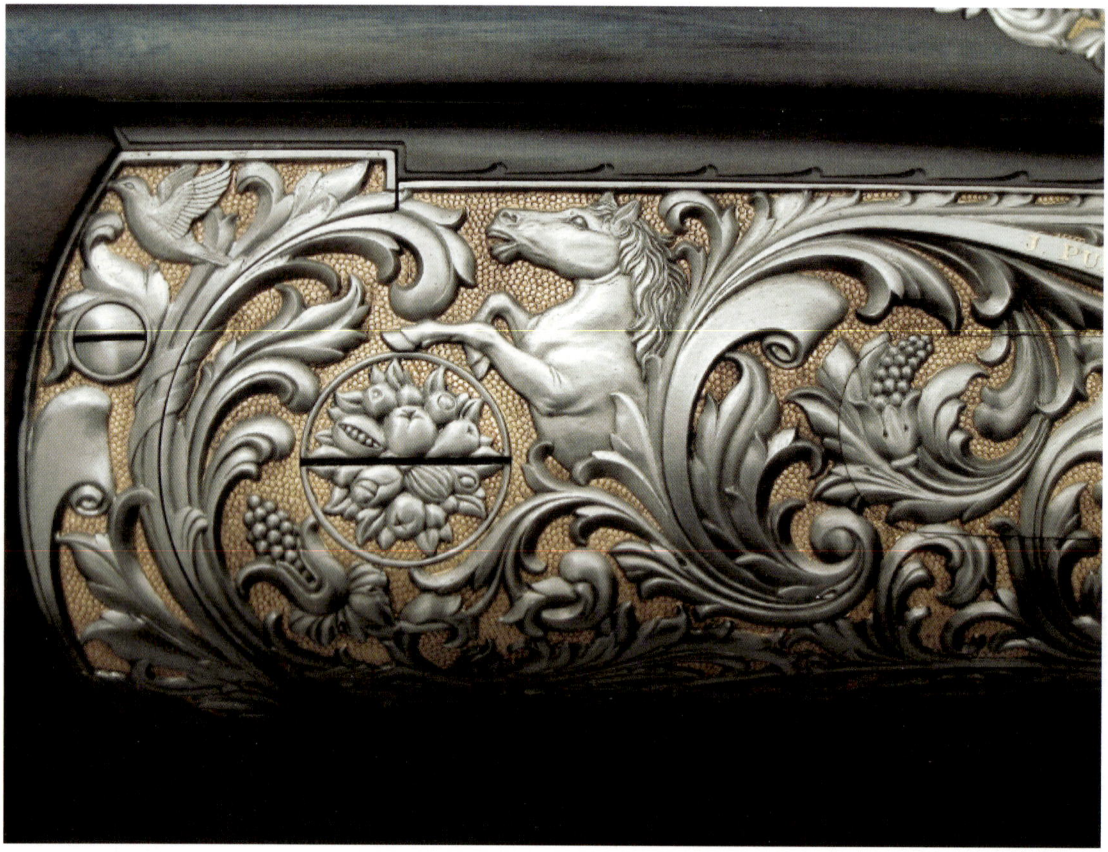

One Man's Gun Quest ~ 123

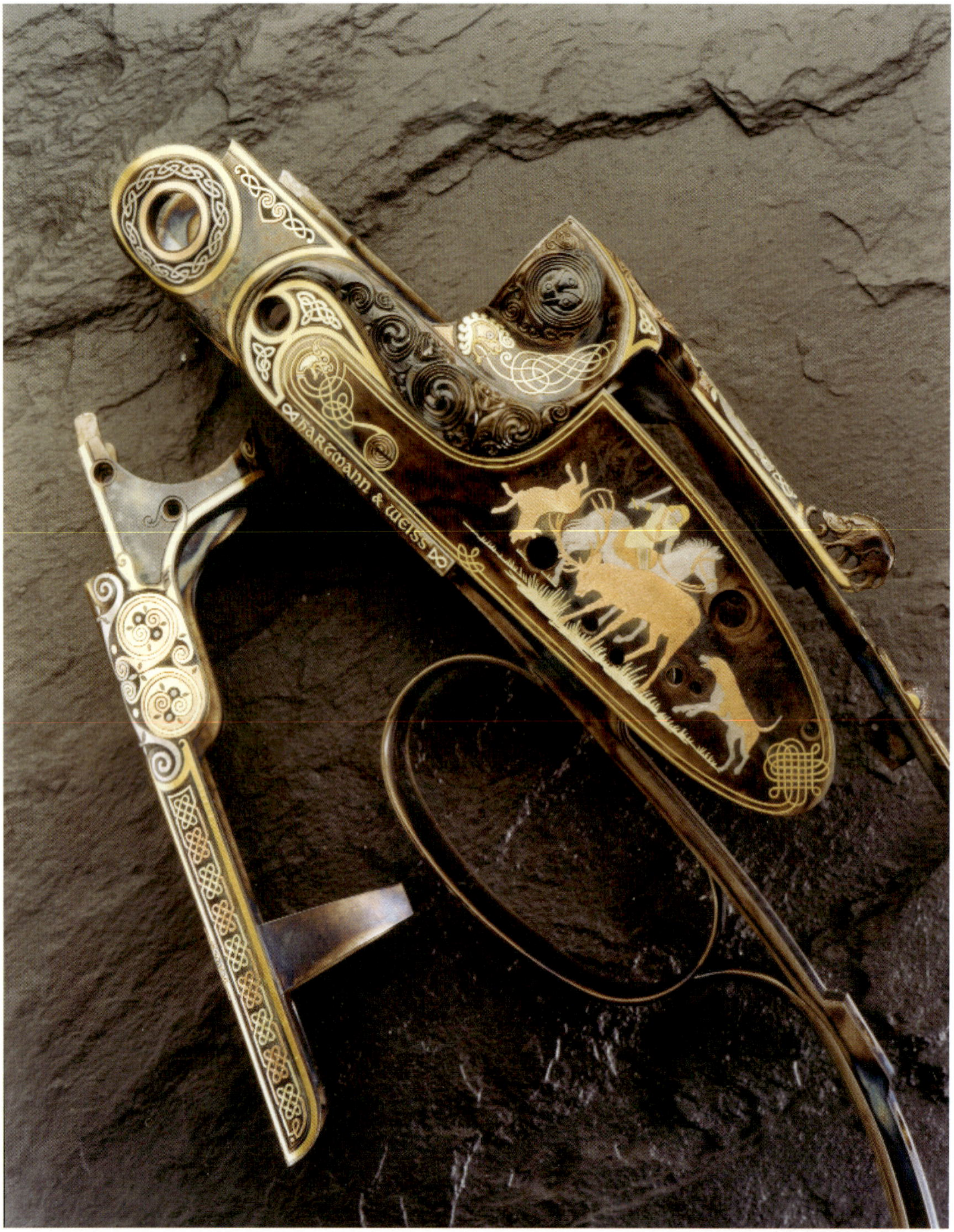
HARTMANN & WEISS

One Man's Gun Quest ~125

126~*One Man's Gun Quest*

Chapter Twenty Two
Twelve Bore Or Twenty

Twenty bores are hard for me to judge: Many people swear by them and claim that despite their smaller shot pattern they can be virtually as effective as a twelve bore with the great advantage of lighter weight and reduced recoil. Somehow I never managed to adapt to twenty bores but the trouble, no doubt, is down to the afterpiece, not the gun! The afterpiece is the man behind the gun!

The recoil of a twelve bore is never noticed during a day's rough shooting but firing continually during, for example, a day at driven grouse the recoil can be a disadvantage: A disadvantage that few of us are fortunate enough to experience!

The great game shot, Sir Joseph Nickerson, experienced many long stints at driven game and was described by The Duke of Wellington, writing in 1994, as "the best shot I ever saw". Shooting at the next butt on Wemmergill Moor to Sir Joseph with his pair or over and under Purdey twenty bores he said "I never saw a man shoot better and his performance convinced me that a twenty bore, provided you shoot straight, is just as effective as a twelve bore and less tiring to use as one gets older".

Eventually Sir Joseph solved the recoil problem by having a trio of twenty-eight bores built for him by Purdeys. He was, of course, one of the few shots with the skill and expertise to use such small bores effectively. After his death I understand that all, or most of, his guns were sold. I wonder why his family got rid of such splendid guns?

In 1955 the Duke of Wellington bought a new pair of Holland and Holland Royal twelve bores as a result of having been left £1,000 by a great aunt.....the price of a pair then! He was delighted with them and used them effectively for about thirty years until Sir Joseph's example on Wemmergill Moor finally decided him to change to twenty bores. They suit him perfectly and he says he would never go back to twelve bores now.

His choice of shot sizes are of interest: In the twelve bores he used a one ounce load of number seven shot. In the twenty bores he uses seven eighths of an ounce of number seven shot. Jim Pillkington in his pair of William Evans twelve bores always used Eley Impax cartridges with fifteen sixteenths of an ounce of number six shot.

Holland and Holland Royals appear to run in the Duke of Wellington's family! His grandfather, the fourth duke and grandson of the original Duke of Wellington of Waterloo fame bought a new pair of Royals in 1893. They are still in excellent order and in use by one of his sons. A later pair now belong to another son.

In 1991 after buying a ticket in the Game Conservancy draw for a pair of Holland and Holland Royal twelve bores for twenty years he finally won! Holland and Holland very kindly exchanged them for a pair of twenty bores.

He was not only a first class game shot but an equally good rifle shot, too. He had shot competitively at Bisley, stalked red and roe deer in Scotland and Germany, chamois in Spain and Austria, mouflon and ibex in Spain. In addition he had shot "the most exciting of all European big game", wild boar, in every Western European country. He described a wild boar travelling at speed through woodland as "the most difficult and, indeed, intimidating target I know".

During the war opportunities for game shooting were inevitably reduced but, even so, throughout the war he carried a .22 rifle and sixteen bore shotgun in the turret of his armoured car!

It is not known if the first duke was a rifle shot but he was a keen game shot. On one occasion shooting on his estate at Stratfield Saye he peppered a woman who was hanging out washing from the first floor of her cottage. Her anguished howls received little sympathy from one of the guests who said to her: "My good woman, you are indeed fortunate to have been shot by no less a person than the Great Duke of Wellington!". She was, however, singularly unimpressed by this honour but a few sovereigns proved as effective as Mary Poppins' spoonful of sugar!

Now from the sublime to the ridiculous! From the Duke of Wellington to the author! The small bores I have enjoyed using are four/tens. This, no doubt, because you are conscious of their limited range and use them with that in mind. Within that range they are delightful little guns to handle.

I had an inexpensive Belgian four/ten double which I thoroughly enjoyed using. It had 30 inch barrels compared to the favourite 28 inch length of modern twelve bores. Both barrels were full choke, making it a surprisingly effective gun.

Perhaps, then, with a twenty bore I was expecting too much of it. What do you think?

Sixteen bores come in between twelve and twenty but I have very little experience of them. I would have thought, however, that you might as well stick with twelve bore or go for the lighter weight of a twenty.

In muzzle loading days all sorts of bores were used including thirteen, fifteen etc. The favourite for game shooting appears to have been fourteen bore compared to today's twelve bore yet many Mantons are in even smaller sizes, twenty bore or thereabouts, for example. Yet they must have been perfectly satisfactory for the people who chose them.

Cased twenty bore hammerless gun by Manton and Co, London and Calcutta.

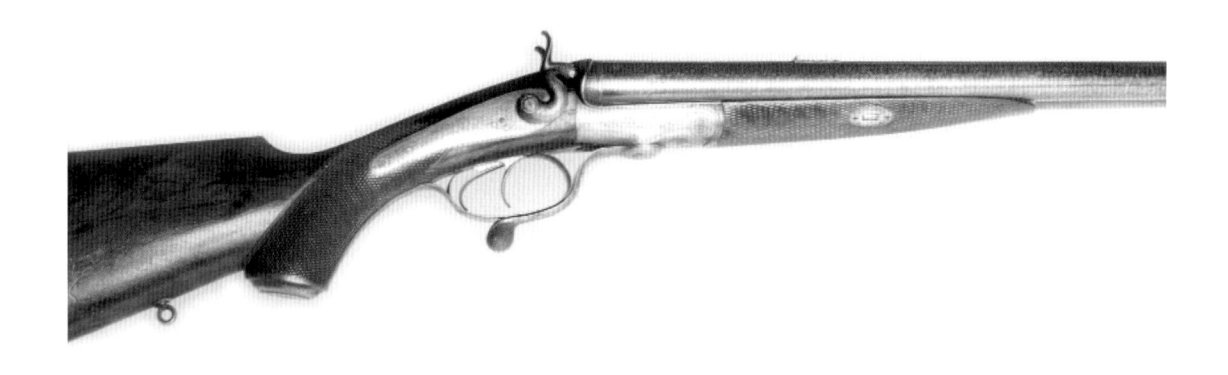

Lieut. Colonel Todhunter's great uncle failed to bag a tiger with this H. Holland .577 in 1876.
The Prince of Wales bags his first tiger in 1921.

Chapter Twenty Three
Richard Ratner and Kit Ravenshear

Kit Ravenshear was another of the fascinating characters in the antique gun world. A handsome man, tall, well built, well spoken. At the time when I met him he had a new, attractive wife, a new baby and a monkey named Peckham! He had two children from his first marriage who lived with their mother.

Kit had done all sorts of things in his time: For several poverty stricken years he had lived as a Highland crofter, shooting winter hinds to eat as a matter of necessity. He then sold Avery scales in the Highlands.

I got on very well with Kit and on one occasion he joined us at Deanich Lodge and shot a stag on the Strouban Ridge, making a good shot at it, too. At Deanich we would chat away about guns and rifles until after midnight.

Among the guns he had owned was a Luger pistol that had belonged to the Nazi Gauleiter of Paris. What a spine chilling story that could have told!

At the time that I met him Kit had recently started out full time in the antique gun business and he did quite a lot of restoration work for me, making a competent job of it. I bought two rifles from him, both double Holland and Hollands in excellent order. One was the .400 Black Powder Express that Marcus Munro of Alladale was to shoot a stag with in October 2002 and the other a .300 rook and rabbit rifle.

I once got a right and left at rabbits with the .300…. almost as rewarding as getting a right and left at stags!

I cannot remember what I paid for the .400, but certainly not more than £100 . I can, however remember the price of the .300……..£50. Ought to have bought a dozen! Snag was that these lovely rook and rabbit rifles were breech loaders, restricting the ability to purchase them as they had to be on Firearm Certificate.

I eventually lost touch with Kit and heard that he emigrated to America; I understand that his second marriage also broke up due to his roving eye for the ladies but how true this is I don't know. I have recently been told that he died within the last year or so.

I knew a firearms dealer in this country at that time who specialised in buying rook and rabbit rifles and selling them to Germany where there was no restriction on ownership…, as in this country today if they are to be held as antiques without ammunition.

But, of course, during all the years when these rifles had to be on Firearm Certificate, so many superlative obsolete rifles of all calibres by the finest English makers were lost from this country.

A friend of Jim Pilkington handed her double Purdey rook rifle in to the Police when told that she no longer had any reason to keep it on her Firearm Certificate.

There was a happier ending for a .577 double rifle that belonged to another friend of Jim Pilkington's. This was the largest calibre of the Black Powder Expresses, made for shooting big game. Lieut. Colonel Todhunter was a friend of Jim's, former Lord Lieutenant of Essex. The rifle was made by H. Holland (predecessor of Holland and Holland) in 1876 for the Lieut. Colonel's great uncle to shoot tiger in India. In the event he never did bag a tiger with it! The rifle had been retained as a family memento in virtually new condition but eventually the Firearm Certificate bogy raised its ugly head and the rifle had to go.

Fortunately Jim Pilkington heard about it in time and asked me if I wanted it for the asking price of….don't laugh…£15. The answer was "Yes!"

Richard Ratner first got in touch with me when he replied to an advert I had placed to sell an antique gun. Negotiations proceeded well enough by letter when, to my surprise, his mother got in touch with me to tell me that he was still a schoolboy: Up to then I had no idea!

But I had described the gun accurately, the sale went ahead and Richard was pleased with his purchase.

Richard was at Epsom College at the time and he went on to take up his career as a stockbroker. His great interest was fine English flintlocks, an interest that never waned. What his collection consists of today I have no idea but he was buying when prices were a fraction of today's so if he has managed to hold onto the bulk of those purchases his collection would be very valuable now.

Richard Ratner, fanatical collector.

When breech loaders took over from muzzle loaders twelve bore became the usual choice but in muzzle loading days smaller bores were the rule. Fourteen bores were popular but guns of around twenty bore were common enough. Joseph Manton made many guns in these calibres. They must, however, have been perfectly adequate for the shooting that was required of them and I have often wondered why. Derek Fearn has arrived at the most likely answer: Despite their small bores, he says, they fired a heavy load of black powder. This would explain the choice.
The gun above is an example: A lovely cased twenty bore by Joseph Manton.

Chapter Twenty Four
Sid Bellamy

Funny how some things stick indelibly in your mind while others are totally forgotten: Sid Bellamy's address, like 1066... has never been forgotten: 367 Laceby Road, Grimsby. On a glorious September day, Edna and I with our small daughter Caroline set out for Grimsby where Sid Bellamy had some Mantons for sale.

Sid was an old timer then, a retired fish merchant and the old established business was being carried on by his son. Laceby Road is the long road that runs into Grimsby.

Sid had four Mantons for sale: Two cased Joseph Manton percussion doubles one uncased John Manton percussion double and a single fourteen bore by John Manton with, unusually, a birds eye maple stock. He was asking fair prices for all of them so I bought all four. In addition, however, he had for sale a remarkable cased rifle: A target rifle of .451 calibre by Sir Joseph Whitworth.

Beautifully made in its original case with all accessories. Among the accessories was a superlative powder flask capable of delivering exact powder charges. In addition to the loading rod was a rod with a hollow brass insert at the end. The object of this was to ensure that every particle of powder was delivered direct to the breech with none sticking to the barrel. To do this the powder charge from the flask was put into the brass tube on the end of the rod and then the rifle was lowered onto the rod. The rifle was then upended so the entire powder charge was deposited onto the breech.

In the early 19th century each engineering works had its own design of screw thread and even bolt head sizes which was an absolute nightmare when any kind of repairs or renewals became necessary.

Sir Joseph Whitworth introduced a standardised screw thread and bolt head sizes that were universally accepted and are in use to this day.

With a breech loading rifle there is no problem in getting the rifling to grip the bullet: Just make the bullet slightly bigger than the bore. But in muzzle loading days this was clearly impossible so the round ball was encased in a small circular piece of cloth, known as the patch which was then rammed down the barrel. This then gripped the rifling but the velocity was restricted because at too high a speed the patch would strip on the rifling.

A simple solution was to rifle the barrel with deep grooves then cast a ball with a belt to fit the grooves so the ball would *have* to follow the rifling.

It was essential, however, to progress beyond the round, lead ball to a cylindrical, pointed bullet. Purdey's answer was the "winged" bullet. This was a cylindrical pointed lead bullet but made with opposite, embossed flat projections. The rifling had a pair of wide, flat grooves to suit so the bullet had to follow the rifling.

Whitworth's answer to the problem was hexagonal rifling so pointed cylindrical bullets could be used. These rifles shot very well and fine quality target rifles were made on this principle that, even today, are shot in muzzle loading competitions at up to 1,000 yards. So to find such a splendid example was an opportunity not to be missed. I bought it for £50.

Years later I saw an almost identical cased Whitworth target rifle. It had been bought by Peter Jacques, another of the "good guys" in the antique gun world. In the case was the original receipt detailing the individual cost of all the accessories, so another unique set.

Always interested in rifles I once bought a .451 muzzle loading target rifle by Gibbs of Bristol, a rifle considered to be superior in accuracy to the Whitworth. Although not cased it still retained its original bullet starter. This is a false muzzle that fits onto the end of the true muzzle with a half turn, like a bayonet. The bullet is put into the false muzzle to ensure that it enters the true muzzle absolutely correctly and not tilted. This to ensure maximum accuracy.

Having finished at Laceby Road we went out to the fish docks. It was a glorious autumn day and I spoke to a trawlerman preparing to embark on the next tide. "How fortunate you are" I said "to be going out to sea on such a lovely day". "It won't be so lovely when we get out there!" he replied, nodding seaward.

The following Saturday I read in the paper the report of a trawler lost off the coast of Iceland: Yes, you're right, it was the very trawler!

Fortunately no lives were lost but the trawlerman was right.......it wasn't so lovely after all!

When I told Harvey Taylor about the Whitworth he was very keen indeed to buy it so I very foolishly let it go for £60 and instantly regretted it. A couple of months or so later I persuaded him to sell it back to me and he did so for £80! Serves me right! From then on it stayed in the collection!

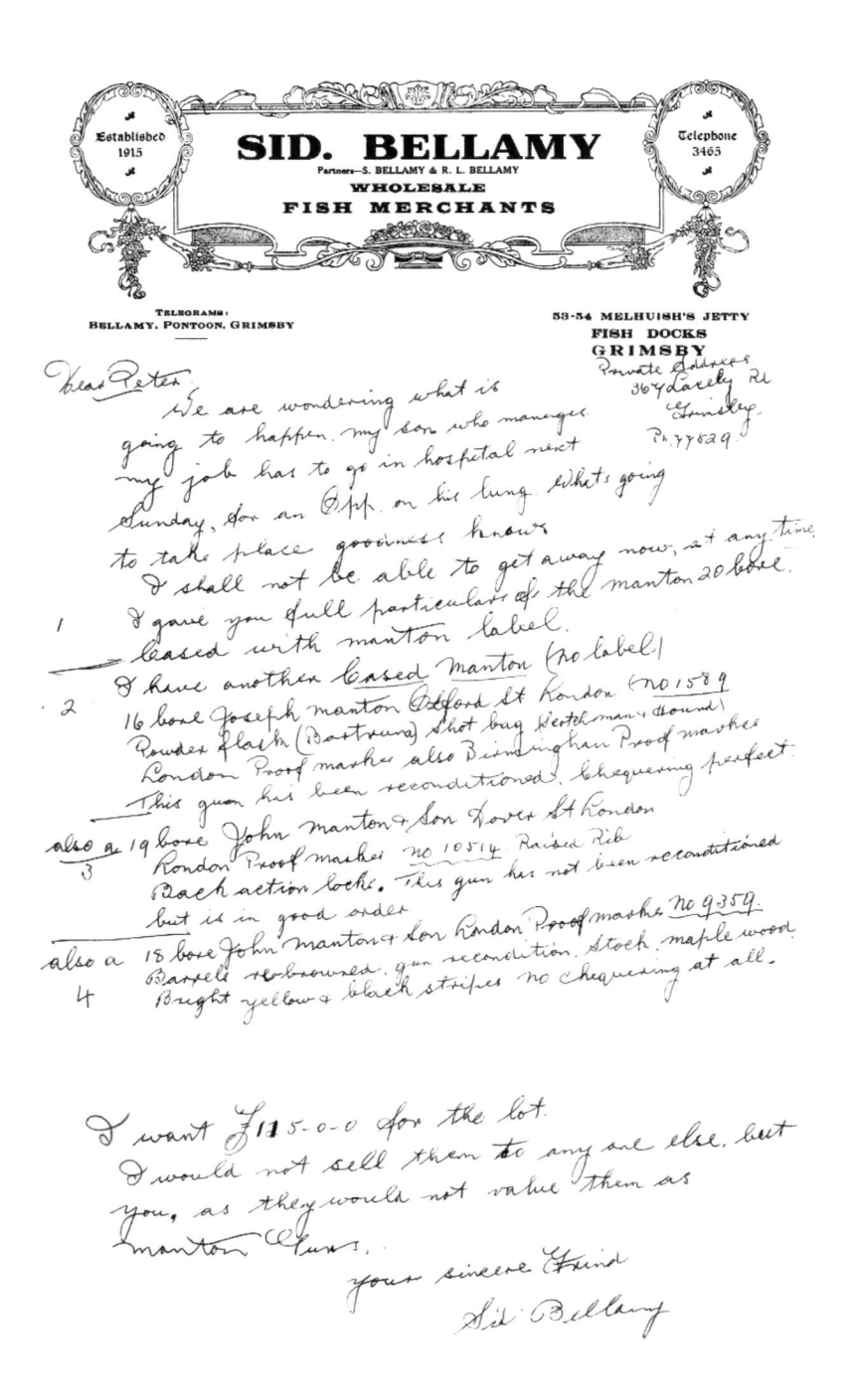

SID. BELLAMY
Partners—S. BELLAMY & R. L. BELLAMY
WHOLESALE FISH MERCHANTS
Established 1915 · Telephone 3465
TELEGRAMS: BELLAMY, PONTOON, GRIMSBY
53-54 MELHUISH'S JETTY, FISH DOCKS, GRIMSBY

Private Address
364 Laceby Rd
Grimsby
Ph. 77529

Dear Peter,

We are wondering what is going to happen. My son who manages my job has to go in hospital next Sunday, for an Opp. on his lung. What's going to take place goodness knows. I shall not be able to get away now, at any time.

1. I gave you full particulars of the Manton 20 bore. Cased with Manton label.

2. I have another Cased Manton (no label) 16 bore Joseph Manton Oxford St London no 1589. Powder flask (Dartrum) shot bag (Scotchman & Hound) London Proof marks, also Birmingham Proof marks. This gun has been reconditioned, chequering perfect.

3. Also a 19 bore John Manton & Son Dover St London, London Proof marks no 10514. Raised rib, back action locks. This gun has not been reconditioned but is in good order.

4. Also a 18 bore John Manton & Son London Proof marks No 9359. Barrels re-browned. Gun reconditioned. Stock maple wood. Bright yellow & black stripes, no chequering at all.

I want £115-0-0 for the lot. I would not sell them to any one else but you, as they would not value them as Manton Guns.

Your sincere friend,
Sid. Bellamy

Letter from Syd Bellamy offering me four Mantons, two of them cased, for £115 the lot! Happy days!

D.B and S.B Forsyths. The first guns in the world to be fired by percussion ignition rather than flint and steel.

Chapter Twenty Five
Forsyth

For centuries the only way to ignite the black powder charge in a gun was by applying an external flame: A glowing match or a spark created by flint on steel. A "match" was a length of glowing saltpetre soaked cord either applied by hand for a cannon or by the hammer for a pistol or musket i.e. a matchlock.

Although the sporting flintlock had been brought to the peak of perfection by the early nineteenth century, drawbacks still remained. Water penetration could never be *completely* eliminated and even dampness in the atmosphere could affect the powder in the pan.

With the flintlock, or any other kind of lock before percussion, the escape of gases via the touch-hole was an insoluble problem with its inevitable reduction in the effective use of the charge.

The chief drawback was the time taken between pulling the trigger and firing the charge, making the forward allowance for a flying bird far greater than it would have been with the percussion system.

The finest sporting flintlocks would fire with only a very small percentage of misfires but this was not, by any means, achieved by poorer quality flintlocks. It has been stated, though surely this is an exaggeration, that military flintlocks would have been expected to misfire as often as seven or eight times out of ten.

The answer, then, was to detonate the charge by percussion i.e. using a substance that would explode by the strike of a hammer, so was such a substance unknown? No it was not!

As long ago as the late sixteenth century it was realised that some substances would explode if struck by a hammer on a hard metal surface. Fulminates of silver or mercury, for example, or gunpowder made with potassium chlorate, rather than potassium nitrate. Samuel Pepys mentioned percussion in his diaries.

Claude Louis de Berthollet (1748-1822) the brilliant French chemist experimented with these substances and others but concluded that such explosives, though powerful, were dangerously unstable, so no practical use could be made of them.

So there the matter rested until the arrival on the scene of the Reverend Alexander Forsyth, minister of Belhelvie, Aberdeenshire, Scotland.

Forsyth was a keen shot and amateur chemist. He claimed that some waterfowl "ducked the flash" i.e. the sight of the flash in the pan of a flintlock alerted them and enabled to dive to safety before the shot charge reached them.

His interest in chemistry prompted him to see if a faster ignition system could be found and between 1800 and 1806 he experimented with different percussion powders and ideas for locks to accept them. Finally, by 1806 he had evolved a workable percussion lock. This lock sounded the death knell of the flintlock era. Every cartridge today is fired by percussion.

The flame from the explosion of the detonating powder shot through the black powder charge, effectively closing the touch-hole, so the Forsyth system not only fired faster but more effectively, too. Not least important was that it was virtually impervious to rain or damp.

The Napoleonic wars were raging so Forsyth offered his invention to the British Government. Lord Moira, Master General of Ordnance, considered that Forsyth's invention might well be applied to military arms and asked Forsyth to develop the system at the Tower of London.

Forsyth was very reluctant to leave Scotland and travel down to London but he eventually obtained leave from the Church, arranged for a substitute to take over at Belhelvie and went to London.

He was allocated workmen to help him in the development of his lock and told that work must be continued in great secrecy. Lord Moira asked him not to apply for a patent to preserve this secrecy.

As with any new idea, development was necessary. Work was carried out using different types of detonating powder. Problems encountered were excessive fouling, too weak an explosion or too fierce. Different locks, too, were designed and made.

Steady progress was made, however, until Lord Moira was succeeded as Master General by the Second Earl of Chatham. He was completely un- impressed by the whole idea of percussion and ordered that all Forsyth's experiments must cease and all his equipment must be removed from the Tower.

As Forsyth's work for the Government was now at an end he immediately applied for a patent in 1807. James Watt, the great engineer, drew up the specification.

The Forsyths.

In June 1808 the *Forsyth Patent Gun Company* commenced business at 10, Piccadilly with James Purdey, formerly with Joe Manton, as stocker and lock filer and Joseph Vicars, who had formerly worked with Forsyth at the Tower, as chief mechanic.

The objective of the business was to make guns with the new percussion locks and with the highest quality of workmanship. From then on the new percussion system was on its way: There were to be many imitators, modifiers, copyists, improvers.

Eventually, of course, the percussion cap was to take over from the loose powder systems but the development from the first Forsyth detonators to the copper cap is immensely interesting and a study in itself.

That the percussion system had signalled the end of the flintlock era was clear to most gunmakers and a number of them were granted permission to make locks on the Forsyth system. Others were to design their own improved versions and start manufacture, though the Forsyth patent provided a blanket coverage.

I once bought, for a modest price, a gun case by Fenton, a name that meant nothing to me. In the case were a number of small, precisely cut, pieces of felt and some totally unfamiliar strikers complete with their springs. I was to find out, years later, that Fenton was one of the gunmakers licensed to make locks on the Forsyth principle and that they were original Forsyth roller primer sealing felts and strikers, a most welcome bonus! But, unfortunately, the gun was long gone!

The above is only a brief précis of the Forsyth story but it is told, in great detail, in *Forsyth & Co: Patent Gunmakers* by W. Keith Neal and David Back.

Over the years I was fortunate enough to acquire two Forsyths: A 10 bore single and a 14 bore double and I must confess that until I had looked closely at the scent bottle shaped roller primer I had never clearly understood how the system worked. So here goes another explanation and a diagram in the hope that it will make it clear to you!

The scent bottle shaped magazine is, in reality, the roller primer and W.Keith Neal disliked "scent bottle", considering that the correct description, "roller primer" should always be used.

You filled the roller primer magazine with percussion powder from a special flask which was enough for about twenty five shots. A half turn deposited a charge in a small indentation in the stub or trunnion upon which the magazine revolved. A hole from this indentation connected to the breech. Half a turn the other way left the roller primer in firing position with the striker in position to fire the charge when the hammer fell.

aneous discharge.

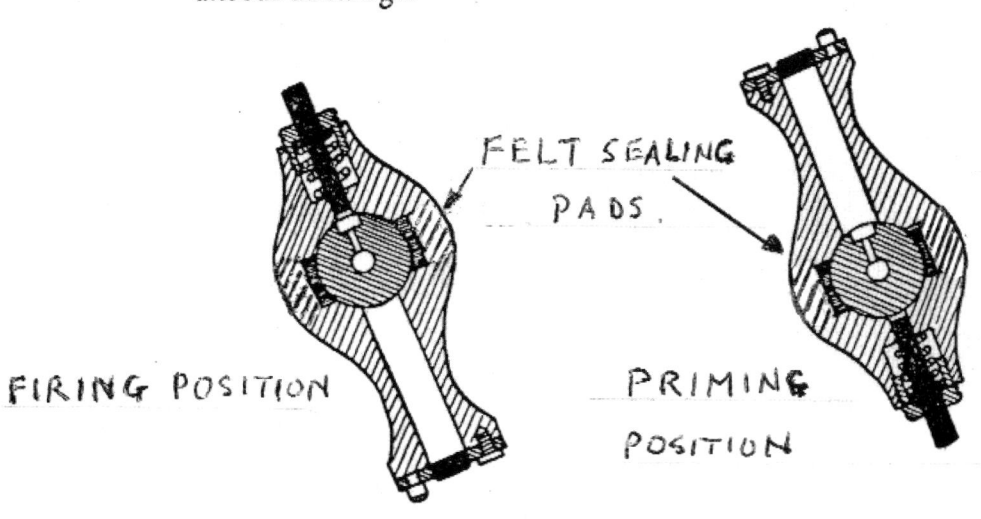

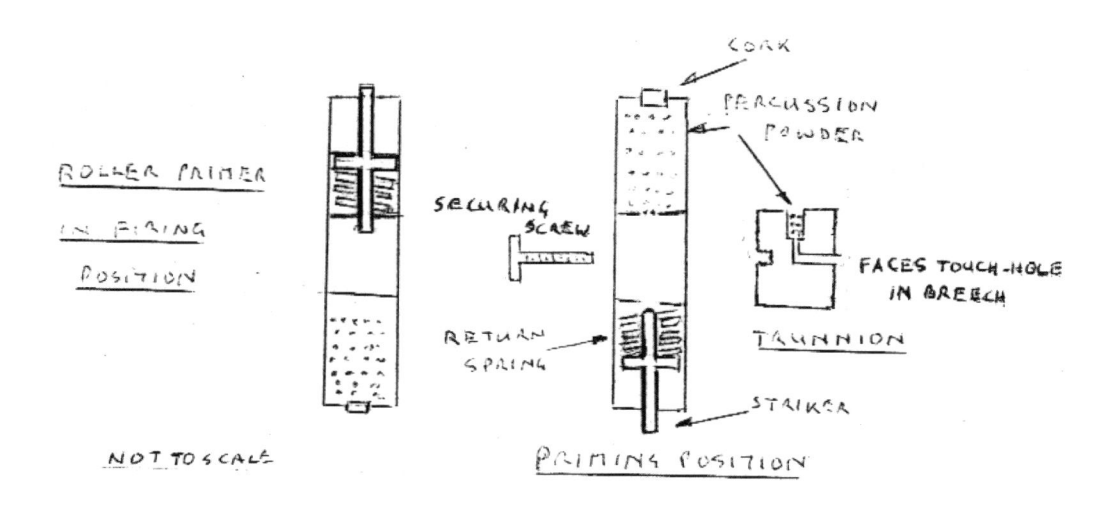

These sketches should make it clear to you how the Forsyth "scent bottle" or, more correctly, roller primer system, worked.

When my daughter, Caroline, was very small, I took her to see a carnival for the first time. She watched, entranced and saucer-eyed, at this amazing colourful spectacle. "Do you like it?" I asked. "Yes" she replied. *But what is it?*

You may well say the same when you look at the photograph of this Lewis and Tomes gun. Yes, you like the look of this attractive and unusual gun, but *what is it?*

For a start, who were Lewis and Tomes? They must have been working together in the period 1810 to 1830 because that was when this gun must have been produced, yet little seems to be known about them.

The best I can come up with is from *Gunmakers of London 1350-1850* by Howard L. Blackmore: "Lewis and Tomes, merchants (probably Edward Lewis, Birmingham and Francis Tomes, New York), Birmingham 1823-1831; New York 1819-1825. Marked guns "London" May have had connections with William Tomes (q.v.) Name also appears on guns of c.1850-1865. This may represent partnership of George Edward Lewis, Gunmaker, Birmingham 1852-1908, and William James Tomes (q.v.)" (q.v. denotes a cross-reference).

All that doesn't really help us a lot! The gun is a loose powder detonator and an ingenious variation of the Forsyth system, so surely it must have been made during the period 1808-1827, which is the period when Forsyth made loose powder detonators. After that they changed to copper cap. It is a simpler system than the Forsyth: you fill the little thimbles with percussion powder and when the hammers are cocked, a hole in the bottom of the thimble deposits a charge of percussion powder in the depression in the trunnion exactly like a Forsyth. The thimble is linked to the hammer so when the hammer falls, the thimble swings forward and the point of the hammer strikes directly into the depression in the trunnion which is now filled with percussion powder.

So a perfectly effective system but much simpler than the Forsyth. The Forsyth patent expired in 1822 so after that date, other makers were free to make their own systems, though before then a number of others had infringed the patent and had to face lawsuits, so was it licensed by Forsyth or pirated? We will never know unless, of course, you have the answer.

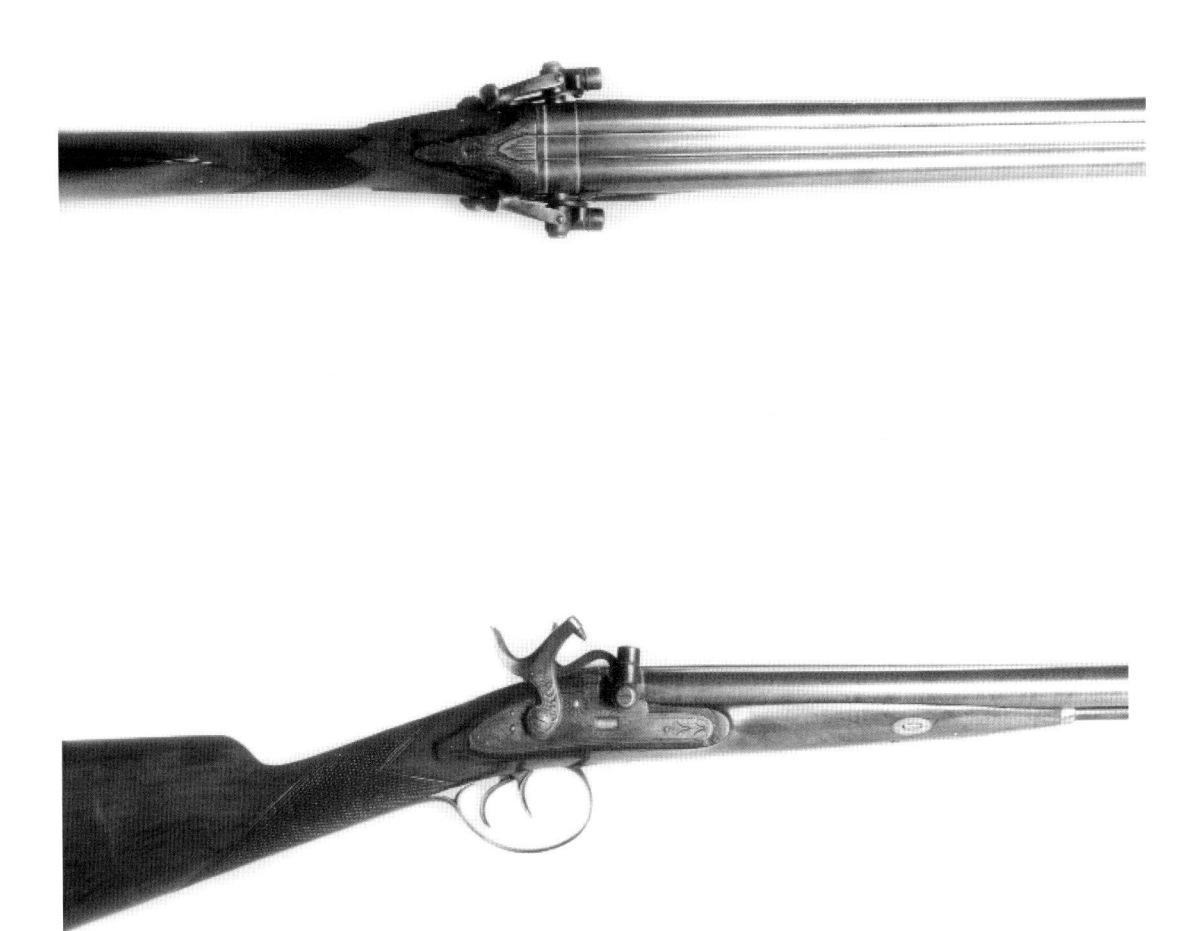

Lewis and Tomes loose powder detonator. A simple variation of the Forsyth principle. The screw-top thimble is filled with percussion powder and with the hammer in the raised position the powder in the thimble fills a U-shaped depression in the trunnion just like a Forsyth. When the hammer falls the thimble moves out of the way and the point of the hammer strikes the percussion powder in the trunnion.

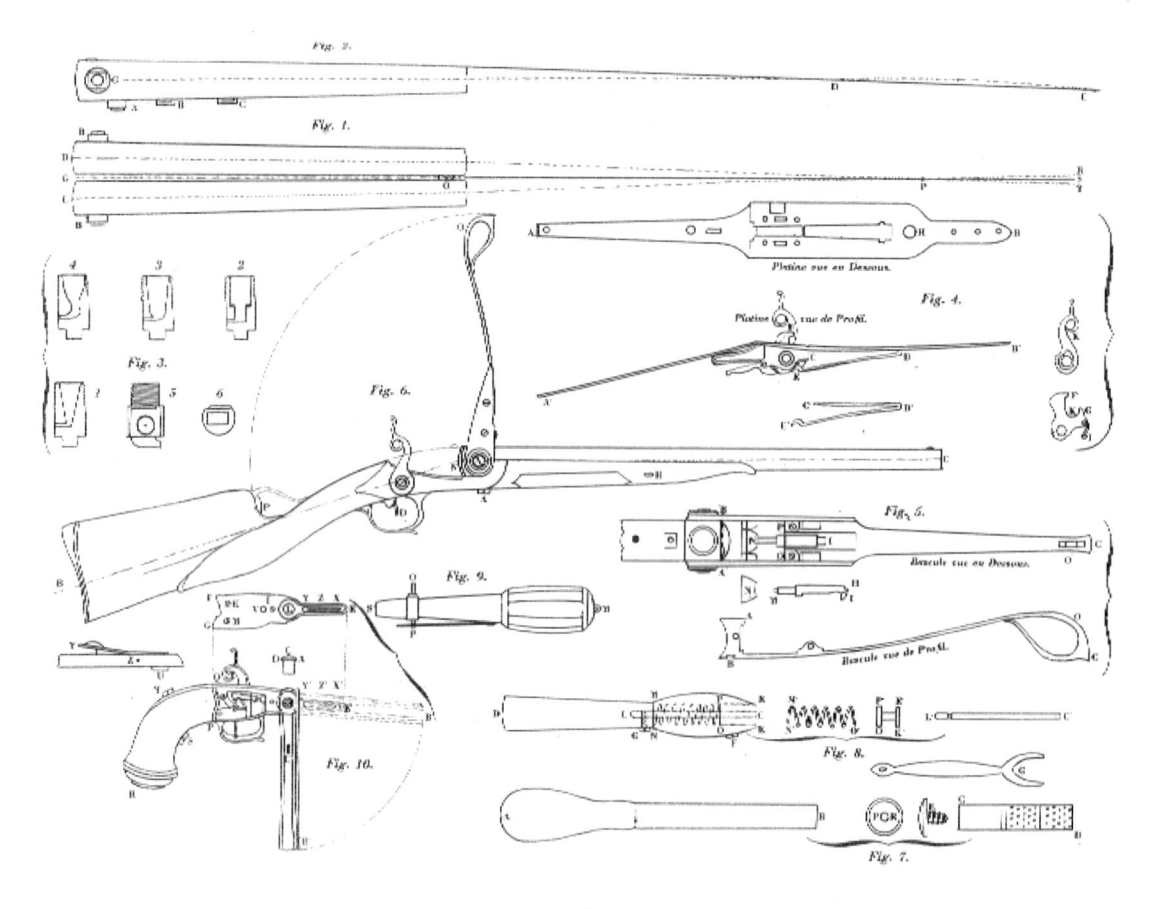

After Henri Roux's Fusils de Chasse

7. Drawing of Pauly firearms, with tools for loading cartridges

So you never can understand diagrams like this? Don't worry, neither can I! In this case it really does take some understanding: Firstly ignore those muzzle loading breeches on the left hand side above the stock as they have nothing to do with breech loading Paulys. Now look at fig 7 in the bottom right hand corner. This shows the brass "rosette" that screws into the cardboard base of the paper cartridge case. The adjoining top view of the rosette is puzzlingly labelled POR. Cannot account for the P and R, but the O is, in fact, the indentation that holds the percussion powder. Getting clearer now? The adjoining fork shaped object is the manual cartridge extractor but the sticking up bits at the ends of the forks that engage the rim of the rosette are not shown. That's just to make it more difficult! DCA in Fig 10 shows the brass cartridge case for pistols. A round lead ball was inserted in the open end. Fig 9 is the percussion powder flask and Fig 8 is the punch for making the hole in the cardboard base of the paper cartridge. Got it all now? Clear as mud!

Chapter Twenty Six
Pauly Breech Loaders

Breech loading was not a new idea in the early nineteenth century: Henry Vlll had breech loading cannon, but ignition had to be in the time honoured manner by slow match or flint and steel. Nor were cartridges new, but a small arms cartridge would be a paper case containing either just the black powder charge or the charge together with the lead bullet.

No cartridge had been made complete with its own system of ignition so that all you had to do, as today, was to put the cartridge into the breech, cock the gun and fire it.

The first man to make such a cartridge i.e. a modern cartridge was a Swiss gunsmith named Jean Samuel Pauly.

Pauly's date of birth is not known but he came to Paris about 1808 and on the 29th September, 1812 he was given a French patent for a breech loading gun that used a self-contained, rimmed, centre fire cartridge. This was the first breech-loader to use percussion ignition.

Many years later, needlefire and pinfire cartridges held sway until centre fire inevitably took over to be universally accepted….but Pauly got there first! It was not until half a century later that the British Army went over from muzzle loaders to breech loaders.

Look at the photograph of the cased Pauly in this chapter and you will see a length of round steel rod. Round this rod you wind a length of cartridge paper, cut to the length of the cartridge you require. (yes, you now know why it is called cartridge paper). You then paste the overlapping ends so that you have a cartridge size paper cylinder.

Next you use a special punch to punch out a circular cardboard disc with a hole in the centre. This is placed in one end of the paper cylinder and the end rolled over with the tool provided to hold it into position.

You then fill the cartridge with powder, cardboard wad, shot charge and overshot cardboard disc in the normal way, finally closing the end with the same roll-over tool.

Now you have your cartridge, all you need is its ignition system! So you take one of the rosettes, (Pauly's description), and screw it into the hole provided in the cardboard disc. You then fill loose percussion powder into the circular depression in the rosette, seal it with some gum arabic, (you have eaten tons of it in Rowntrees fruit gums), and there you are with a cartridge ready to fire.

Look at the breeches in the barrels of your modern shotgun and you will find that they are counterbored to accept the cartridge rim and chambered to accept the cartridge. The Pauly barrels are exactly the same yet they were designed almost two centuries ago.

Your modern shotgun is centrefire….. so is the Pauly. The external levers on the Pauly are cocking levers operating internal strikers, not hammers, so the Pauly is a hammerless centrefire. A design far ahead of its time.

The Pauly cartridge with its rosette and consumable paper case could not be expected to be 100% gastight so the small vent holes in the bassinet (hinged breech) allowed for any escape of exploding gases. Pauly explained that the rosette fitting into the breech did help to reduce the escape of gases and, in addition, ensured that the cartridge was exactly positioned and did not go too far into the barrels.

In Pauly's later 1816 British patent he was well aware of the need for a gastight joint at the rosette and suggested that it could be made of "some plastic or yielding substance, turned or cast in a mould". The cartridges for his pistols, however, were entirely of brass, like a modern cartridge, so you would have expected them to be far more gastight than the rosettes. Other than the question of expense there was nothing to prevent shotgun or rifle cartridges being made of brass.

In July 1814, at a meeting of La Societé, the society for the encouragement of national industry in France, the committee published a report on Pauly firearms. The committee was composed of highly regarded men of science: M.M Bardel, Humbelot, Regnier, and Brillat-Savarin who recognised the many advantages of the Pauly system. They concluded that "Your Commission thinks the Pauly gun should be given first place among firearms that are known in this day".

Napoleon was an artilleryman, fully conversant with guns of the day. Had the French army faced the British flintlock muskets at Waterloo with the immensely superior firepower of the Paulys, the result could have been different. Another enormous advantage of the Pauly, also pointed out by the committee, was that the Pauly could not be double loaded… a problem with muzzle loaders in the heat of the battle.

So why did Napoleon reject the Pauly?

He would have been well aware that in the hands of a leisurely sportsman shooting September partridges the Pauly would be infinitely superior to any flintlock, but in the hands of an ordinary soldier in the heat of battle with a complex and unproved new gun? Surely better to stick to the rugged, simple and well tried flintlock musket.

The Ministry of War was against the change chiefly because of the high cost and the danger of using one kind of powder for ignition and another for the propellant. They do not appear to have realised that complete, ready primed cartridges would have been issued to the army and there would have been no question of the soldier in battle reloading them.

In any event Napoleon had said, though not in connection with the Pauly to which it equally applied: "Inventions coming before their time remain useless until knowledge in general comes up to their level". As pointed out earlier when Faraday demonstrated the generation of electricity to Queen Victoria she said: "Very interesting, but what use is it?"

Pauly guns were, however, used at Waterloo, Some French officers used their own privately owned Pauly pistols. The first ever guns with 'modern' cartridges ever used in war.

Very few Pauly guns, rifles or pistols have survived and only small numbers could have been made. Some are only marked Pauly but others were made on the Pauly principle by other makers. Some are marked "Pauly & Cie" and others have the names of Pauly's successors: Roux, Pichereau and Lefaucheux.

The original Paulys were, of course, made before the invention of the copper cap but in 1829 Pottet patented a modification of the rosette to take a copper cap so that all you had to do was substitute the Pottet head, which took the paper cased cartridge, in place of the original rosette.

Pauly's inventive genius did not end with the invention of his breech loader and he took out several British patents. One in 1814 and another in 1816 were for compressed air ignition. Other inventors were to take out patents for such guns but Pauly was the first.

The idea, which was perfectly sound, was to compress air with a piston operating in what Pauly called a "syringe" then force the heated air into a small hole in the base of the cartridge enabling the "caloric" to ignite the charge. Had Pauly thought of this idea earlier, before Forsyth's loose powder detonators, he would have been the man to have made flintlocks obsolete.

Pauly came to England about 1814 and used the Christian names of Jean Samuel and Samuel John. In 1822 it was confirmed that he had lived in England for several years but apparently he had died by 1828.

The famous London gunsmith, Durs Egg, was also a Swiss and he and Pauly joined forces in 1815 to obtain the first ever British patent for a flying machine. The machines were described as "Certain Aerial Conveyances and Vessels to be steered by Philosophical or Chemical Mechanical Means". Philosophical in those days meant scientific.

The design was for a fish shaped balloon with a wooden frame which would have carried a "Gondola, boat or car". There was to be a movable tail and movable "fins, feathers, fans or wings" to steer the machine from side to side or up and down". They would be operated by machinery which was claimed to be extremely simple and could be made by any practical mechanic. The machinery to be powered "either by manual or mechanical means using, in the latter case, any first mover which may be applicable to the purpose".

There would be a water filled barrel moved either forwards or backwards by pulleys to raise or lower the nose of the craft with the water also doubling as ballast. A silly idea? Not at all! Count Zeppelin used it in his first rigid airship almost a century later.

It was named the "Dolphin" and in 1816 a shed was built 100 feet long and over 30 feet high and construction commenced. Tickets were sold at a guinea each to see "one of the ascensions" but, of course, none ever took place.

The project was said to have cost Durs Egg ten thousand pounds before it was finally abandoned and he died about 1828.

J.E. Hodgson wrote in more detail about it all in his book, written in 1924, *The History of Aeronautics in Great Britain.*

So this brings us to the end of what we know about this amazing man. Was there a Mrs. Pauly or any baby Paulys? On this, history is silent but, as you know, "When nature creates a genius, she breaks the mould".

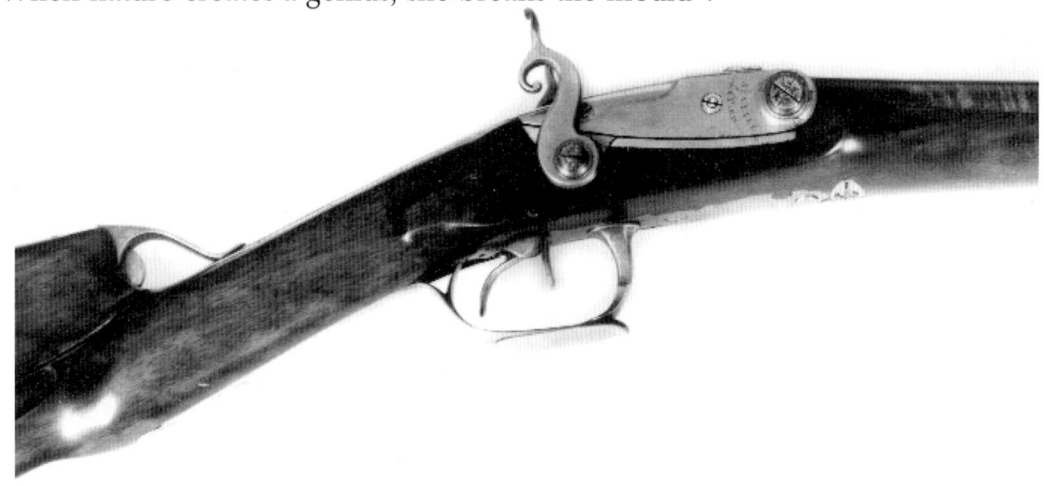

The 1812 Pauly Breech Loader.

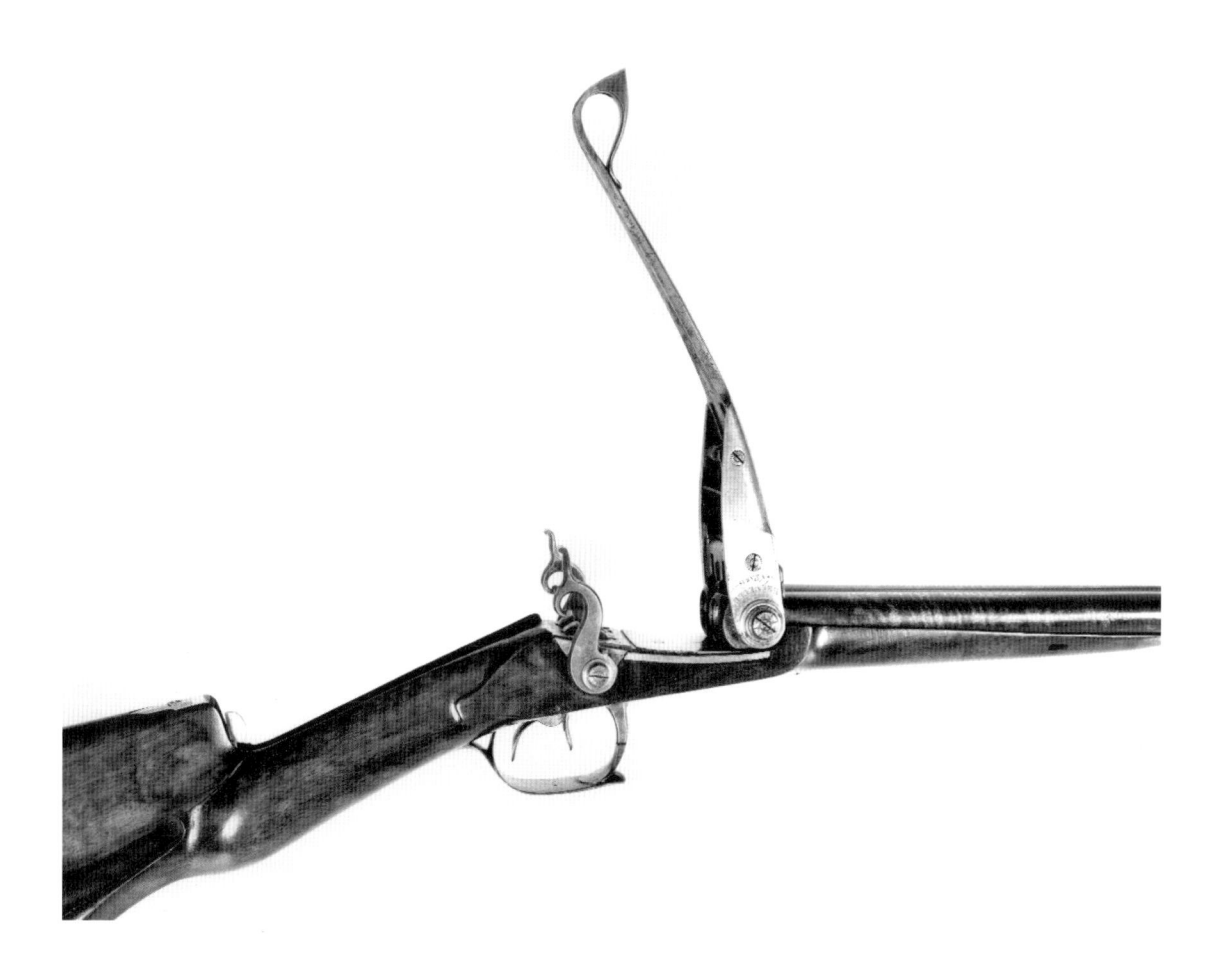

The 1812 Pauly Breech Loader. The first gun to fire a self-contained cartridge with its own percussion element, as today.

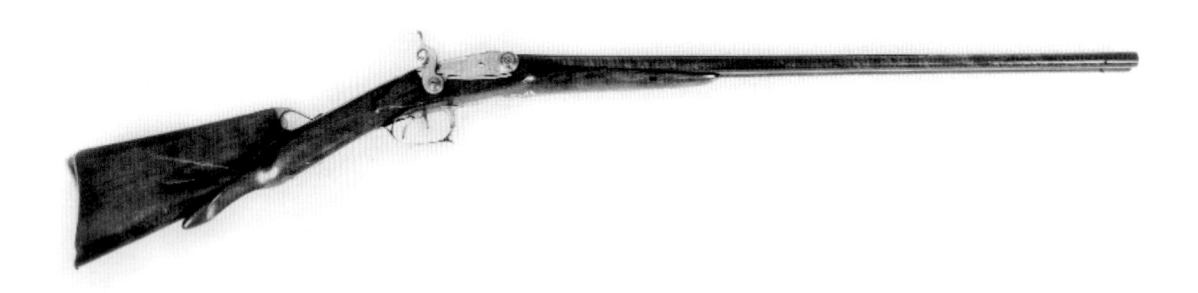

Another view of the 1812 Pauly Breech Loader and case.

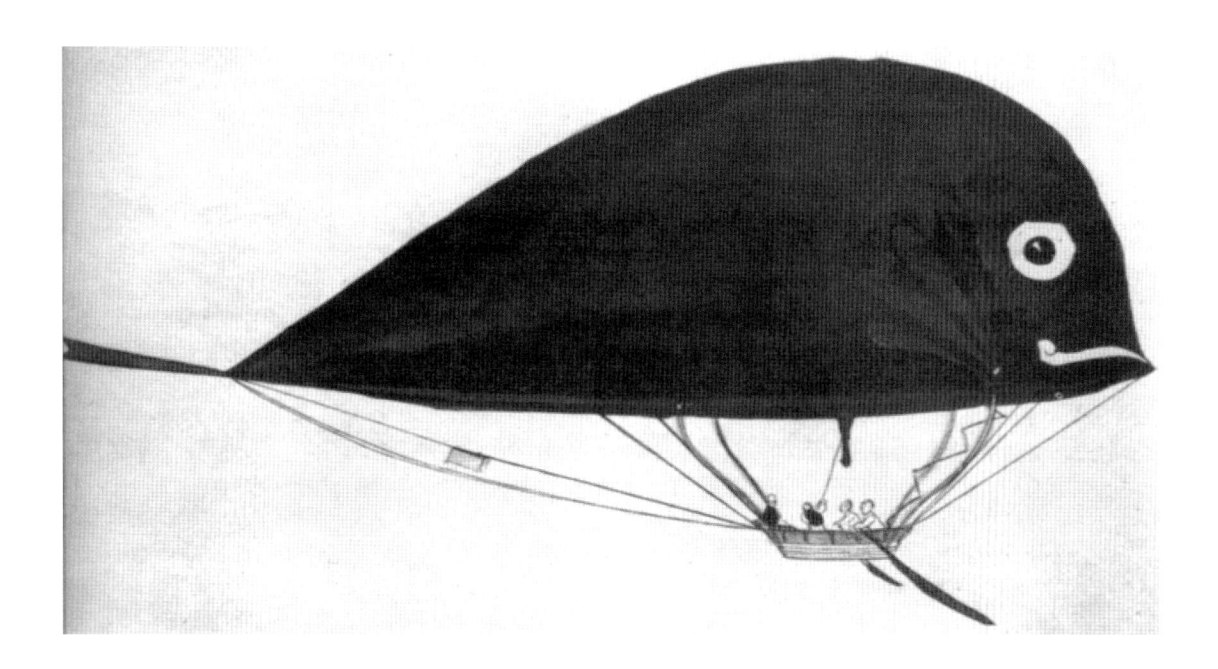

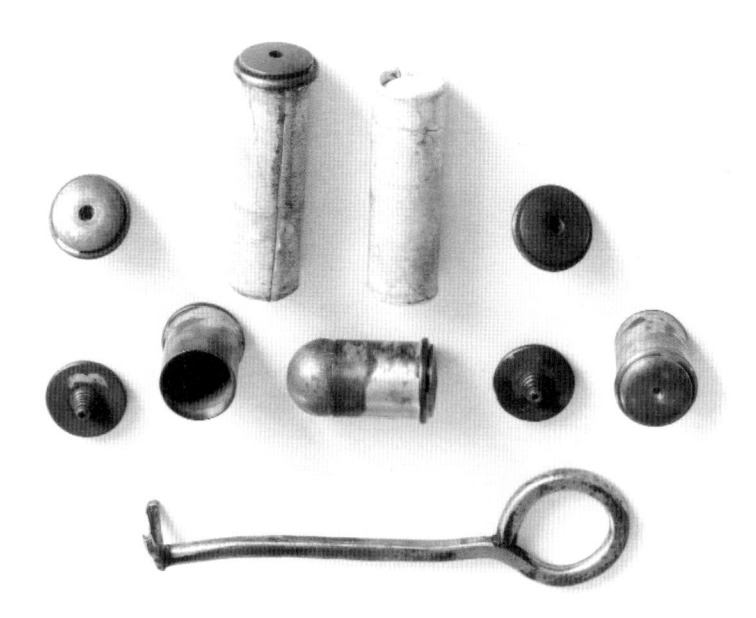

Pauly and fellow Swiss, Durs Egg, designed this flying machine in 1816 but although construction was started it was never completed.
Cartridge extractor, rosettes, paper cartridge cases with and without rosette, brass pistol cartridge cases.

Derek Fearn with a pair of shotgun barrels prepared for the centre rib to be relaid.

Chapter Twenty Seven
Derek Fearn, Master Gunsmith

A few years ago I was told about an extremely talented gunsmith who lived not far from me. His name was Derek Fearn and he worked in one of the outbuildings at Catton Hall near Swadlincote, South Derbyshire.

I went over to see him in his workshop which was a revelation! The kind of scene that would have been just the same a hundred years ago.

Not only is the whole place crammed from floor to ceiling but *including* the ceiling with every kind of gunsmiths impedimenta: All kinds of gun parts in every state of repair, or disrepair, including barrels, stocks, actions, tools and equipment of every kind. Junk to the uninitiated but an absolute treasure trove for anyone interested in guns and shooting.

Derek is one of the good guys of this world, one of the most fortunate of men whose work is his hobby. He runs a one-man business whose main concern is the repair and maintenance of modern guns and rifles but, in addition to that, he is immensely skilled in the restoration of antique guns and rifles. He has even made several double rifles. How many gunsmiths could achieve that?

He has another remarkable talent: An encyclopedic knowledge of the whole world of guns and rifles, ancient and modern, that few could match. So much so that if anything unusual, unheard of or baffling turns up in the Birmingham gun trade the word goes out: "Ask Derek!"

Was it Confucius or Joe Bloggs who said: "If you have time to spare, don't spend it with someone who hasn't". So when visiting Derek's workshop you have to resist the urge to stay and chat. When there is the opportunity to talk, however, when visiting him at home, for example, then his range of knowledge never fails to astound you: When was the Birmingham Proof House opened? Derek will know. Date the .22 rimfire long rifle cartridge was introduced? No problem. How many pellets of number six shot will a full choke sixteen bore barrel put into a thirty inch circle at thirty five yards? Easy-peasey! So much to learn when talking to Derek.

Vintage rifles are a special interest so the Black Powder Expresses retain a great appeal. He has several examples in his collection and has shot deer with them in England but not Scotland. No shortage of striking energy which is acceptable for both England and Scotland but in Scotland there is, in addition, a requirement for a bullet velocity that no black powder rifle can achieve. You have a huge black powder rifle that will stop a charging African buffalo? Fine, but you cannot use it to shoot deer in Scotland.

But despite Derek's skill, talent, ability and knowledge he remains a very modest man.

Winston Churchill, discussing his political opponent, Clement Attlee said: "He is a very modest man and he has much to be modest about!" Derek, on the contrary, is a modest man with *nothing* to be modest about.

When I first met Derek Fearn I had three Manton and Co., London and Calcutta SB screw breech rook and rabbit rifles that I had owned for years. All of them had bits and pieces missing and all required restoration.

Now Derek is far too busy to tackle this kind of work but you know the saying: "If you want a job done, ask a busy man. A lazy man never has the time!" So Derek, always prepared to go out of his way to help a fellow enthusiast, undertook the task and made an excellent job of them all.

His masterpiece was the restoration of a .450 Purdey double Black Powder Express rifle after a century of neglect, but more of this later.

I count myself very fortunate indeed to know such a remarkable man and as I tell him, and any of his customers I meet, whatever he charges it's worth double!

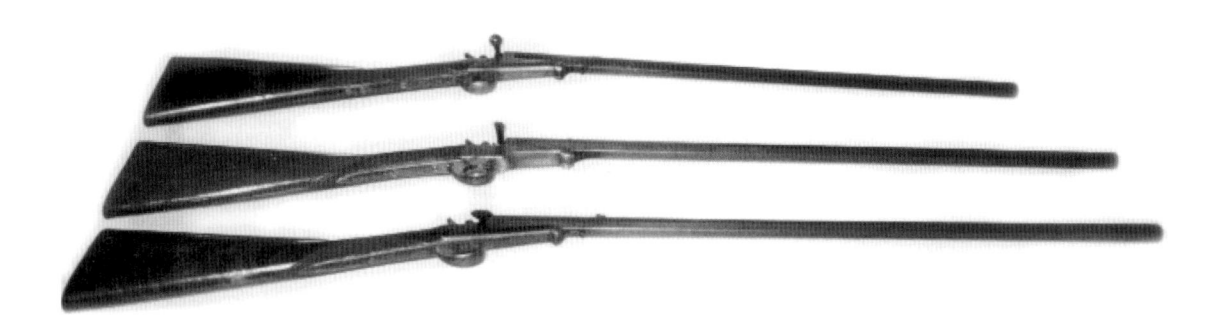

Three Manton and Co, screw breech needle fire rook rifles restored by Derek Fearn.

Derek Fearn heats the barrels of a D.B. shotgun to melt the solder and secure the rib.

Entrance to the Birmingham Proof House.

Chapter Twenty Eight
A Visit To The Birmingham Gun Quarter

At one time the Birmingham gun quarter was a rabbit warren of premises divided into dozens of rooms, each occupied by a specialist worker: Barrel filers, stockers, engravers, colour hardeners, lock filers and every possible branch of the gun trade.

They all worked together and the result of their work was finally assembled into the finished gun.

Those days are long gone but a remnant of the gun trade continues in Price Street, Birmingham. Some of the old buildings do survive, now restored and, in addition, there are new buildings, too.

The tradition of specialist craftsmen working in their own rooms continues and they all co-operate.

Every Friday morning for the last twenty five years Derek Fearn the superlative gunsmith from Catton Hall, has made the trip to Price Street and, if necessary, to the Birmingham Proof House to deliver and collect work.

He had promised to take me with him one day and on a bright February day that day finally arrived.

Derek had made a beautiful job of restoring a .450 D.B. Black Powder Express rifle for me. It had languished, rusting away, in Purdey's cellar for half a century or more before being given to an old friend of mine and fellow Manton enthusiast, Michael Weaving. Michael passed it on to me for £5 about 1960 and some time later I lent it to a keen black powder rifleman to get a new fore-end made. (The piece of a gun or rifle you hold with your left hand).

The years went by and I forgot the name and address of the chap I had lent it to but by a series of coincidences, thirty years later, I located him. Yes, he still had the rifle. No he had never managed to get a new fore-end made and, as he was an honest man, yes, I could have it back.

Derek Fearn, master gunsmith, collects a de-activated Tommy Gun and other rifles from the Birmingham Proof House. Wayne Massey is behind the counter.

Wayne Massey and pony tailed Laurence High in the Birmingham Proof House. In the foreground is a Remington rifle in for English Proof.

 All it needed now was fitting into the correct Purdey guncase. Fortunately I had one that would suit complete with its original Purdey label into which the rifle fitted loosely. Now it required to be fitted correctly.

 At Price Street there is still, believe it or not, a gun and rifle guncase maker, Robert Hayden, a man I had to see to explain exactly how I wanted the Purdey fitted into the case, so on the appointed date off we went to Birmingham in Derek's little green van.

 First stop the Birmingham Proof House, one of the most famous and historic places in the world of gunmaking. Derek had several guns for re-proof and others for de-activation certificates. Guns to collect including three de-activated Tommy Guns. "Not for me," said Derek hastily "they're for another dealer…..they're not my scene!"

 A very pleasant man named Wayne Massey was dealing with Derek and I asked him if it would be possible for me to go inside, ask some questions and take some photographs. The answer was a hesitant "Yes", on the understanding that I could only photograph under his supervision, but that was fine.

 Some guns and rifles for re-proof were in short racks so Wayne very kindly lined them up for me to photograph. Other items pointed out, too, for example a vast array of proof gauges. Two huge stacks of World War Two M30 automatic carbines were verboten! They all looked like scrap to me but Wayne told me that some were for re-proof and others for de-activating but, of course, the re-proofed ones could not be owned privately in Britain.

Derek Fearn discusses a job with master stocker Barry King.

About half a dozen World War Two de-activated Bren guns in very shabby condition were also on the forbidden list but would, no doubt, be re-furbished before resale.

Much more to see then on to a long room where a lady was crouched over, examining a gun. "What's the gun that lady's examining?" I asked. The lady straightened up….. it was Laurence High, a man with a pony tail and a broad smile! Profuse apologies offered but, as I pointed out to him, with a hairstyle like that mistakes were going to be made! He was, in fact examining a new Remington rifle, one of a batch in for English proof.

On, then, to Price Street, the gun and rifle Mecca. On the way we passed an innocent looking row of shops behind which two teenage girls died when caught in gang warfare crossfire the previous New Year.

All premises under strict security with push button locks. You have to press a button and announce who you are before the outside door is opened. Then up flight after flight of stairs to reach Robert Hayden's eyrie at the very top of the building.

Robert is a small chap with a very pleasant personality who listened patiently to my requirements for the Purdey case and suggested several improvements which were most welcome. Acceptable price quoted and the case left with him for Derek to collect in a couple of weeks. He showed us a massive leather covered oak case by Purdey for a pair of guns. Stamped on the lid was "Prince Frederick Duleep Singh". It had been bought by a Canadian collector from Sothebys for two thousand pounds and this, remember, for an empty case.

The Maharajah Duleep Singh was one of the legendary characters in the nineteenth century shooting world. One of the very finest shots who still holds the record for the most walked up (not driven) grouse shot in one day (at Grandtully, Perthshire.) He gave the Koh-I-Noor diamond to Queen Victoria…..but later regretted it. He was the owner of the famous Elveden estate in the south of England.

He had two sons, Prince Frederick and Prince Victor, also excellent shots and fine cricketers, known as "The Black Princes". So this case was for Prince Frederick's pair of Purdeys……….but what happened to the guns?

The Black Princes are known to have shot over the land at Newton Park Farm when it was part of the huge estate owned by Lord Chesterfield.

On, then, to the next building and up the stairs to Barry King's room. Barry is a stocker and was working on a fitting a new stock to a fine sporting shotgun. Would he re-stock a muzzle loader? "No, not at any price!" He had done them in the past but nowadays it would be completely unfamiliar so he stuck with work he knew.

Superb engraving prior to colour hardening.

The .450 Purdey put in his gun safe for safekeeping then he chatted away imparting all kinds of information. He showed us the action and specification of a system patented in Austria at the end of the nineteenth century. Your right hand gripped the gun in the normal manner but instead of triggers you pressed buttons, one for each barrel. The buttons projected downwards so your fingers pressed them upwards. The idea was to prevent the jerking that can spoil your aim with conventional triggers. All new to me, but the nineteenth century produced literally thousands of inventions in the gun world, some to gain lasting fame, many destined to be never heard of again.

Next to the colour hardeners. ………this firm run by Ray St.Ledger and his two sons, Richard and Robert. They showed me two actions kept as workpieces to demonstrate their work. Both of them works of art in variations of colour that would enhance the finest gun or rifle. They then showed me two actions for new guns that were absolutely encrusted with gold, beautifully engraved.

One was for an over and under double rifle, the other for a 12 bore shotgun. Colour hardening is produced by heat, so why didn't the gold melt? The answer is that the treatment is produced in an electric furnace and the heat can be precisely controlled *lower* than the melting point of gold; but what a responsibility!

Robert Haydn, guncase maker in his eyrie.

The degree of colour can be to the customer's choice and the high colour of these two actions seemed over the top to Derek and I but, as Richard and Robert said, you would have to see the completed gun to make a correct judgement and they were sure that you would finally approve.

So who was the maker of the guns for which these actions were destined? Pass! Not to be disclosed for reasons of confidentiality.

When "Dallas" was essential viewing on television sets throughout the world, Larry Hagman, the infamous "J.R.", commissioned an unique twelve bore double shotgun from Holland and Holland. Nothing quite like it had ever been seen before or since. The engraving must have cost as much as the gun!

Portraits of all the leading characters from the series were inserted in circular discs: J.R. himself, of course, Sue-Ellen, Lucy, Ray, Des Barnes, Miss Ellie……..the lot!

All the colour hardening had been carried out by Ray and his family. But how would you dare to actually use such a gun? No doubt, however, the objective was not to use it but keep it as an unquestionable work of art.

Next, then, to Philip Duffill the engraver. Again his workshop was very small but in keeping with all the others was spotlessly clean. Philip had "picked up" the engraving, where necessary, on my .450 Purdey rifle.

Robert Haydn shows the Purdey gun case owned by Prince Frederick Duleep Singh one of the two "Black Princes", great cricketers and shots, sons of the legendary Marharajah Duleep Singh.

He was re-engraving a Dickson of Edinburgh muzzle loading double rifle. Strangely enough Derek Fearn is, at the moment, doing some work on a very similar Dickson double rifle of mine that was made as a muzzle loader but was later converted to .500 Black Powder Express.

The breeches, false breech, lock plates, trigger guard, hammers etc had been badly rusted but it had been possible to take a rubbing and Philip was carefully reproducing the original design. He was working on one of the hammers, now completely filed up and polished. "Surely it will take you days to complete one hammer?" I asked. "No" said Philip "less than a day". He showed me the completed false breech, i.e. the piece immediately behind the barrels and he had beautifully duplicated the original engraving.

On a plain workpiece he engraved a scroll freehand, then engraved an identical one about half an inch below it. No measuring, no marking out. He then set a pair of dividers against them both and the size was identical! What skill!

On his bench he had a circular stainless steel device about the size and shape of a two and a half litre paint tin. On the top was a small vise to which he transferred the same workpiece. Holding his engraving tool against the workpiece he rotated the device by hand and made an identical scroll *without moving the engraving tool!*

Then, to my amazement, he lifted the whole thing off the bench! The circular, rounded base fits into an identical shape, like a ball and socket.

So a morning absolutely packed with interest and, as a bonus, during the journey both ways there was so much to learn chatting to Derek. On guns and shooting, ancient or modern, his knowledge would be hard to equal.

Wayne Massey at the Birmingham Proof House.

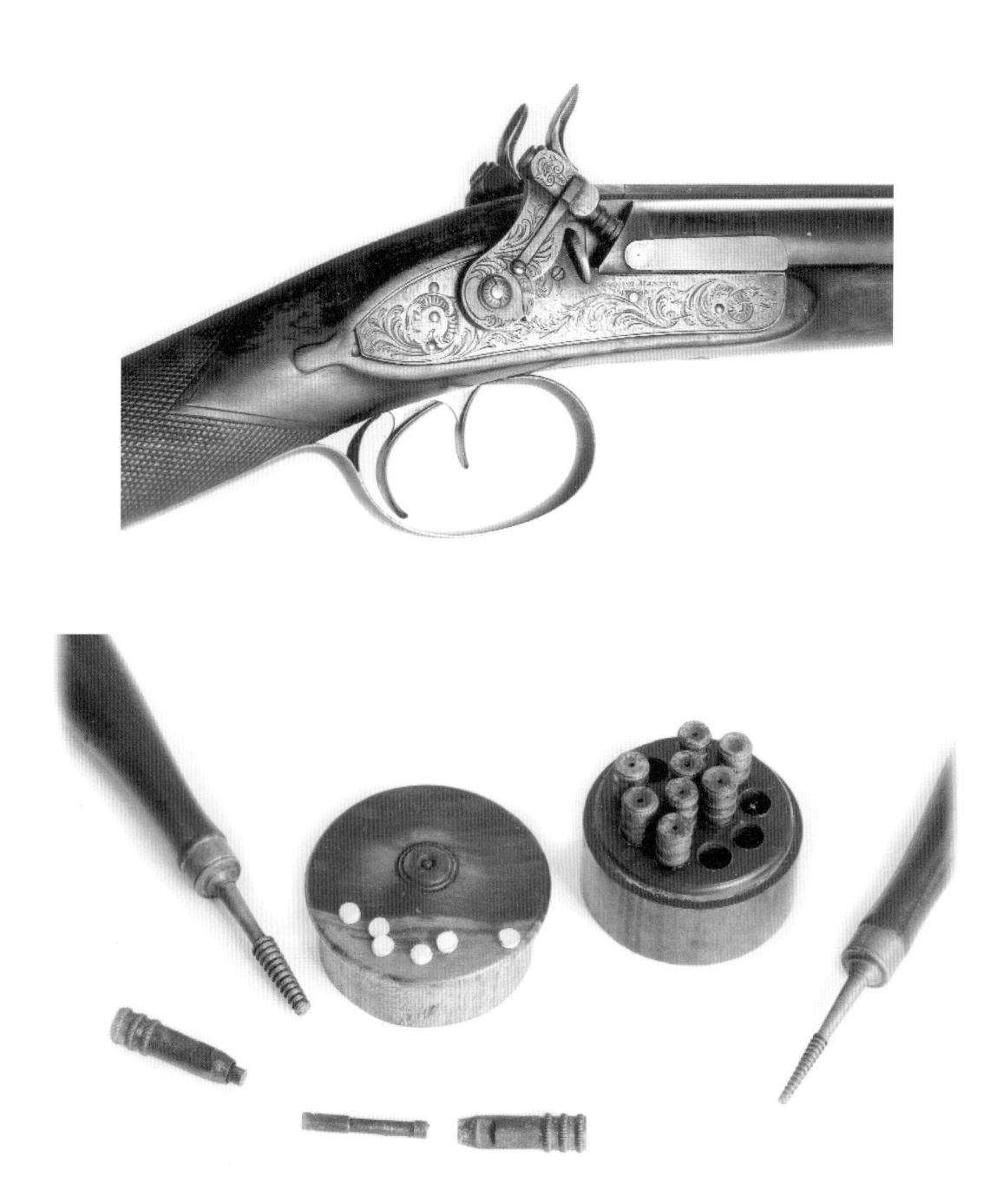

Joseph Manton pelletlock no. 8063. An important and hugely under-estimated improvement in the development of percussion ignition.
Strikers in their holder. Cleaning jags for hammers and strikers. Paper caps which replaced pellets.

Chapter Twenty Nine
The Joseph Manton Pelletlock

In 1816 Joseph Manton invented his pelletlock and for the first time a sportsman could fire a shot, remove the fired striker with a twist of his fingers, take a previously primed striker from a container in his pocket and simply snap it back into the hammer ready for the next shot.

This was an enormous advance on the loose powder detonators such as the Forsyths and their followers. This, remember, before the percussion cap had arrived.

The importance of the Joseph Manton pelletlock on the evolution of the percussion system has, unfortunately, been largely overlooked.

With the Forsyth and other loose powder detonators the percussion powder had to be kept in a separate flask which was potentially dangerous. Re-filling the magazine during a day's shooting was not only messy and time consuming but also risky.

The pelletlock eliminated all of this so why has its importance been unrecognised?

The reason is down to Joe Manton's questing, innovative brain: Only two years after the invention of the pelletlock he invented the tubelock and it was a case of out with the old, in with the new.

The tubelock eliminated the chore of cleaning the pelletlock strikers and hammers after a day's shooting so Joe Manton, never a man to look back, discarded the pelletlock in favour of his new system.

Conventional wisdom has branded the pelletlock a failure *but this is untrue*. It worked perfectly well during the time that it was in use. It is important to remember that less than three hundred were ever made.

I discussed this with the great gun collector and authority on antique guns, W. Keith Neal. Both he and I had fired Joseph Manton pelletlocks and we had found them perfectly satisfactory. I now refer you to Hawker's diaries in which he records shooting with pelletlock no 8111 presented to him by Joseph Manton on October 26th 1816:

Oct 26th. Received a detonating double gun (No.8111) value 100 guineas, presented to me by Mr. Joseph Manton.

Oct 27th. Went out with this elegant gun, and notwith-standing an incessant pour of rain, I killed, in 15 shots - 9 snipes, 3 partridges, a spotted gallinule, and a water rail. The one shot that I missed was far beyond a fair distance.

Nov 4th. Drove to Andover, walked from the town down the river, and bagged - - 19 snipes and jack-snipes, besides two shot and lost, making 10 and a half couple, without having missed a fair shot.

Nov 6th. 2 partridges and 4 snipes. Tried the effect of the detonating gun at birds which "duck at the flash" and found it to answer admirably, by killing dabchicks swimming at a considerable distance.

Nov 20th. In consequence of the death of our lamented Princess Charlotte, I had laid aside my gun, and prohibited every kind of sport, till this day . Her mortal remains having been last night committed to the tomb, we may now, without indecency, endeavoured to divert our minds from the universal affliction that has been produced by this severe calamity!

The next diary entry is not until December 30th and we have no idea if he continued to use 8111 but, even so, it is quite clear that the gun's performance was perfectly satisfactory.

Joseph Manton pelletlock number 8063.

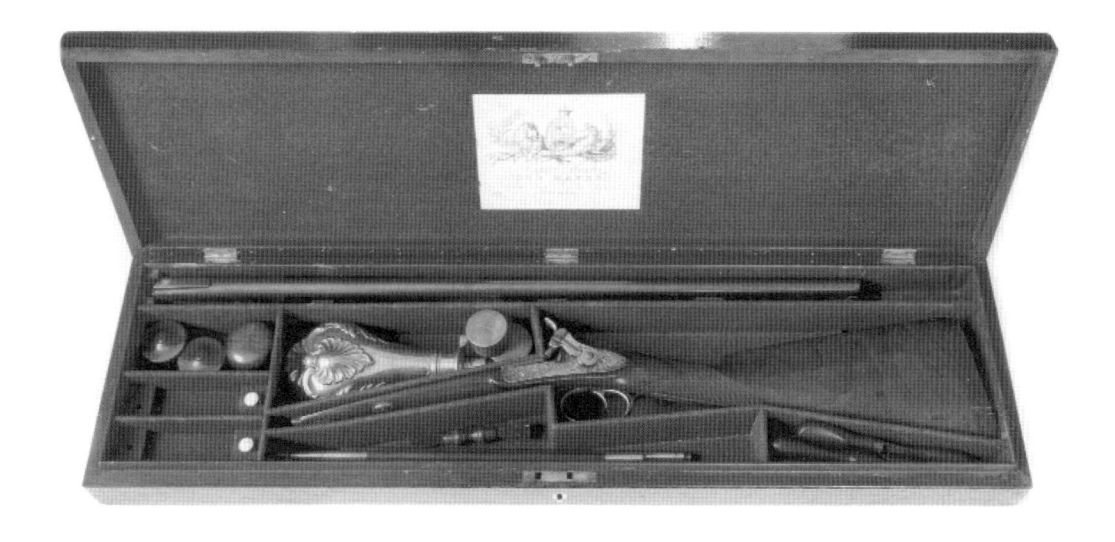

Joseph Manton pelletlock no. 8063 complete in case. Accessories from case: pricker to clear touch-hole. Of particular interest is the steel scraper that screws into the ramrod to clean the small aperture that leads to the breech during a day's shooting. Surely a throwback to the flintlock days when patent breeches shot a tongue of flame through the charge to ensure more efficient ignition, but rendered unnecessary with percussion ignition.

"Mantons are meant for men of tone but Eggs are good for poaching". So wrote Byron: A little harsh because the Egg family made fine guns.

Durs Egg was a Swiss who set up in business in London in 1772, going on to become "Gunmaker to His Majesty". The Prince of Wales having become George IV in 1820.

You will remember that it was Durs Egg who joined forces with his fellow compatriot, Pauly, to design their airship.

Joseph Egg, Durs' nephew was in business at 1 Piccadilly, firstly in partnership with Henry Tatham and then on his own. Joseph Egg claimed to have invented the copper percussion cap and stated this on his trade label.

Brothers Charles and Henry Egg were Joseph's sons. They bought the Joseph Manton business in 1838 and the Egg business continued up to 1880.

This 14 bore SB gun was originally made as a flintlock but converted to pelletlock by Charles Moore. The pelletlock was invented by Joseph Manton but there were many imitators.

The system is quite different from Joseph Manton pelletlocks and has been beautifully done. The barrel is engraved Joseph Egg Piccadilly London. The new pelletlock breech, however, has a platinum insert stamped "C Moore London Patent". The lockplate is signed "C Moore London". Complete in its original case from the time of conversion with its trade label "Charles Moore 77 St James Street London".

There have been enough gunsmiths named Moore in London over the years to fill an almanac!

Charles Moore was established in Regent Circus in 1821 and was well known for his pelletlock guns based on the Westley Richards pelletlock patent of 1821 no. 4611. He did not move to St James Street until 1825 by which time you would have thought that the percussion cap had taken over from the pelletlock. Evidently, however, this was not the case and there was still some demand for pelletlocks though the inventor, Joseph Manton, had abandoned them in favour of his new tubelock as long ago as 1818.

The firm eventually became Moore and Woodward.

Detail from the 8063 case. But what are the little holes in the detachable lids for? My guess is that it was to allow some air circulation to the cleaned strikers under the lids unless of course, you know different!

Although Joseph Manton invented the pelletlock system, many other gunmakers designed their own. This is Charles Moore's version.

174~One Man's Gun Quest

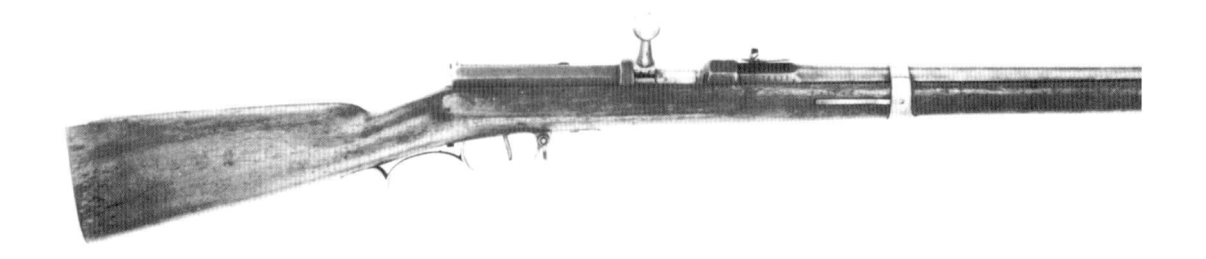

The rifle that changed the world: The 1842 Prussian Dreyse needlefire rifle, the first breechloading rifle to be adopted by any country.
This is an example of a screw breech needlefire rook and rabbit rifle. The rifle is by Manton and Co., London and Calcutta but is typical of the needlefire rifles produced by many other makers.

Chapter Thirty
Needlefire

Pauly in 1812 created the first centrefire breech loader so you would have thought that subsequent development would have followed this lead. After all, full bore cartridges today are centrefire. When Dreyse, who had worked for Pauly, invented the needlefire system, that too, was centrefire.

There was, however to be a diversion when the pinfire appeared before centrefire finally took over, but more of this later. Prussia was the biggest and most powerful of the independent German states and when they adopted the needlefire in 1842, they were the first country in the world to change over from muzzle loading to breech loading.

But the needlefire system was disadvantaged by having the long, thin firing pin or needle penetrating through the powder charge to strike the flat copper percussion disc situated behind the lead bullet.

The needle was subjected to the flame of the charge resulting in corrosion and early failure, so replacing the needle in the heat of battle must have been a difficult, dangerous and frustrating task.

The cartridge was paper, not cardboard, and was supposed to burn away when fired. This, too, must have caused problems with unburnt paper fragments remaining in the chamber, as did gas sealing at the breech.

Even so, the needlefire was to give Prussia an enormous advantage that resulted in the unification of the German states into the single nation of Germany and enabled Germany to defeat France in 1871.

This victory stimulated Germany's subsequent advance and sowed the seeds of the 1914/1918 conflict, so the Dreyse needlefire rifle shaped the world we live in today and I was fortunate enough to acquire an example.

The French Chassepot needlefire rifle faced the Dreyse in the 1871 conflict and, in the opinion of many experts, was superior to it. But the French lost!

The British Army never followed the needlefire route and when the change was made to breech loading, the muzzle loading Enfields were converted to centrefire by the Snider system.

The advent of the "new" breechloading needlefire system created a vogue for rook and rabbit rifles. Quite a lot of them survived and in the 1960's they could be bought for a few pounds. Many were on the screw breech system i.e. the breech was closed by the half turn of a screw that screwed into the breech. They all look very similar to me so were they all made in Birmingham and engraved with the names of different makers?

I acquired several by Manton and Co. of Calcutta and I'm sure that these all came from Birmingham.

Needham was one of the finest makers of needlefire rifles and shotguns with his own design screw breech and flat bolt handle that pre-dated the Mannlicher style. I did have a Needham rook and rabbit rifle that was a little gem, high quality and beautifully engraved.

But although these screw-breech rifles were all described as "needlefire" they were not identical to the Dreyse. Their paper cartridges had a cardboard base and the percussion cap was placed backwards! The firing pin, much shorter, of course, than the Dreyse, struck into the back of the percussion cap. So, in reality, they were centrefire, not true needlefires. Too late, however, to change their description now!

But in between the needlefire and centrefire came pinfire, so let's look at that in the next chapter.

Screw-breech needlefire rook and rabbit rifle.

274   VARIETIES OF SHOT-GUNS, ETC.

Needham's bolt being raised in passing through a hedge, which may happen to the striker of any of the locks constructed on the ordinary pattern. After the above description, it will at once be apparent that in the act of opening the breech, the lock is cocked, and that before closing it, the bolt ought to be lowered so as to show the word BOLTED, or else the gun is in the same dangerous state as it would be if on full cock in the ordinary kinds of gun. This precaution is of great importance to the safety of the sportsman who uses Mr. Needham's invention, and as the bolt can be raised by the left hand at the moment of taking aim, there is never any necessity for carrying this gun cocked, or I should rather say unbolted.

The cartridge-case employed is a much cheaper and more simple affair than that used for the Lefaucheaux gun, being

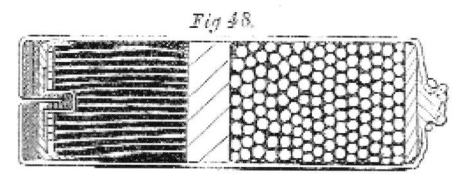

Fig 48.

SECTION OF LOADED CARTRIDGE.   (FULL SIZE.)

composed, however, of the same elementary parts, with the exception of the brass pin, whose office is here performed by the needle. Every part, however, is modified, and there is not nearly so much difficulty in constructing it. Besides this, the case is not withdrawn after being used, so that there is not the same necessity for its fitting the chamber easily, as in the French gun. The most important part is the arrangement of the wad and cap, which must be examined attentively, in order to comprehend their offices (see figs. 48 and 49), in which these parts are represented in

Fig 49

LOADED CARTRIDGE.   (FULL SIZE.)

From "The Shotgun and Sporting Rifle" by "Stonehenge", 1859. This is a shotgun needlefire cartridge. The rifle cartridges were the same but loaded with a solid bullet. Note that the percussion cap was "backwards" and the "needle", unlike the earlier Dreyse, did not penetrate the powder charge.

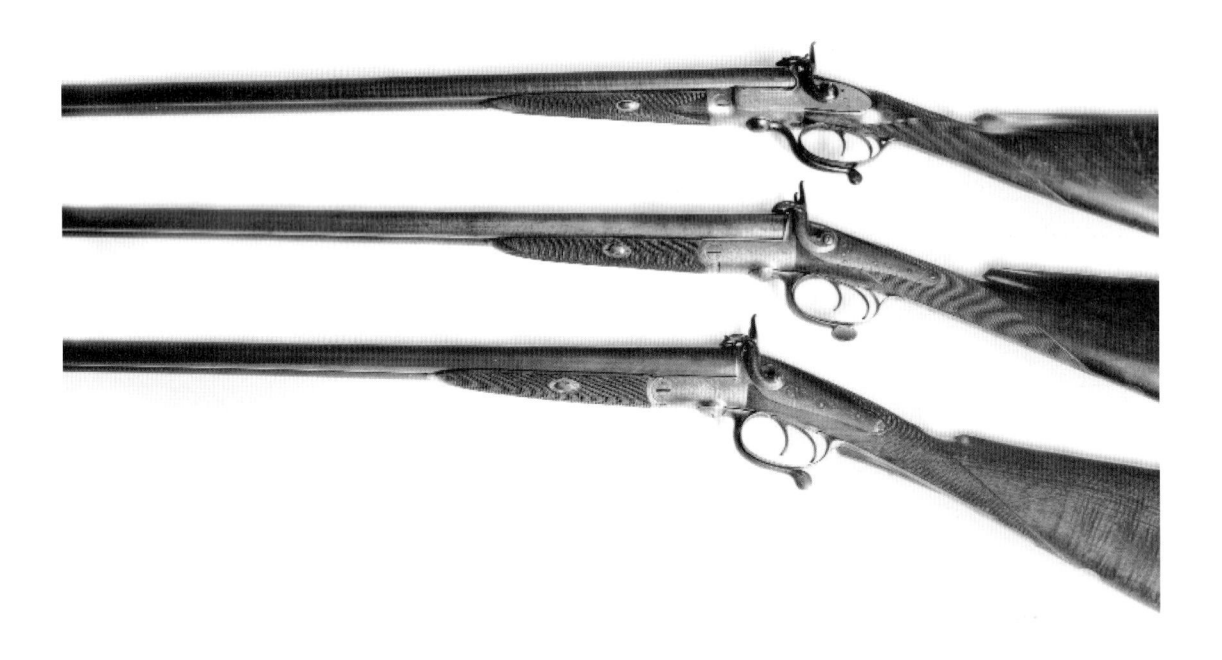

Three lovely pinfires:
John Manton pinfire conversion from muzzle loader.
15 bore original pinfire by Orlando Smith of London Road, Derby, about 1860. One of the finest provincial gunsmiths of his day. Just compare the quality of his work with the Mantons.
Original John Manton pinfire with grip safety.

Chapter Thirty One
Pinfire

The pinfire system was invented by the Frenchman, Lefaucheaux and, for a time, was surprisingly successful. Lefaucheaux had also worked for Pauly and yet, once again, Pauly's true centrefire system was again ignored.

Introduced by Lefaucheaux in France in the early 1830's but not generally known in England until shown at the Great Exhibition of 1851. A percussion cap was used but instead of being struck by the firing pin it was situated inside the breech end of the cartridge. A pin rested in the cap which protruded out of the side of the cartridge. The barrels of the gun had slots at the breech to accept the pin and the face of the hammer struck the pin to detonate the cap.

Loading the gun with cold fingers must have been something of a fiddle because the cartridge had to be inserted into the breech with the pin correctly fitted into the slot provided for it. Potentially dangerous, too, because if a cartridge was dropped onto a hard surface and the pin struck the ground there could be an explosion.

But despite its disadvantages the pinfire system was very popular for a considerable time, especially for shotguns, and many were made. In England, however, pinfires continued for considerably less than two decades before being finally superseded by centrefire.

"You never see a poor quality English pinfire gun." So said Oliver Nightall and there is a lot of truth in that. Pinfires came into use at the time of the increase in popularity of the back action lock and to compliment the back action lock the breech tang was usually very long indeed. To make a stock to fit was a highly skilled task but the final result of this precision fitting gave you a beautiful stock.

Over the years I acquired a number of pinfires by various makers including several by John Manton. In the early days of our marriage when my birthday came round Edna used to go to see Mr. Ellis the gunsmith, who lived in St. Albans Road Derby to buy me a gun. He knew my interests and would always find a gun for me at the same price....£5.

One year she bought me a 15 bore double pinfire by Orlando Smith of London Road Derby, a beautifully made gun retaining most of its original barrel browning. Made in the early 1860's, the gun has spent all its life in Derbyshire.

John Manton pinfire.

Orlando Smith was considered to be one of the finest provincial gunsmiths of his day. "Stonehenge" writing in his book, *The Shotgun and Sporting Rifle*, in 1859 said:

"The price of percussion double guns varies from £4 or even less, to 50 or 60 guineas, which Purdey, Lancaster, Manton and one or two other fashionable London makers, obtain for their articles. At the lowest price here mentioned the iron used in the barrels would be twopenny, or perhaps sham damn. Keepers guns are sold at all prices; but a good useful one, with barrels of charcoal iron, should cost from £10 to £15. No safe gun can be purchased for less than £20 if tolerably well finished, and none, in my opinion, ought to cost more than 35 to 40 guineas complete in case, and I believe that for the latter sum as good a gun as can be built can be obtained. At the same time I confess, that if I were offered my choice, regardless of price, I should select a gun of Mr. Purdey's make, believing that he is supremely careful that every part is of the very best quality, and that the workmanship is the best which can be obtained by money or care.

I have reason to believe also that all his guns are actually tried at brown-paper targets, those only being passed which perform to his satisfaction. But though I thus place them at the head of the list, I would not give £5 more for a gun of his make than for one built by Pape of Newcastle, or Dougall of Glasgow or Henry of Edinburgh or O. Smith of Derby, all of whom turn out guns which handle well, look well, and *perform well*, and who charge from £35 to £40 for a double gun in case complete. Prince and Green, Fuller, Jackson, Reilly, and some others in London, may be mentioned as selling excellent guns at about the same price, or perhaps a trifle higher, and among these I would specially call to attention the gun patented by Mr. Prince, of the firm of Prince and Green, on the principle of elevating the left barrel higher than the right, which has been already alluded to at page 223. *(i.e from The Shotgun and Sporting Rifle")*

That demonstrates the high regard in which Orlando Smith's guns were held at the time of their manufacture.

Few of Orlando's guns survive today but Derby museum have a cased percussion pistol made by him and a local enthusiast, Bill Hodgkinson from nearby Etwall has a twelve bore pinfire double that he used to shoot. Others may well have survived and if you know of one I would be delighted to hear from you.

Little seems to be known about Orlando Smith. He was in business in Derby from 1856 to 1863 at 14 London Street (now London Road) when the premises and business were taken over by another famous Derby gunsmith, Frederick Gates, who had served his apprenticeship with H.J. Holland of London. H.J. Holland was later to become Holland and Holland.

But where did Orlando come from? Where did he serve his apprenticeship and did he die or retire when the business went over to Gates in 1863? If you have any answers or any further information, please let me know.

In *The Field* trials of 1859 there were two classes and both muzzle and breech loading guns competed. A 15 bore muzzle loader by Orlando Smith came first in the lighter class and, believe it or not, a long obsolete 16 bore Joe Manton muzzle loader came a creditable fourth.

There are quite a lot of pinfire shotguns around and I had some excellent examples by John Manton but pinfire rifles by any maker are comparatively rare. Never did acquire a pinfire rifle by John Manton and pinfires were after Joe Manton's time.

J.R Ewing's Holland and Holland

The T.V. series, Dallas, appeared from 1978 to 1991 and was one of the most successful in history. Larry Hagman played the charismatic bad guy, J. R. Ewing, and about 450 million people round the world viewed it every week.

When the series ended, Larry Hagman commissioned Holland and Holland to make a superlative twelve bore double to commemorate the series.

The gun was to be of the finest quality reflecting the wealth, glamour and power of the Ewing dynasty. All work, including the engraving, gold inlay and colour hardening to be of the very highest standard of workmanship.

The medallions depicted all the leading characters in the series.

The gun took three years to build and cost Larry Hagman a huge sum, though he could double it if he put it on the market today. It is not merely a visual delight but is as usable as any other Holland and Holland.

J R Ewing.

One Man's Gun Quest ~ 183

THE BASE OF THE ACTION

This is engraved with a gold mounted portrait of Larry Hagman as J. R. Ewing. The word Dallas is inlaid in gold together with the head of a Texas longhorn steer surrounded by gold-inlaid border.

THE FORE-END IRON AND TRIGGER GUARD

The base of the fore-end iron bears Larry Hagman's signature. Inlaid on the trigger guard are the initials S.F.

184~One Man's Gun Quest

Leonard Katzman
Producer

Lucy Ewing
played by Charlene Tilton

Ray Krebbs
played by Steve Kanally

Pamela Ewing
played by Victoria Principal

Bobby Ewing
played by Patrick Duffy

THE RIGHT LOCK
The lock is embellished with gold-mounted vignettes against a coloured background portraying main characters from the cast. The leg of the lock plate shows the Dallas skyline in raised gold inlay. On the knuckle is the yellow rose of Texas. The lock plate is surrounded by a gold-inlaid border.

One Man's Gun Quest~185

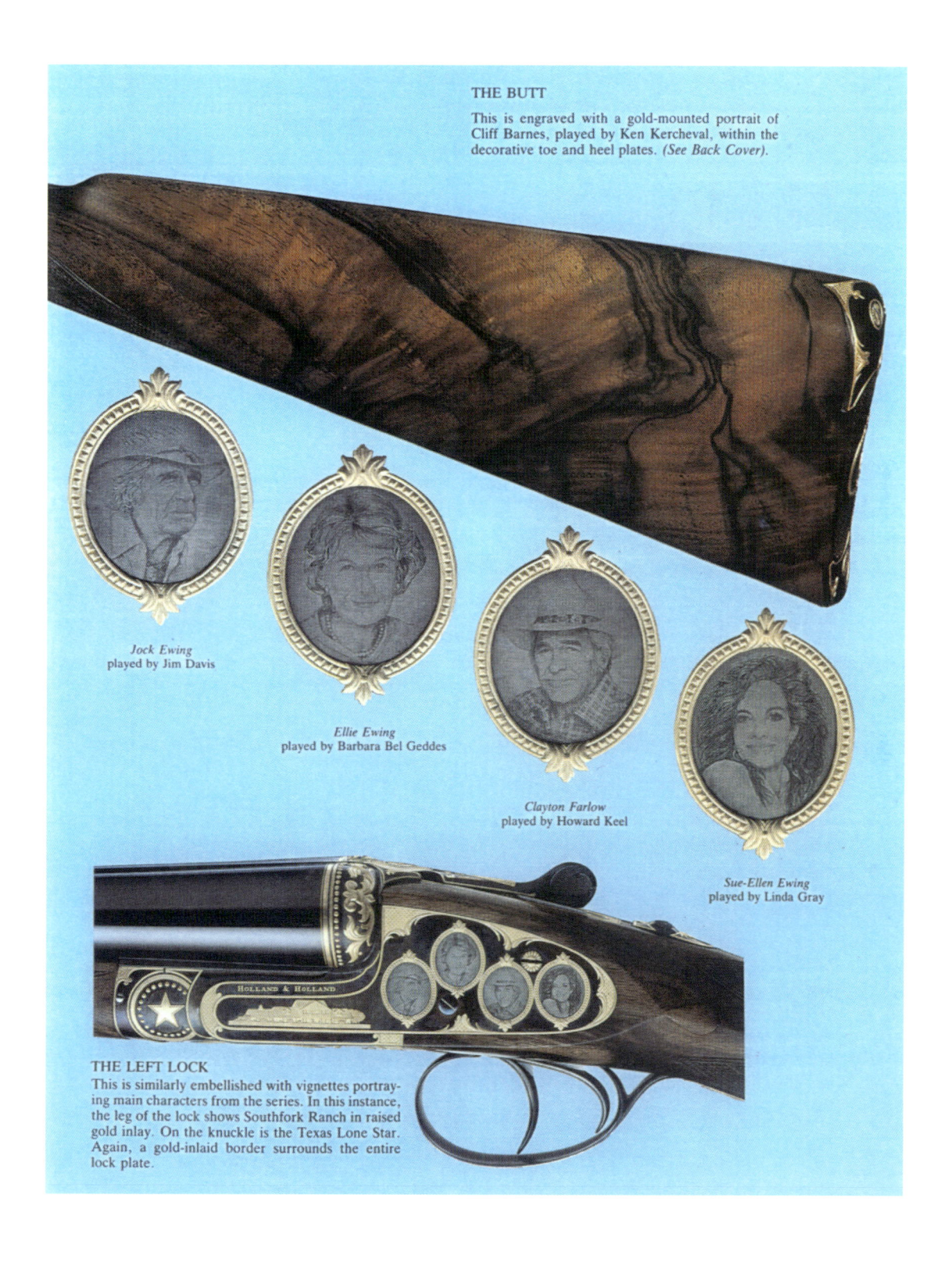

THE BUTT

This is engraved with a gold-mounted portrait of Cliff Barnes, played by Ken Kercheval, within the decorative toe and heel plates. *(See Back Cover).*

Jock Ewing
played by Jim Davis

Ellie Ewing
played by Barbara Bel Geddes

Clayton Farlow
played by Howard Keel

Sue-Ellen Ewing
played by Linda Gray

THE LEFT LOCK

This is similarly embellished with vignettes portraying main characters from the series. In this instance, the leg of the lock shows Southfork Ranch in raised gold inlay. On the knuckle is the Texas Lone Star. Again, a gold-inlaid border surrounds the entire lock plate.

186~One Man's Gun Quest

Chapter Thirty Two
Shooting At Bisley

Alan Kirk of Naseby, Northamptonshire, is an early breech loading rifle enthusiast, in particular the rook and rabbit rifles of the late nineteenth century. He organises a shoot for them once a year at Bisley in the Spring and another in the Autumn in the Midlands.

As mentioned earlier, my father would have nothing to do with guns, having seen more than enough of them in World War One but, even so, he was always very proud of having been selected to shoot at Bisley on, I believe, a musketry instructor's course. The unique atmosphere of Bisley is absolutely captivating with the period colonial buildings an unique reminder of the great days of Empire. Most of the finest rifle shots of the nineteenth century shot with distinction at Bisley: Walter Winans demonstrated his expertise at the running deer target, Horatio Ross shot in the Scottish team and many more.

Alan had organised three categories: Pre 1900 black powder only, pre 1919 centrefire and pre 1946 rimfire. He very kindly sent word to me asking me to attend at the Sunday April 5th shoot and Derek Fearn said that I could accompany him.

Derek usually travels down to Bisley on the morning of the shoot but as it is on the far side of Heathrow and 140 miles I decided that it would be far better to travel down the evening before in my car, so that we could be fresh for the day's shooting.

We stayed at the Holiday Inn, Woking but at 3.40 am every TV set in every room burst into life with fire alarm bells that could have awakened the dead! I simply couldn't believe that there was a fire as there was no smell of smoke but, of course, had no alternative but to get up and get dressed. In no time at all Derek was knocking on the door to tell me that everyone was racing downstairs, some in their pyjamas.

Down the stairs we went to an emergency exit only to find that despite the arrival of two fire engines it was, in fact, a false alarm. Only possible to doze after that so our objective of arriving at Bisley refreshed after a good night's sleep was not to be realised!

Peter shoots the .300 double Holland and Holland.
The shooters inspect their targets.

Top picture .310 Martini action Cadet.
Bottom picture B.S.A. 1907 training rifle in foreground. Alan Kirk on extreme left.

But what an experience! Bisley is the rifleman's Mecca, famous throughout the world and on arrival you would be forgiven for believing that rifle shooting was Britain's favourite sport. Ranges of every kind and distance all set in glorious, wooded, Jane Hunter Dunn country, beloved of John Betjeman. Every range appeared to be occupied and a continuous crackle of rifle fire enhanced the unique atmosphere.

Steady east winds had brought us a welcome spell of dry, sunny weather but, although the day was dry, it was, unfortunately overcast and chilly. Better than rain, of course.

About thirty of us had turned up to shoot with all kinds of rifles of around .300 calibre. One or two .300 Holland and Hollands though mine was the only double of any kind. It was much admired! A favourite rifle was the Martini action .310 Cadet, a training rifle made for the Australian Army by B.S.A. which shot very well. Young Army man, Chris McEvoy, shooting next to me got every shot in the bull at 50 yards and was, understandably, very pleased with his marksmanship.

One of the oldest rifles there was a .380 Snider, very like the Manton and Co. Snider I used to own, probably made in the 1860's. The owner, Robert Williams from Kegworth, told me he had spent quite a lot of time getting it to shoot at its best. "Now it's down to the afterpiece." he said with a smile. Yes, he had read my previous book!

In the vintage .22 category a number of interesting rifles had turned up, my Model 12 BSA target rifle among them. In early Lee Enfield days for target practise the .303 was reduced to .230 centre fire by inserting a "Morris tube" in the barrel. When I was a boy old sweats from World War One often talked of the Morris tube. Later the barrels were sleeved down to take .22 rimfire but still referred to as the Morris tube.

No Lee Enfield Morris tubed rifles, however, turned up at the shoot but in the early days of the twentieth century the Army produced a .22 miniature rifle not based on the full sized service rifle. I had never seen one in use but two turned up at the shoot and they shot very well indeed .

The tremendous advantage of attending a shoot like this is the opportunity to meet and chat to so many interesting and knowledgeable people. In between the shooting not a moment is wasted and there is much to learn.

So the great moment arrived when I was to fire in competition at Bisley with my lovely .300 Holland and Holland; a rifle equal in quality to any of the opposition. So did I sweep the board? Sadly, no! But did I enjoy the shooting? Yes, enormously! Possible score was 140. Derek scored a creditable 120 but I came nowhere!

Walter Winans at the Bisley pistol range. Walter Winans was a superlative shot with pistol and rifle. In Scotland he shot running stags at anything up to two hundred yards.

When it came time to shoot the .22 Model 12, however, I was getting the hang of things.

The Holland and Holland. had vee sights but the Model 12 had the enormous advantage of aperture sights……far kinder to my ancient orbs! Five of the last ten shots were in the bull boosting my score in the .22 category to 105. Derek didn't do as well with his .22 as he had in the previous round, scoring 110.

An excellent lunch at the Honourable Artillery Company's clubhouse for a very modest £6 rounded off an excellent day.

So a memorable experience adding a new dimension to my shooting saga.

Mutton chop whiskered muzzle loaders shoot at Bisley in the nineteenth century. I am sure that the rifle on the right is a .451 Gibbs.

Derek Fearn at Bisley shots the .300 rook rifle by Daniel Fraser of Edinburgh. Made about 1880 with its Daniel Fraser telescopic sight. The eye-piece is spring loaded to avoid any recoil striking the eye.

194~One Man's Gun Quest

ESTABLISHED 1824   Telephone : CENtral 7665

WARD & SONS
HIGH CLASS GUN MAKERS ETC.
2 ST. MARY'S ROW
BIRMINGHAM, 4

Anson and Deeley Ejector Gun

No. 1

ANSON and DEELEY no extension, Southgate Ejector, steel barrels, ANSON rod fore-end, engraved lined border.
Price £

No. 1a
Anson and Deeley Hammerless Gun (Non-Ejector)
No extension, steel barrels, snap fore-end, straight or pistol hand stock, engraved lined border.
Price £

Anson and Deeley Cross Bolt (Non-Ejector)

No. 2

Hammerless ANSON and DEELEY cross built extension, steel barrels, rod fore-end, engraved finished drop points.
Price £
No. 2a   Ditto but Ejector £   extra

Anson and Deeley Cross Bolt (Non-Ejector)

No. 3

Hammerless ANSON and DEELEY action, cross bolt extension, steel barrels, engraved in game, finished drop points.
Price £
No. 3a   Ditto but Ejector £   extra

Side Lock Ejector

No. 4

Side lock ejector, Southgate, Scott spindle, no extension, double Sear locks, best rod fore-end, fine scroll engraved, best figured stock.
Price £

410 Bore Folding Gun

No. 5

Single barrel Top Lever Hammerless 410 bore with automatic Safe. "Safe" inlaid in silver. The action is strong and and reliable. The extractor has long leg to ensure perfect extraction of cartridges. The folding device is simple and efficient. The barrel is chambered to take the "Fourlong" case **nitro proved.** It is a sound, reliable gun, and guaranteed in every particular.
Price £

Sales leaflet for Ward guns.

Chapter Thirty Three
Scott Motorcycles And The Gun Trade

What are Scott motorcycles doing in a book about antique guns, you may well ask. Don't panic, as Corporal Jones might have said…….I can explain everything!

St Mary's Row in the old gunmaking quarter of Birmingham had seen the manufacture of guns from the earliest days.

In one of the old, rambling buildings, 2 St Mary's Row, gun trade workers had plied their trade in every room and, latterly, Ward Guns were made there.

Wards made all kinds of guns and were one of the last makers to supply the African trade. You will see from their sales leaflet that their modern breech loaders appear to be sound, well made guns…..wish I had one! Note that no name was engraved on the guns shown on the leaflet, nor were prices quoted. I take it that this was because the leaflet was intended for the trade: Local gunsmiths or ironmongers would be able to order from the leaflet and have their own name engraved on the gun.

So J. O. Bloggs, Ironmonger, High Street, Wobbling-on-the-Wolds could have a gun made by Wards with his name and address, less the "ironmonger" bit, engraved on the barrel rib and tell his customers that with the expenditure of countless gallons of midnight oil he had manufactured it with his very own hands in his workshop behind the shop.

Some time after the War the premises were bought by Matt Houlder, one of those colourful eccentrics that only England can produce. Originally a silversmith and keen Scott enthusiast. The Ward Guns name went with the premises in which Matt made all kinds of metal items but he did not, as far as I know, continue to make guns and eventually sold off all the remaining guns.

A Scott motorcycle enthusiast from pre-war days he bought the Scott business when it eventually folded. He did manufacture some Scotts from the premises, but never on a grand scale. They were always known as "Birmingham Scotts", Not to be confused with the original Shipley machines. He was later to buy Velocette and Royal Enfield when they too, folded. Edna and I *almost* bought Velocette and their entire spares stock but that's another story……. you will have to wait for the next book!

The St. Mary's Row premises were eventually demolished as part of the re-development scheme but, thankfully, Price Street, part of the original gun quarter remains.

I met Keith Fuller in the nineteen sixties and we had a lot in common. He was an antique gun enthusiast and a motorcycle fan, having started his career working at the Hastings branch of King's of Oxford, one of the biggest motorcycle dealers in the country at that time. We also shared a common interest in World War One aviation.

During his boyhood he had been privileged to examine several Purdey Black Powder Express rifles and these classic rifles had triggered his interest in antique guns.

At that time Keith was married with two young children and had the nucleus of a muzzle loading collection including a SB percussion 9 bore. They stayed with us several times and Keith was able to shoot the 9 bore at Ousley Wood.

He had been in the RAF at one time but when I met him he was a trainee manager at Marks and Spencer though he was later to re-join the RAF and remain there until retirement.

I once bought a D.B. percussion John Manton in very poor condition for £3.10s. I later sold it to Keith for £6. He never did get round to restoring it and when he was posted abroad he sold it back to me for £10.

Now you can't make a silk purse out of a sow's ear and this sow had been badly ill treated anyway. Even so I took pity on the brute and had it restored. It was never destined to achieve first class status but it did come out as a respectable John Manton. It cost me £500! This was before the days of "a thousand pounds, Peter!" and was not one of Peter Dyson's jobs.

At a later date I sold it for the price of restoration, £500 and, believe it or not, took pity on it yet again and bought it back for £500! It then stayed permanently in the collection.

I lost touch with Keith over the years and we did not meet again until he got in touch with me having read my book *One Man's Motorcycles*. By that time his two children had grown up and it was an enormous pleasure to meet him again. His marriage had broken up but he is now married to the lovely Claire.

He had never lost interest in antique guns, ancient aviation or motorcycles and was the owner of two four cylinder Danish Nimbus motorcycles made in the 1930's.

One Man's Gun Quest ~ 197

A Birmingham Scott.

198~One Man's Gun Quest

The 1936 25/30 Rolls Royce Barker bodied owner/driver saloon we bought from Wilkinsons of Derby. This is the actual car illustrated in "Those Elegant Rolls Royce" before it was superlatively restored by Wilkinsons.

Chapter Thirty Four
Peter Gavuzzi, Wilkinsons And The Classic Rolls Royce

Wilkinsons of Stafford Street, Derby, were an old established firm with large premises. Eventually taken over by Frank Gilbert and his father who specialised in the restoration of vintage motor cars. Rolls Royce and Bugattis were great favourites of theirs.. On one occasion they completely restored a pre World War One Rolls Royce Silver Ghost for an Australian customer. About ten years later he decided that it needed re-spraying so he shipped it back to Wilkinsons.

Frank is a Bugatti owner and also a vintage motorcycle enthusiast. He is now semi-retired and the Stafford Street premises have been sold but the Wilkinson tradition of excellence continues in new premises by one of Frank's protégé's, Andy Jones.

In the mid 1980's Frank had restored a beautiful 1936 25/30 owner driver Barker bodied saloon Rolls Royce, even down to new headlining, carpets and new blue leather upholstery. It was featured, for all time, in *Those Elegant Rolls Royce*.

When the work was done, however, the owner asked Frank to sell it for him. I saw the car and decided that it ought to be bought at the asking price of £13,000.

It was an incredible experience to drive that 1930's Rolls: Back in time to when the Rolls Royce really was the best car in the world. Only synchromesh between third and top……..after all, wasn't synchromesh only for wimps? But a delight to get those gearchanges exactly right.

We used it for one summer, just for fun, then sheeted it up in one of the farm buildings for the winter. It had an aluminium body and when we got it out again the following spring I noticed telltale traces of corrosion beginning to start on one or two edges. Clearly, if we were going to keep it we would have to house it in a heated garage. Rather than do that, we decided to sell.

I had decided to accept £13,500 so to allow some leeway for negotiation I advertised it for £15,000.

An extremely pleasant chap, Brian Corser from Shrewsbury came to see it. He owned a 1926 Rolls Royce Phantom One open tourer but wanted, in addition, a Rolls that would be more practical for all weather use. The Phantom One was the first overhead valve Rolls Royce.

Brian drove the car, liked it and offered, believe it or not, £13,500.

However I stuck out for £14,000 until we finally reached deadlock. "Right," I said "what we will do is to toss up for that £500. You toss and call. If you win you pay £13,500 for the car. You lose and the price is £14,000.

"Well," said Brian "I have done some strange deals in my time but I have never tossed up for £500. But, O.K., I accept".

The coin spun and I won!

Brian was another of the "remarkable" people I met. He had inherited a large piece of land with views across Shrewsbury to the Welsh hills. He sold most of it to the Shrewsbury local authority on the understanding that he would retain the highest portion and build a house on it. In return the local authority undertook never to destroy his view by building too closely to the house.

Brian was a bachelor and had built a superlative "motor-house". The entire ground floor consisted of garaging for his car collection and the living area was on the first floor with the benefit of a marvellous view.

At one time he had owned a fleet of a dozen or more Jaguars, all with a racing history. On occasion Jaguars would borrow them for display.

When we delivered the Rolls to Shrewsbury I drove it and Edna followed in our car. Halfway along the motorway I suddenly realised that she was no longer on my tail. Nothing for it but to turn off at the next intersection and go back to the turn-off where I had last seen her.

No sign of her so no alternative but to turn off at that intersection and park the car. I then walked back up the slip road until I could see across the motorway. Across the motorway on the opposite slip road Edna's head popped up! She had done the same!

A tyre had gone flat and she couldn't undo the wheel nuts but a good Samaritan in a Reliant had stopped to change the wheel for her.

On, then, to Shrewsbury where Brian made us welcome and very kindly gave us a run in his 1926 Phantom One.

But what has all this got to do with Peter Gavuzzi and guns? Patience, gentle reader, all will be revealed!

Peter was a radiator repairer who rented a workshop at Wilkinsons. An extremely pleasant character, one of the good guys. He was also a gun enthusiast who later opened a tiny shop in Friargate, Derby, selling guns, cartridges,etc. Modern guns, mostly, but antique guns as available.

Arguably the fastest of all shotgun opening systems at the start of the breechloading era in the 1860s and 1870s was the Purdey Thumbhole. The generous trigger guard was provided with a thumbhole through which you placed your thumb to press a lever and the breech flew open. Other makers produced this system under license.

Visiting Peter's shop one day I saw one of these rare Thumbhole Purdeys in the rack behind the counter. I asked to see it, the price was fair so I said I would have it. "I have got the pair to it in the back," said Peter "would you like to see it?" Indeed I would!

The price was the same so I bought that, too. "Now would you like the case?" said Peter..................!

I was amazed that anyone would want to split up a pair of Purdeys but he told me that he thought he would have a better chance of selling them singly rather than as a pair.

This is by no means unusual and so many pairs have been broken up over the years which is much to be regretted today. A pair was often split up to give to two brothers and this happened to a friend of mine, Jim Pilkington. When Jim's grandfather died he left one of his Purdeys to Jim's father and the other to his other son, Jim's uncle, who was not a shooting man. Two years or so later Jim's father asked if he could buy back the other Purdey only to be told that it couldn't be found. Obviously it had been sold so the guns were never re-united.

A similar thing happened to a leading Derbyshire family, the Shields who once owned the Donington Park Estate. Grandfather owned a pair of Purdeys and in a surprisingly generous gesture he gave one to a farming tenant on the estate. Years later the son of the original owner asked if he could buy the gun back but, again, was told that it could not be found!

Among my bits and pieces I had a superb leather covered oak case for a pair of Purdeys, numbers 10649/50. But what happened to the guns?

After the War Jim Pilkington wanted a pair of guns and asked a gunsmith friend to look out for a pair of Purdeys for him. Shortly afterwards the gunsmith rang to say that a pair of guns by William Evans had turned up. They were in splendid condition and with long stocks that would suit Jim perfectly. Jim bought them and shot very well indeed with them despite his description: "Absolute carthorses!"

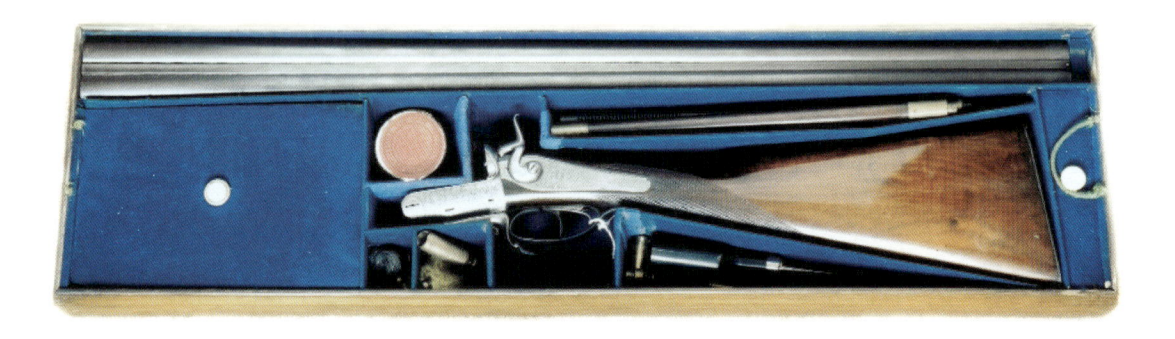

The cased pair of "thumbhole" opening Purdeys I bought from Peter Gavuzzi.

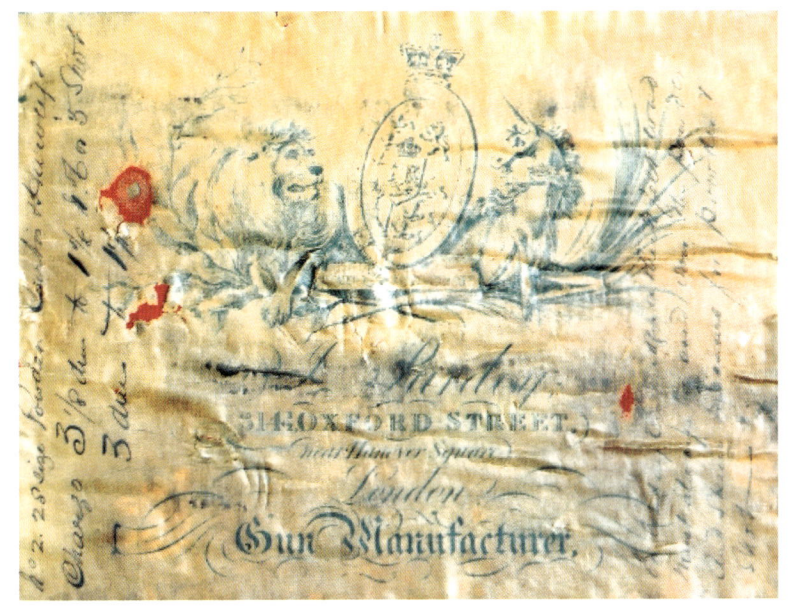

Purdey trade labels.
Walter Winans' 16 bore. 2½ drams powder, ¾ oz. shot.
The 12 bore thumbhole Purdeys. 3⅛ drams black powder no. 2, 1⅛ oz. shot.
When smokeless powder arrived, many sportsmen swore that black powder no. 2 shot faster.

Thorburn's famous portrait of Francis MacNab the twelfth Laird - Uncle of Archibald MacNab the thirteenth and last MacNab.

Chapter Thirty Five
Some Special Mantons

Over the years I managed to acquire a number of rare and unusual Mantons. Among them was one that I consider to be very special indeed:

The gun is a 14 bore S.B. in splendid virtually unfired condition and in its original case with its accessories but there is no trade label. The barrel retains its original browning and is simply engraved "Haymarket".

The gun is clearly by Joseph Manton so why the curious barrel inscription? At Joseph Manton's bankruptcy sale Joseph Lang of the Haymarket, London, bought a lot of finished and unfinished guns and this is, without doubt, one of them, hence the Haymarket address. As far as I know it is the only Manton that can be identified as having been sold at the sale.

In the collection was a flintlock double made for the MacNab of MacNab by Joseph Manton. On the side of the stock is a silver plate with the clan crest engraved on it together with a savage's head and the inscription "Timor Omnis Asbesto" (Let fear be far from all). The plate is engraved:

Archibald MacNab of MacNab
13th and Last Chief, Son of Robert
MacNab of Bovain by his Marr. 8.Jany
1782 with Anne. Dau. of Archd. Murdoch
of Gartincaber (1706-89) died in
France 12.Aug. 1860 giving his gun
To Archd. Burn-Murdoch. W.S. (1836-1916)
Who gave it to GARTINCABER

Archibald MacNab, "The Last Laird", by Roland Wild 1938 tells the strange story of Archibald MacNab. His uncle Francis, the twelfth chief was the subject of Raeburn's famous portrait that adorned countless biscuit tins! Archibald succeeded him as the thirteenth and "Last Laird".

In April 1825 84 members of the Clan MacNab set sail for Quebec on a voyage that took 38 days. Archibald's plan was to re- establish the clan in Canada under the same feudal system that had survived in Scotland. An experiment that was, of course, doomed to failure. He took this gun, no. 6926, with him.

This gun had been very simply converted from flintlock to percussion by the plug and nipple method. A cylindrical plug was screwed in to the touch-hole, a nipple was screwed into it at right angles, flintlock hammers replaced with percussion hammers and that was it! In this conversion even the bases of the flintlock pans had survived intact so it was a very simple job to put it back to original and even a pair of correct flintlock hammers were located.

Some muzzle loading purists hold up their hands in horror at the very idea of putting a flintlock back to original and in some cases, perhaps, this is understandable.

Strangely enough this reasoning does not apply to vintage or classic cars or motorcycles and to restore to original is considered to be absolutely the right thing to do. It is certainly not frowned upon for destroying the character of the conversion.

Parry Thomas' huge 21 litre Liberty engined car, "Babs", was built to make an attempt on the land speed record on Pendine Sands South Wales. The Liberty Engines were designed in America towards the end of World War One to provide more power for the planes of the day.

The car was driven by a massive chain but, tragically, during the attempt the chain snapped, decapitating Parry Thomas. Babs was buried in the sands at Pendine.

Approaching three quarters of a century later Babs was dug up and a massive restoration project was but in hand so now Babs can be seen again as she was when Parry Thomas attempted to take the Land Speed Record. But would a similar project be frowned upon in the world of antique guns?

Another MacNab Manton I acquired was a military flintlock rifle, barrel length 29½ inches, .650 bore, but made to the highest standard by John Manton for Lieutenant Alan MacNab of the Queens American Rangers. The rifle is full stocked and was used in the American War of Independence. It is engraved on the butt plate. As he was a member of the Perthshire Clan MacNab I wonder if he ever had a shot at a stag with it?

The only British rifle regiment before 1800 had Continental troops with Continental rifles and it was not until just after 1800 that a rifle regiment with British troops was formed armed with the new rifle designed by Ezekiel Baker. All other regiments had smooth bore muskets. As this rifle's barrel length and bore is so similar it has always been considered to be the forerunner of the Baker rifle.

A Highlander of the Clan MacNab he had, no doubt, shot stags in Perthshire so instead of using the military issue smooth bore Brown Bess he commissioned John Manton to make a special rifle with what was to become the Baker bore. A John Manton flintlock rifle of the highest quality.

Lock signed Manton in block letters on a gold inlay. John Manton platinum inscription on the breech.

Stock of American style with square back trigger guard. A single set trigger with intercepting cut-off.

Engraved patch box in the butt and the butt plate engraved "The Queen's American Rangers   Lieutenant Alan MacNab."

Barrel octagonal with multiple leaf sights and, unusually, a "telegraph" aperture sight that is a work of art in itself.

Platinum bar at breech and platinum vent.

Date of manufacture before 1800. No serial number, unfortunately, as early John Mantons were not numbered.

The history of lieutenant Alan MacNab is authenticated.

One of the rarest and most desirable of all John Manton rifles.

The cased S.B. Joseph Manton sold at his bankruptcy sale.

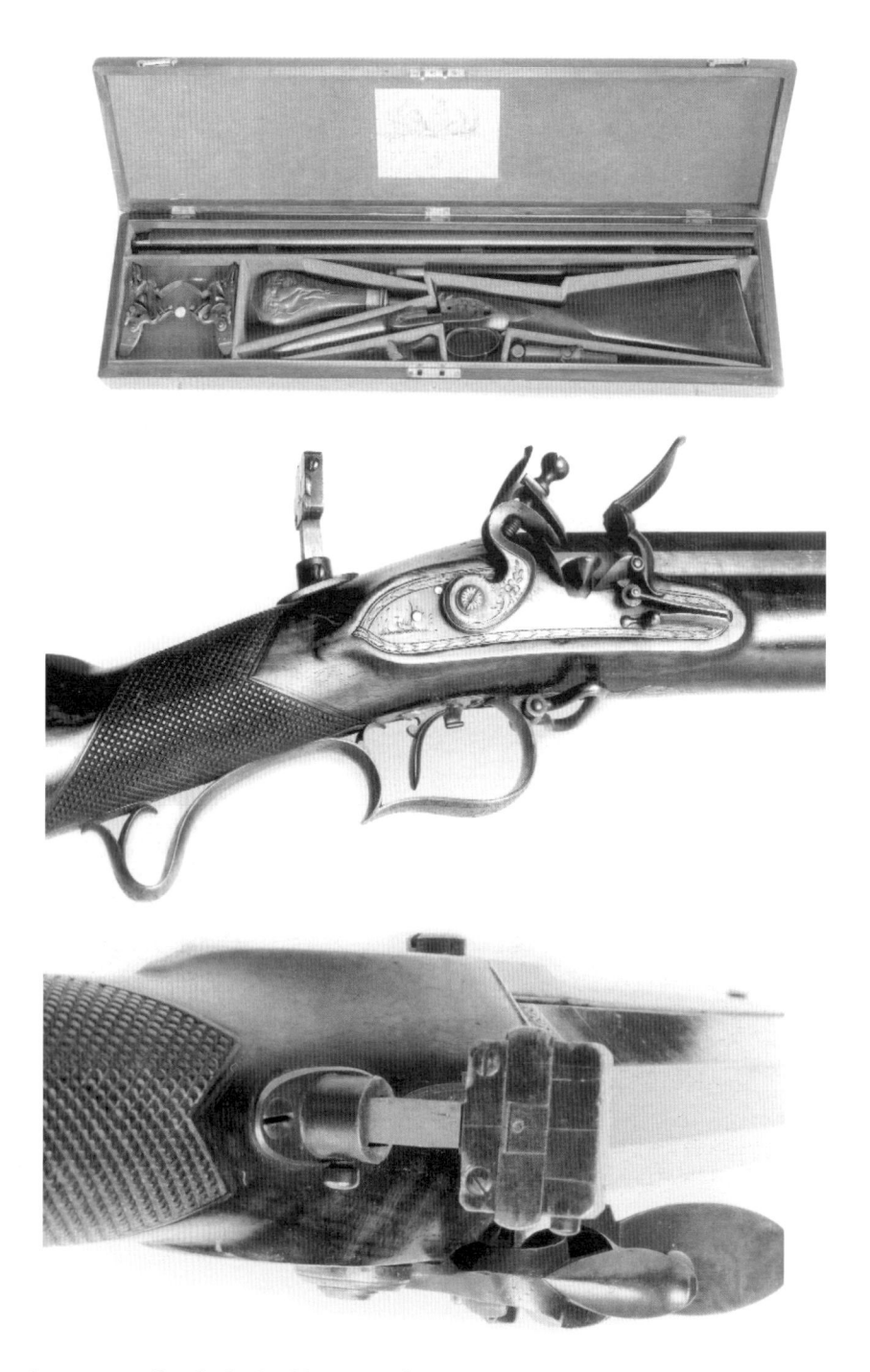

The Joseph Manton flintlock double made for the MacNab of MacNab and the John Manton "Baker" rifle made for Lieutenant Alan MacNab of the Queen's American Rangers.

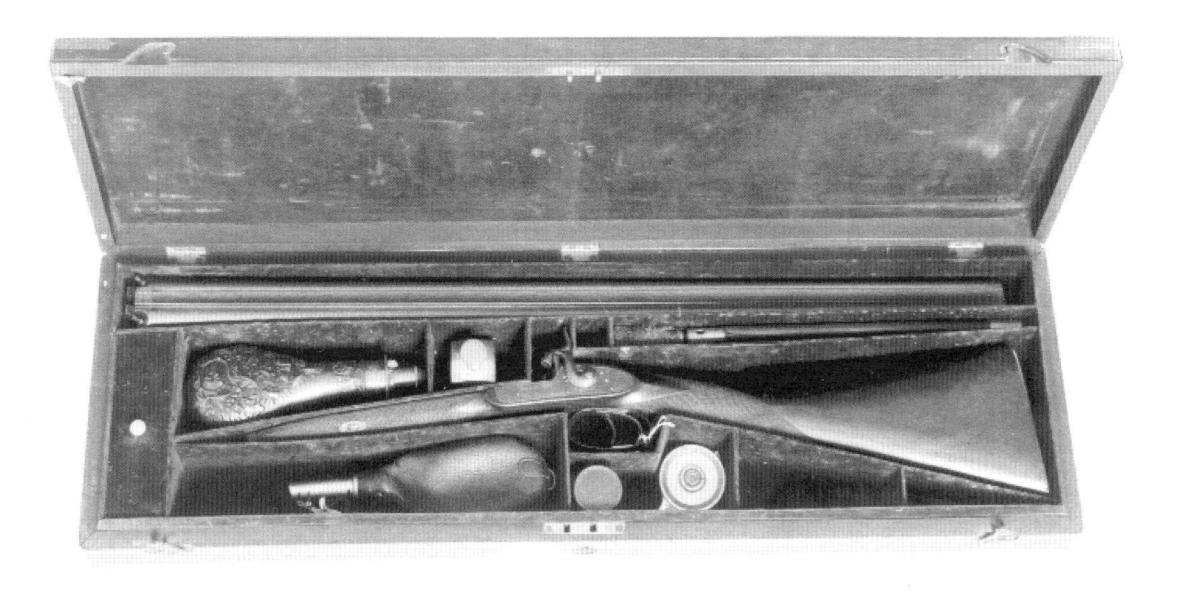

The rare D.B. percussion Joseph Manton with the Oxford Street address made for the Dakins family of Derbyshire.

MANTON & Cº.

Gun Makers.

63, Cossitollah Street.

CALCUTTA.

TO H.R.H. THE DUKE OF EDINBURGH.   GUN MAKERS BY SPECIAL APPOINTMENT.   TO H.E. THE VICEROY OF INDIA.

MANTON AND COMPANY

PRESENTATION FANCY SWORDS & DAGGERS.

GUN, RIFLE & PISTOL MANUFACTURERS.

REGULATION SWORDS FOR EVERY BRANCH OF THE SERVICE.

ESTABLISHED IN INDIA BY THE LATE JOSEPH MANTON.

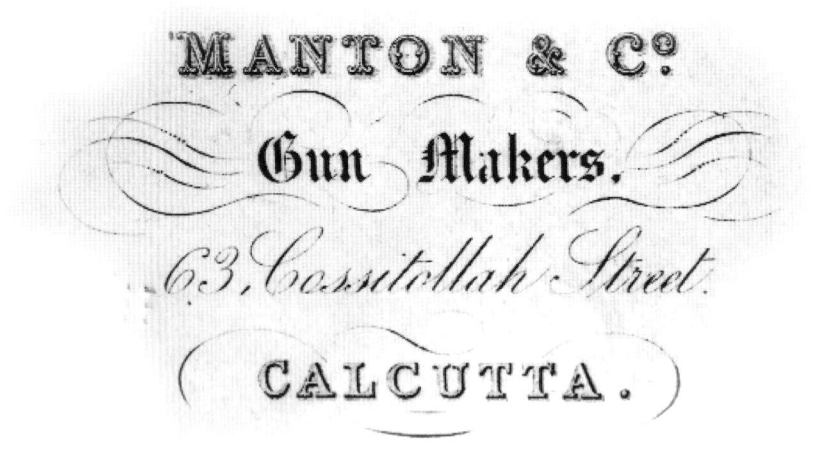

13, OLD COURT HOUSE STREET, CALCUTTA. ESTABLISHED 1828.

& INCORPORATED WITH THE FIRM OF SAMUEL NOCK, OF REGENT CIRCUS.

The top trade label is an early one from the cased needlefire and Snider rook rifles. The large label is much later from the time when Manton and Co. were long established.

Chapter Thirty Six
Manton And Co. London And Calcutta

A motorist in the south of Ireland stopped to ask an old Irishman driving a donkey cart if he was on the right road to Dublin. "Well" replied the old timer, scratching his head "if you're going to Dublin, this is a bad place to start!"

It's rather like that when starting to write about the origins of Manton and Co., Calcutta, as a number of misconceptions have been accepted as fact.

So let's start with a letter written by Manton and Co., Calcutta about 1900:

"Frederick Manton was sent to India by his uncle to start the firm in Calcutta. On the death of his uncle all the books connected with the firm of Joseph Manton were sent to India. These have been entirely destroyed by white ants. The most valuable book was the stock book, from which we could trace for whom any gun bearing the name of Joseph Manton was originally made, but even this has been destroyed. We now have in our possession the several weapons mentioned in the enclosed list. These were also sent to India when Mr. Joseph Manton died. The pair of flint pistols were presented to the senior partner of the firm by an old constituent."

In the past it has been assumed that the letter was incorrect and as Frederick was Joseph Manton's son it was Joseph who sent him out to India. Sifting all the evidence, however, it is perfectly clear that it was, indeed, Uncle John who sent Frederick to India to start the Calcutta firm in 1826.

In 1826 Joseph Manton was in dire financial straits and was, in fact, declared bankrupt in that year so it would have been impossible for him to have financed the setting up of a business in India. No, it was Uncle John who sent out his nephew Frederick.

Frederick started the Indian branch under the name "Manton and Co., London and Calcutta" at 10, Lall Bazaar and ordered guns as required, presumably from Uncle John. Frederick left in 1828 and another of Joseph's sons, John Augustus took over, remaining until 1833 when, at his father's request, he returned to England to start out in business with him.

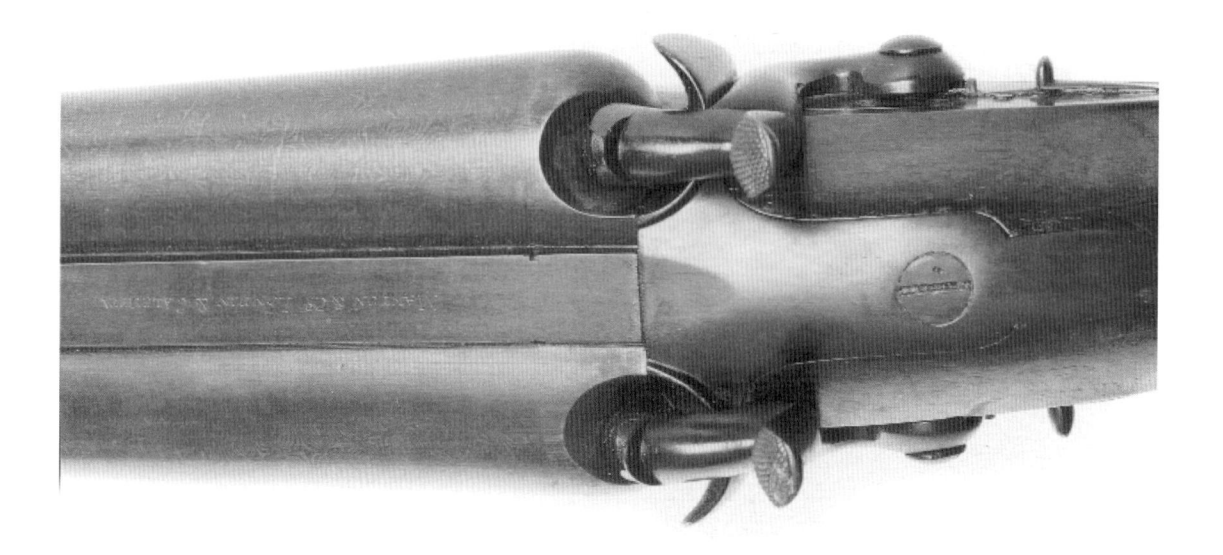

Massive twelve bore Manton and Co. muzzle loading double rifle in virtually new condition.

.380 Manton and Co. Snider action rook rifle.

John Manton was furious and "apparently the quarrel that broke out between the two brothers was as fierce as any they had previously had". This also confirms that it was John who had financed the Calcutta venture.

John then sent out his own son Edward to run the Calcutta business from 1833 to 1846. John died in 1834, Joseph in 1835 and it was at some time after John's death that the Joseph Manton books and guns mentioned in the 1900 letter were sent out to Calcutta confirming, once again, John Manton's connection with Manton and Co., Calcutta.

Back in England "Joseph Manton and Son" opened in 1834 at 6 Holles Street, Cavendish Square with Joseph as "acting manager" to his son.

It appears that in 1837 Manton and Co. moved to 63 Cossitollah, Calcutta and later to their final address 13 Old Court House Street, Dalhousie Square, Calcutta, apparently before 1850, though I have been unable to find a date for this. The Manton interest was to end in 1846 when the business was taken over by W. R. Wallis who continued to trade under the original name, Manton and Co., London and Calcutta.

Established before 1850 their London business was carried out from 116 Jermyn Street.

W. R. Wallis retired in 1878 and the Calcutta business was continued by his son John. In 1935 a branch was opened in New Delhi and the firm still continued under the same name, surviving until after the Second World War. It did not finally close until 1966 and the historic premises were demolished in 2002.

So the firm saw the changes from muzzle loading through needlefire, pinfire and up to modern breech loaders.

Their guns were "bought out" and despite London proof marks on many of them they were, without doubt, made in Birmingham but engraved with the Manton and Co., London and Calcutta name so not on a par with the work of Joseph and John Manton. Even so, however, worthwhile collectors items. Those I have seen are of sound, serviceable quality clearly aimed at the British in India market, not at the very top end of the scale like those of Joseph and John Manton.

Back in the 1860's screw breech needlefire rook and rabbit rifles by Manton and Co. could be bought for ten or twenty pounds and I was fortunate enough to acquire several including cased examples. Lovely little rifles of around .400 calibre.

They fired "self consuming" cartridges i.e. the paper case was supposed to burn away on firing but it must have been a hit or miss affair with fragments of half burned paper often left in the chamber.

These screw breech needlefires as explained, did not have a needle that penetrated right through the powder charge to strike a flat percussion disc behind the lead bullet but had a firing pin that struck a rearward facing percussion cap in the base of the cartridge.

As the Snider breech was introduced as an interim measure to convert the Enfield muzzle-loading rifles to breech loading, you would have thought that the case for sporting Sniders would never have been considered. Surprisingly, however, I had two in my collection, both by Manton and Co. One was an original Snider, the other a conversion from muzzle loading.

The delightful rook and rabbit rifle was in its case with trade label. Made as an original Snider, not a conversion from muzzle loading. The other was a sporting rifle for bigger game which takes the .577 military Snider cartridge but this is a conversion from muzzle loading with a patch-box in the butt. Clearly, then, sporting Sniders were produced.

Few muzzle loaders by Manton and Co. have survived but I had one, a 12 bore double rifle in practically new condition that had seen very little use made, no doubt, for shooting big game in India. If only it could talk!

The other Manton and Co. was a cased double hammerless twenty bore that Edna and I gave to our son Ross for his eleventh birthday. Ross did get some use out of it but soon graduated to a twelve bore.

With one exception the Manton and Co. examples I was fortunate to acquire were rifles. The earliest was a twelve bore double caplock muzzle loading rifle in excellent virtually unfired condition, probably made in the 1840's for shooting tiger in India. Next in date of manufacture were the screw breech needlefire rook and rabbit rifles all around .400 calibre probably made in the 1850's. Four in all, virtually identical, one of them cased and in original condition.

Next came two Sniders made in the eighteen sixties. Inspired, without doubt, by the adoption of the Snider system by the British Army as their first breech loaders.

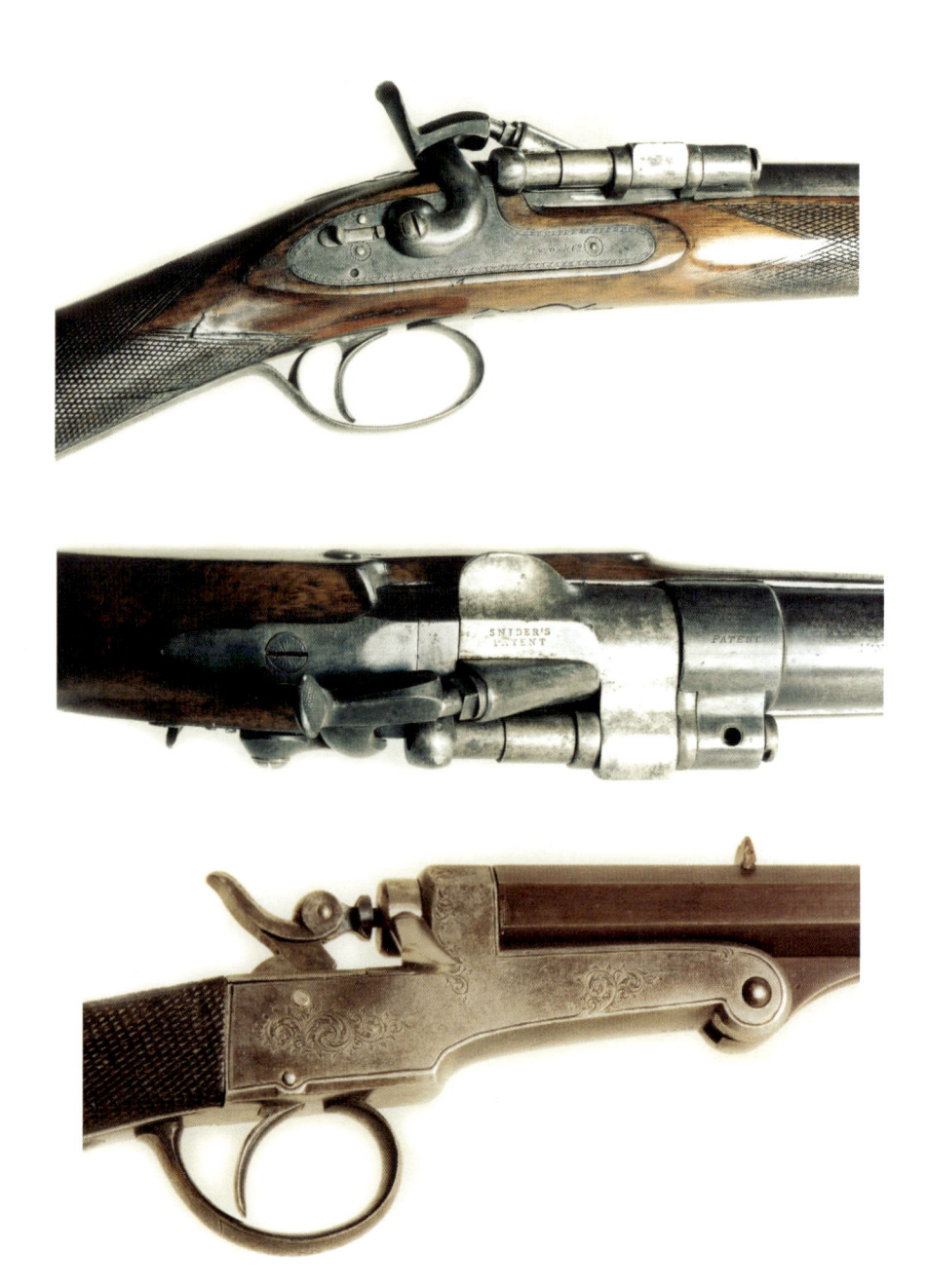

.577 Manton and Co. Snider action sporting rifle. Originally a muzzle-loader with a patch box in the butt, but converted to breech loading with the Snider breech. Can't be many of those about.
Close up of typical Manton and Co. screw breech rook rifle action.

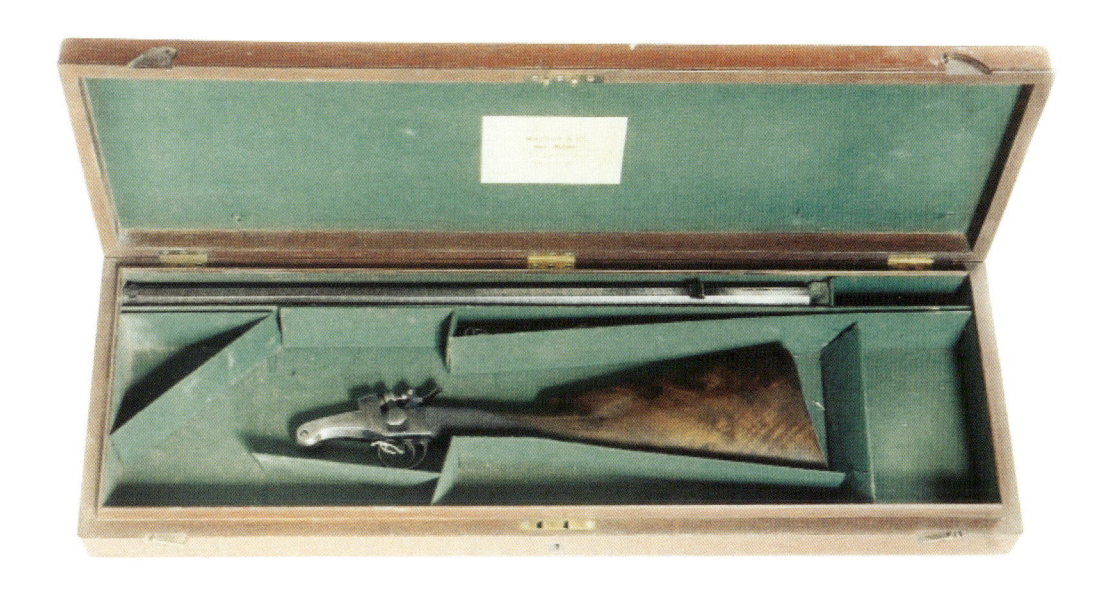

Cased Manton and Co. .380 screw breech needlefire rook rifle.
Four rook rifles. Snider at the top, rest are screw breech needlefire. All three were restored by master gunsmith, Derek Fearn.

218 ~ *One Man's Gun Quest*

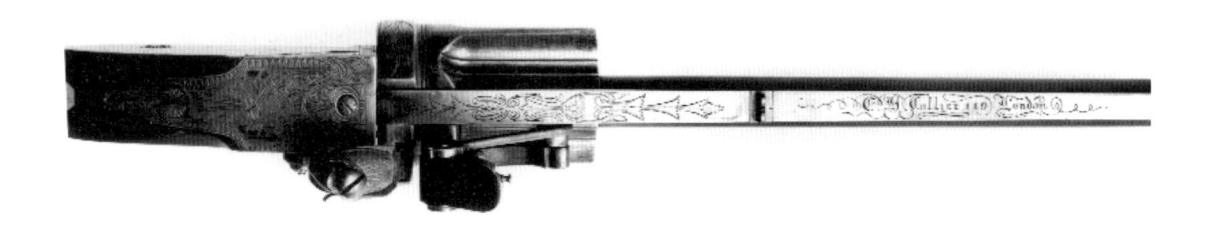

Multiple fire: *This has always been the Holy Grail but always out of reach until the advent of breech loading and the metallic cartridge. In flintlock days, however, there were many attempts to secure that Holy Grail. Probably the most gallant failure was the Collier.*

Chapter Thirty Seven
Exotica

Elisha Haydon Collier was an American engineer from Boston. He took out English and French patents for a revolving flintlock in 1818 and 1819. They were evidently based on the design of another American, Captain Artemus Wheeler, Gunmaker, 6 Herberts Passage, Beaufort Buildings, Strand, London.

Collier revolving pistols and rifles were made by Wheeler, Collier and others for a number of years so must have enjoyed a measure of success.

The cylinder was revolved by hand and a magazine that contained the priming powder was linked to the cylinder to deposit the correct amount of priming powder in the pan. As each cylinder came in line with the barrel it was locked in position.

I imagine that as percussion took over the Colliers would be made in percussion form, rather than flintlock.

To fire the rifles your left hand went under the cylinder: Further along the barrel and you would lose your hand if all cylinders flashed across and fired all at once!

My rifle is no. 119 and only .400 calibre so, presumably, a rook and rabbit rifle, or could it be a rat and mouse rifle! Excellent order and one of the greatest rarities in the world of guns.

Once at an arms fair in Nottingham I saw a pair of guns that were of absorbing interest. They were by Jos. Heinige of Vienna and said to have been made for the Emperor Franz Joseph of Austria. They were not a pair but were in identical style, clearly two out of a set. One was 20 bore, and the other was 16 bore, They both carried the imperial cipher and the engraving, gold inlay and workmanship was to the highest possible standard.

Actions gold inlaid and superbly engraved. One set of barrels original browning, the other re-blued. Nothing that could not be put right....at a price!

The guns had been made with watchlike precision and you opened them by sliding sideways a delicate lever under the fore-end.

My great interest is fine English guns and rifles but the sheer quality of these guns was an irresistible draw. I believe I am right in saying that they were the most expensive guns at the fair!

Franz Joseph was one of the finest shots in Europe. The family was touched by tragedy when his son, heir to the throne, took his own life in a suicide pact with his mistress at the family hunting lodge at Mayerling. This has been the subject of many plays and films. These guns would have been in the gun-room at the time.

At the end of World War One Austria became a Socialist state and all the Royal Family's estates and possessions reverted to the state.

The guns were being offered by a Leicester man, a cheery chappie with a most likable personality. A day or two after the fair I rang him and asked if the guns had been sold……they hadn't! I asked him to bring them round to see if my first impressions would be confirmed…..they were! I bought them and they were to remain in the collection until it was passed out of my ownership.

So what did I pay for them? A lot of money at the time though, mercifully, I now have no idea what that figure was!

The Emperor Franz Joseph of Austria, one of the finest shots in Europe. Note the bare knees also favoured by Walter Winans. I wonder what the full stocked carbine style rifle with external hammer was? No doubt of the finest quality.

A sixteen bore and twenty bore gold inlaid and of the finest quality made for the Emperor Franz Joseph. They are both numbered and reputedly from a set of ten.

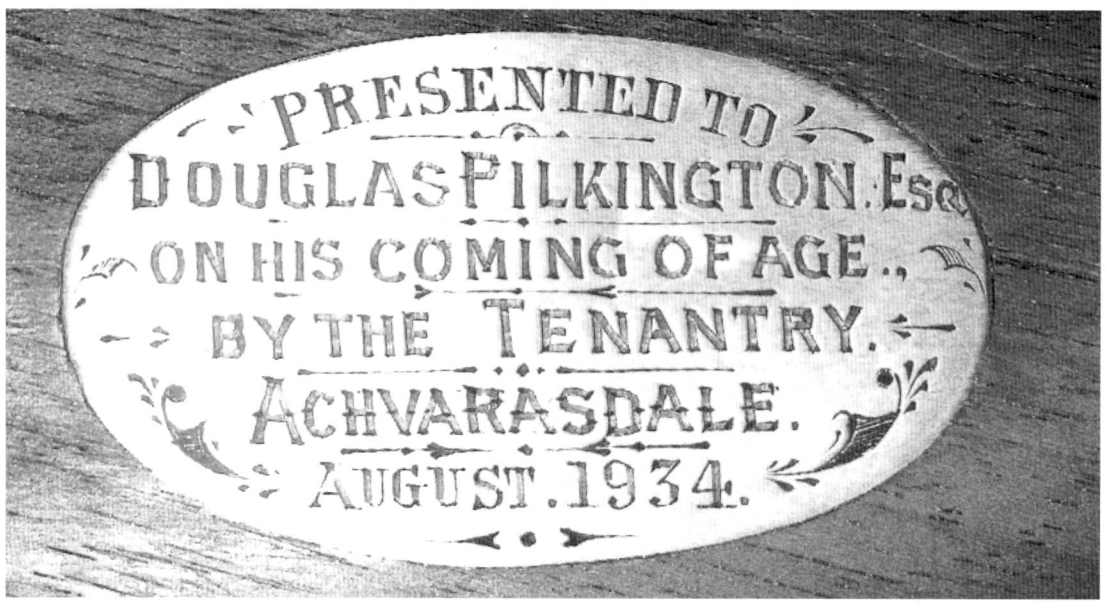

Derek Stimpson, rifleman and collector extraordinaire, with the rare BSA design .260 which fired belted rimless cartridges. Presented to Douglas Pilkington on his 21st birthday (August 1934) by the tenants of Achvarasdale Estate, Sutherland. The old stalker/fishing gillie from Amat, Jack McNichol, was at the celebration party with his father. They were stalkers on the neighbouring Shurrery Estate, also owned by the Pilkingtons in those days.

Chapter Thirty Eight
Stalking Rifles

The evolution of the stalking rifle is covered fully in my previous book *One Man's Scotland* together with the great characters who made stalking history:

Scrope whose book *Deerstalking* helped to start the vogue for deerstalking in the early 19th century and whose muzzle loading rifles still survive at Blair Castle, Perthshire, home of the Duke of Athol.

Roualeyn Gordon Cumming, aristocratic Highland poacher and first African white hunter who ventured into "darkest Africa" having been told that it was twenty to one against him coming back alive. He took with him his muzzle loading double rifles by Purdey, William Moore and Dickson of Edinburgh finding them just as effective against African game as Scottish stags.

Horatio Ross, legendary rifle shot and considered to be the world's finest pistol shot. He accepted a wager to shoot ten brace of flying swallows in a day and managed it before breakfast at his home, Rossie Castle with a pair of John Manton rifled flintlock pistols that eventually ended up in W. Keith Neal's collection.

He was equally proficient with shotgun or stalking rifle from muzzle loading days to the Black Powder Expresses.

In those days the two great shooting clubs in London were the Red House Club and the Old Hats Club. "Very Old Hat" meant very exclusive. The target was live pigeons and huge sums were wagered. Horatio asked Joe Manton to make him a gun that would be virtually impossible to beat. Joe made him an extremely light, handleable S.B. nine bore tubelock. Shooting against the flintlocks of the day Horatio could not be beaten.

Shooting was at live pigeons, not clay ones! The pigeons would be released at 25 or 30 yards and to be counted as a kill they had to fall within a given boundary. On one occasion shooting at the Red House, Horatio killed every pigeon, though one or two fell outside the boundary.

In my collection was a light S.B. nine bore Joseph Manton tubelock in splendid condition reputedly made for Horatio Ross. At this distance of time the ownership cannot be proved but the gun was, without doubt, made for shooting live pigeons at the Red House and the Old Hats Club. A notable addition to any Manton collection.

Sir Charles Ross (no relation) was the owner of the Balnagown Estate, Ross-shire, that stretched right across Scotland. Another superlative rifle shot and inventor of the straight pull Ross Rifle. Eccentric, womaniser and with a hatred of paying income tax! So have you? But not nearly as much as Sir Charles!

Walter Winans, the American millionaire who leased a string of forests from coast to coast in Scotland to indulge in his favourite sport of shooting driven stags. He enjoyed shooting running stags "leaping and bounding" at two hundred yards! The stags, not Walter! Superb pistol shot, too and a talented wildlife painter.

You can read very much more about these amazing characters in *One Man's Scotland*.

In 1954 the purchase of *With a Gun to the Hill* by Stephen Pilkington decided me to start deerstalking in Scotland and a suitable rifle was required. The choice was a new .303 BSA built on the incomparable ex-German Army 1898 Mauser action: A good, strongly made accurate rifle that served me well.

In the 1950's the most popular choices for deerstalking were the 6.5mm (.256) Mannlicher and the 7mm (.275) Mauser. I eventually changed over to the Mannlicher attracted by its slim elegance, light weight, watch-like precision of manufacture and its unique Schonauer rotary magazine.

Nearly all my stalking was done with this rifle which was a delight to use. My choice was always an aperture sight rather than a vee sight because, firstly, you have a much longer sight base and secondly you only have the foresight to line up on your target.

With a vee sight you line the foresight into the vee sight and line this on your target. With an aperture sight all you have to do is place the foresight onto the target. Yes, you are looking through the aperture but your eye automatically looks through the centre of the aperture, you do not have to line it up: Much quicker and easier, in my experience.

I still feel that for a Sassenach with good eyesight a rifle with iron sights provides much more rewarding stalking, though read more about this in *One Man's Scotland*. For the professional stalker, however, the rifle is the tool of his trade and nowadays the telescopic sight is essential.

After many years I finally gave in and bought a rifle with a telescopic sight, the incomparable David Lloyd. The David Lloyd is, in my opinion, the

Prince of stalking rifles. Hand made using the same ex German Army 1898 Mauser action as my humble BSA.

David Lloyd was a practical stalker who designed his rifle with the telescopic sight virtually built as part of the rifle. It is screwed direct to the rifle and cannot be taken off or adjusted. It is claimed that David Lloyd rifles can be thrown onto a concrete floor without disturbing the sight. I can believe it! My rifle has sustained some severe knocks on the Hill but has never gone "off song". Young and old can pick it up and shoot straight with it.

The Highlands of Scotland were cleared of their crofting tenants in the late 18th century to make room for huge sheep walks. From about 1830 it was realised that it would be more profitable to let them for shooting so the sheep were cleared off to make way for deer.

Although flintlock rifles and muskets were used to shoot deer from the earliest times the percussion era had begun before the vogue for stalking, as we understand it today, finally got under way.

The favourite rifle at the time had not, of course, been designed with deerstalking in mind but it was usually a 16 bore S.B. caplock rifle. The round lead ball was placed in a cloth patch and rammed down the barrel to grip the rifling. Quite close spiral rifling was used so the bullet velocity was restricted: A large powder charge creating a higher velocity would just cause the bullet to "strip" i.e. skip over the rifling grooves without gripping.

Various ideas were used to attempt to solve this problem and mechanically fitting bullets were the obvious answer. Belted balls were used with the rifling consisting of two deep spiral grooves which were reasonably successful. Purdey went one better with his "winged bullet." At last a pointed conical projectile replaced the round ball with raised sections either side to accept the rifling. These rifles shot very well.

But the real breakthrough came when in the mid 1850's Purdey designed his "Express Train" rifles. Originally muzzle loaders in 40 bore i.e. .500 calibre with a much slower rifling spiral to allow higher velocities and flatter trajectories. Such small bores were considered revolutionary when calibres of .400 were not unusual for shooting rooks.

The muzzle loading Expresses were soon superseded by breech loaders and, at last, the problem of getting the rifling to grip the bullet was solved: All that had to be done was to make the bullet slightly larger than the bore and the rifling *had to grip*.

Although some of the first breech loading Black Powder Expresses were pinfire, most makers skipped the pinfire option and went straight to centrefire. They were considered to be the limit of power and accuracy in sporting rifles until the advent of cordite.

To put things into perspective, the .400 Black Powder Expresses produced a velocity of 1,900 feet per second with a 235 grain bullet. Sighted for 100 yards they shot one inch high at 80 yards and one inch low at 120 yards: A performance that any stalker would find acceptable. True, a long shot to stop a wounded stag would make life difficult, but all the more important to make that first shot count.

Contrast this with the first British cordite magazine rifle of the 1890's, the .303 Lee Metford: The Mark VI bullet was not that much lighter at 215 grains and the velocity was not so much higher at under 2,100 feet per second.

To shoot the Black Powder Expresses today is a delight with that huge plume of black powder smoke. Black powder gives more of a push than a jolt so the recoil is pleasantly less than you would expect. Ronnie Ross, shooting the .400 Holland and Holland, pronounced the recoil less than that of a modern rifle.

Derek Stimpson again, this time sans head, with his splendid Dougal "Lockfast" 12 bore double rifle. Note the "Lockfast" lever at front of lockplate.

Live pigeon shooting with flintlocks at Hornsey Wood House.

228 ~ One Man's Gun Quest

*Deerhounds. An indispensable adjunct to stalking in black powder days.
The rifle that went with them. .500 muzzle loading Black Powder express rifle by Alexander Henry with every conceivable extra.*

Chapter Thirty Nine
The Search for Black Powder Express Cartridges

Please, dear reader, let me divert for a moment.

The World's Fair is the newspaper devoted to the interests of the fairground community and at one time I was often able to read a copy. The fairground people, not without good reason, refer to themselves as "Grafters" and the page I always turned to first contained a column called "Grafters Corner". It was written, of course, by "The Grafter".

Grafters Corner was always hilarious but one issue always stuck in my mind: The Grafter was discussing honesty and was working out how many truly honest people there were in England.

He got out his pencil and paper and at the top he wrote down the number of people in jail. Next the wrote down the number of people who ought to be in jail if they had been found out! Quite a lot!

Next he added the number who had fiddled their expenses followed by those who had been less than honest about their income tax calculations.

On he went, not missing a thing: Those who had fiddled pencils or stationery from work, cheated on their time-sheets, dodged paying train or bus fares, avoided parking charges......and so it went on.

At the end he added all the numbers up and deducted them from the total population to reach the conclusion that there were only two honest people left in the country......The Grafter and you, the reader of the column!

Tongue in cheek? Of course. But there was one more honest man who, if The Grafter had known him, he would have unhesitatingly added to the two remaining to make three.

That man is Martin Golland.

For many years we stalked at Deanich and Alladale forests by Ardgay, Bonar Bridge Ross-shire (now Sutherland), Scotland. Our stalking there is well described in *One Man's Scotland.* Richard Munro was head stalker but when.

he died of a heart attack his son Marcus gave up his job as a keeper in the north of England and took over at Deanich and Alladale.

Marcus truly merits the description "remarkable" in the best sense of the word. His mother died when he was eight years old but he and his father enjoyed a remarkable *rapport* and could communicate without speaking. We had known him since he was born and had the great privilege of watching him grow up: A marvellous youngster who would join us on our fishing and stalking expeditions.

Marcus grew up, got married to the lovely Jennifer and they now have four beautiful children, all under eight: Cameron, Annie-Rose, and twins Hamish and Jessie. Hamish couldn't wait to get to hospital in Inverness and was born in the ambulance at the viewing spot overlooking the Kyle on Struie Hill.

Marcus is, as you would expect, a superlative rifle shot who shot his first hind at the age of seven. He has gone on to develop and even manufacture, with the assistance of an American gunsmith, space age rifles with a huge cartridge case necked down to .22. Flat trajectory from here to eternity! These rifles have stainless steel barrels and telescopic sights of anything from fifteen to twenty five power magnification.

Surprisingly, however, Marcus had never shot a deer with anything but a rifle fitted with a telescopic sight.

One Spring day, Marcus rang me and said that he would like to fulfil his ambition of shooting a stag with one of the old Black Powder Express rifles. Could I help? The answer was "Yes". The ideal rifle for him would be the .400 double Holland and Holland from my former collection. The rifle is in excellent condition with an aperture sight fitted from new....surely the next best thing to a telescopic sight.

So the search was on to find .400 Black Powder Express cartridges.

We think that all .400 Black Powder Express cartridges are the same but this is far from the case. There are different case lengths, even different case shapes. Probably up to half a dozen different cartridges all nominally .400 calibre.

So where do you find cartridges that were obsolete over a century ago? The name that immediately sprang to mind was Peter McGowan of Ruddington, Nottingham.

Peter is one of the remarkable characters I met in the antique gun world. A muzzle loader, of course, but also immensely knowledgeable on early breech loading guns and rifles, He has several John Manton breech loading shotguns and more Black Powder Express rifles than anyone else I know. He must have about a dozen from .360 upwards. Many of them with the desirable Farquharson and Alexander Henry falling block actions.

An authority on cartridges Peter once published a magazine on obsolete cartridges, so he was the man to ask, which brings me back to Martin Golland.

Peter had examples of all the cartridges though none surplus but he did know a man on Humberside who was an obsolete cartridge dealer who would be sure to help.

"Is his name Martin?" I asked " and does he have only one eye?" "Yes." answered Peter in some surprise.

"In that case he is the man to whom I lent a Purdey .450 Black Powder Express double rifle about thirty years ago. Has he still got it and, if so, would he let me have it back?" Peter said he would get in touch with Martin and let me know.

As explained earlier I bought my first Manton in 1954 from Michael Weaving of Ayot St. Peter, Welwyn, Herts. Michael bought and sold Mantons and modern Purdeys on a part time basis.

He was on very good terms with Purdeys and one day in the late nineteen fifties they hauled out of their cellar a long forgotten Purdey .450 Black Powder Express double rifle with fore-end missing that had been gathering rust for half a century or more.

When cordite rifles took over from black powder the old black powder rifles were as obsolete as yesterday's newspaper….and about as valuable! Strictly speaking, as a breech loading rifle, it should have been on a Firearm Certificate but as it was only considered to be an incomplete long forgotten curio Purdeys, knowing Michael's interest in antique guns, gave it to him.

Some time later Michael decided that it was not for him so he passed it on to me for £5. Should have bought a dozen! Once again the rifle was put on one side and I never did get a fore-end made.

About 1970 I met a farmer from Humberside at a Weller and Dufty firearms auction in Birmingham. He was a very keen early breech loading rifleman and he thought that he could get a new fore-end made for the Purdey so I lent it to him to see what he could manage.

Once again the rifle was forgotten as was the borrower's name and address! All I could remember was that his christian name was Martin and that he had lost one eye in an accident some time before.

So Peter got in touch with Martin Golland, the surname I had forgotten, and, as I said earlier, still had the rifle. He very kindly, let me have it back.

So The Grafter would have most certainly added Martin to the two honest men making it up to three!

Martin was sure that he could find some cartridges for the .400 and Peter McGowan very kindly offered to take me over to see him to collect the .450. The date was fixed, I picked up Peter from his home in Ruddington and off we went with the .400 Holland and Holland and two of Peter's .450 Black Powder Expresses with Farquharson actions.

It was a glorious Spring day and Martin and his wife made us most welcome. The cartridges required were .450/400 and Martin had in stock the correct paper patched bullets of 235 grain. Marcus Munro is a Registered Firearms Dealer so he was able to purchase them.

As previously explained, at one time all breech loading rifles had to be on a Firearm Certificate even if only required as collectors items; of recent years, however, rifles that were made for long obsolete ammunition are excluded from this requirement *provided* that they are not to be used and no ammunition is required.

If you wish to shoot them, however, and require ammunition for that purpose then they have to be on a Firearm Certificate.

Martin farms about 600 acres of good land on Humberside but, in addition, he is a cartridge dealer of note, travelling to the Continent and the United States to buy and sell obsolete cartridges.

So the three rifles were tried out to see how they would perform against a backstop of old railway sleepers. We fired two shots each with the Holland and Holland and found that it grouped very well at 50 yards. It was shooting about five inches higher than the point of aim so where would it be at 100 yards? My guess was that it was set for 125 yards but I knew that Marcus would find out and adjust the sights accordingly.

I was only wearing a shirt and light pullover but found the rifle a delight to shoot with no unpleasant recoil: Just the job for Marcus! Peter and Martin also fired the two .450s and very kindly gave me a shot, too.

A lovely lunch laid on by Martin's wife and an opportunity to briefly look over Martin's bewildering collection of rifles and cartridges.

On the drive to and from Humberside I had the chance for a long chat with Peter for the first time in years. Like so many people in the antique gun world I found him to be a most interesting companion, witty and knowledgeable on a vast range of subjects from cartridges to cars. He was, to my amazement, even knowledgeable about vintage Alfa Romeos so we had a marvellous and most enjoyable day.

The .400 would be perfectly legal to shoot deer in England as it exceeds the minimum striking energy requirement but, believe it or not, not in Scotland. In Scotland rifles for deer must not only have adequate striking energy but, in addition, must have a minimum velocity of, I understand, 2500 ft/sec.

You might have a breech loading black powder rifle perfectly capable of stopping a charging African buffalo but you cannot shoot a deer with it in Scotland.

So how would Marcus be able to use the .400 Holland and Holland to get his stag? Martin is an expert on Black Powder Expresses and their cartridges so he had the answer: He explained that the heavy barrels of the Black Powder Expresses are perfectly capable of coping with cartridges loaded with modern nitro-cellulose powder so the increased velocity can easily be achieved.

Marcus is a dedicated hand-loader, loading his modern rifle cartridges to precise measurements, so re-loading the .400 cartridges with nitro-cellulose powder would be no problem. He went on to shoot two stags with it and that's a story in itself !

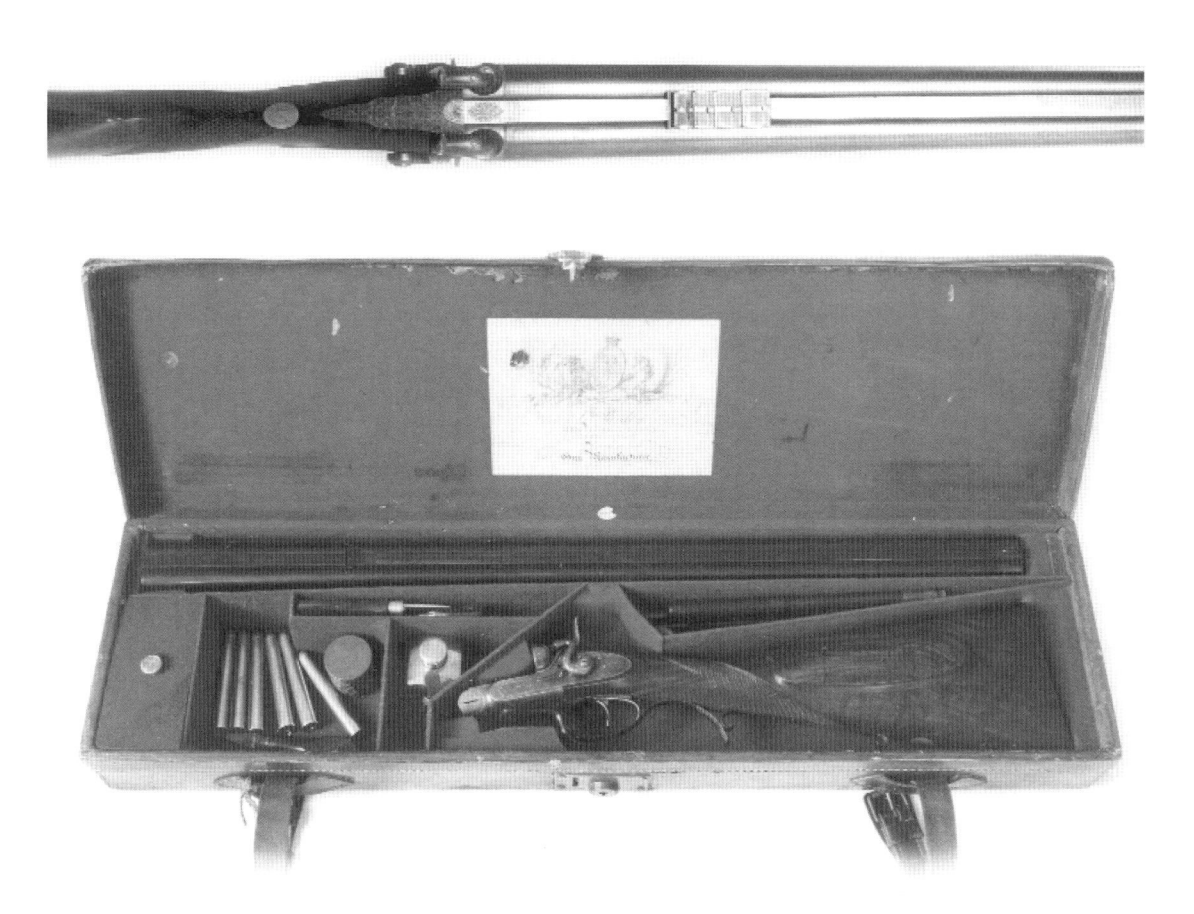

The first "Express Train" rifles were .500 muzzle loaders, but breech loading soon took over. This .500 muzzle loading Express is by Williams and Powell. The breech loader is the .450 Purdey.

The .450 Purdey Black Powder Express awake again after its hundred year sleep. Clive hands two cartridges to Marcus Munro at Deanich ready for him to fire it.

Chapter Forty
Derek Fearn And The Four Fifty Purdey

Having got the Purdey home from Martin Gollands, I checked the serial number in the Purdey book and saw that it was one of a pair of .400's sold new in May 1865 and the next day I took it in to Derek Fearn, master gunsmith.

He is a true enthusiast with an enormous knowledge of antique guns and has a collection of his own. Black Powder Expresses are a special interest of his and he has shot deer with his own .450.

He is, then, one of the most fortunate of men whose work is his hobby. The only problem is that he is so busy with work on modern guns that he has very little time to spend on antique work.

The day after I had taken the rifle in to "Sherlock" Fearn he rang me: He had seen instantly that the rifle had been originally made as a muzzle loader as it had a patch box in the butt……obsolete when breech loading came in. He had also looked at the Purdey book and confirmed that it had, indeed, been made as one of a pair of .400 calibre *muzzle* loaders, though it was now a .450 *breech loader*. Price for the pair £168.

The rifle has underlever action with non-rebounding locks so I had assumed that it had been converted to breech loading not long after it had been originally made but Sherlock Fearn did not instantly jump to this obvious conclusion. The whole thing was covered in rust so he rubbed off the rust covering the name and address on the barrel rib and found that it was South Audley Street. Purdeys did not move to that address until 1883 so the conversion to breech loading was done at that date or later.

Curiouser and curiouser! In the early days of brass rifle cartridge cases the technology had not been invented to make extruded brass cases so Colonel Boxer designed a case made out of a ribbon of brass i.e. the "ribbon cartridge". This was, of necessity, a parallel case and it was not until the extruded brass cartridges came in that it was possible to make tapered or bottleneck cases.

The new .450 barrels had been made long after the Boxer ribbon cartridge had become obsolete so surely they would have been bored to accept the current, tapered extruded brass cases? But, no! They were bored to take the obsolete ribbon cartridges. This really is a puzzle, but if you have any ideas, please let me know.

First problem, could Derek find a second hand fore-end that would fit? "Well," said Derek "I have a drawer full of fore-ends but they never fit anything else!" When the rifle was in Martin Golland's hands he once tried a fore-end from a Purdey rifle only four numbers away, but it was nothing like a fit! In those days they were hand made, not duplicated by machine. To make things even more difficult an Anson fore-end would be required i.e. with a spring loaded button at the tip to release it, not just a simple snap-on.

But, at the end of the day, Derek set to and made a fore-end including the tricky plunger mechanism at the tip. He found a piece of walnut to match the stock, cut it all to shape and now the rifle has a fore-end beautifully chequered and completely in keeping with the original workmanship. He even made a new horn fore-end tip.

He went on to restore the rest of the rifle and has made a superlative job. Part of the butt plate had completely rusted away but Derek welded in the missing piece and filed in the missing cross hatching *by hand*. I had volunteered to file up and polish the barrels ready for blacking, but what a task! When originally put in Purdey's cellar the bores had been greased so they had been preserved but the outsides were rusty and pitted. Whenever I had an hour to spare through the summer I would file away at these hard steel barrels but the undersides, in particular, were a very difficult task.

So the rifle is now completely restored and shooting again after its sleep of a century or more.

All that remained was to put the rifle into a correct gun case. I had in my possession a leather Purdey guncase with trade label, of the correct period, that had been made for a breech loading gun or rifle with underlever action. The Purdey fitted in it loosely so the gun and case were taken to Robert Hayden, guncase maker of Price Street, Birmingham. Yes, incredibly enough, there is still a professional guncase maker in Birmingham. Robert fitted the rifle correctly into the case, making an excellent job at a surprisingly modest price.

I wonder if its sister, no. 6933 survived? As no. 6934 languished for half a century or more in Purdey's cellar, this seems highly unlikely unless, of course, you know different!

Stalker Marcus Munro, shoots the .450 Purdey. Note how a Highland stalker keeps his head well down to present a minimum view to the deer.

Looking down on Deanich Lodge from the "South Side." Son Ross in the foreground.

Chapter Forty One
Deanich Lodge 2003

In August 2003 we took Deanich Lodge, by Ardgay, Bonar Bridge again where we had spent so many happy days stalking and fishing in earlier years. Read all about it in *One Man's Scotland*.

During the time we were there the Deanich and Alladale Estates were sold to a Lister family trust for a reputed £3.25 million. David Lister was the young family member chosen to run the estate. He was in his mid thirties with a wife and two small children and we were fortunate enough to meet them.

Clive, Iain, Adam, Marcus and Peter with the .450 Purdey Black Powder Express, the .400 Holland and Holland Black Powder Express, .22 rimfire Brno and Marcus' state-of the-art centrefire .22 Max with powerful telescopic sight and silencer.

David is an enthusiastic businessman and ocean yachtsman. The family bought a failing marina on the Isle of Wight and turned it round into a profitable business. He intended to use the same skills at Deanich and Alladale.

David's uncle successfully ran the huge conglomerate, M.F.I and David was tackling this estate with boundless enthusiasm.

The key solution was government grants. The marina changed direction to concentrate on giving sailing experience to the disabled for which government grants were available. While we were at Deanich David Lister had brought in experts on forestry and environmental grants and I understand that other grant possibilities were being explored.

It appeared that the ultimate aim was to largely replace the deer by forestry planting. Alladale Lodge was to be thoroughly updated with en-suite bedrooms to cater for the very top end of the market. A full time chef was to be employed and the kind of clientele expected were those looking for executive holidays and corporate entertainment. The lodge, as far as possible, was to be kept busy all year round.

Huge changes, then, in prospect for Marcus Munro, the Head Keeper there, but he was looking forward to the challenge and happy to go along any route that was proposed.

Historically, Highland estates lose money…..Lots of it! Undaunted by historical precedents, David's objective was to make the place pay and we wished him well. No lack of enterprise and new ideas, he was starting with a blank sheet. The stalkers were to become "Rangers", far more politically correct! Marcus was to be promoted to "Manager", his colleague Innes to "Head Ranger".

Since then, however, I understand that David has been replaced by his cousin Paul, son of Mr and Mrs Noel Lister.

The previous owners, the Macaires, had previously raised the price of a day's stalking to what we considered to be an incredible £500 and this, of course, did not include the rental of the lodge which was not cheap! But this figure is bound to rocket when all the new work has to be paid for. Yes, I agree, *One Man's Scotland* is already history!

Taking Deanich Lodge was an opportunity to show my grandsons, Adam, then almost twelve and Clive aged nine what it was like to stay in the remote Highland Lodge that we know so well.

Daughter, Caroline with son-in-law Iain were with us, of course, and Iain's mother made up the party.

My son, Ross, was only able to stay for a few days and on the first morning Clive woke him up at 6.15 am to go fishing in the River Carron.

To catch trout is not so bad as they eat when they are hungry but salmon are an entirely different proposition. For a start they do not eat in fresh water, so why do they tackle a fly or lure? Don't know, but they will only do so when conditions are exactly right, when the river is rising or falling and the water temperature is favourable. It also helps if Saturn is in conjunction with Uranus, the weather is not too bright, there is not a cold wind on the water, you have your lucky rabbit's foot in your pocket and, of course, you are holding your feet right!

But that morning conditions were absolutely wrong: The river was dreadfully low and no salmon had been caught by any estate on the entire length of the River Carron for weeks.

In no time at all Ross hooked a good trout and gave the rod to Clive to land it: A good start. Shortly after, Clive shouted "I think I've got something, Uncle Ross". "Then reel it in", Ross replied.

Under Ross' instructions Clive successfully reeled it in and it was safely landed: A seven pound salmon!

Clive was, understandably over the moon! Not only his first salmon but the first fish he had ever caught. The fishing gods were smiling on him that morning and for the rest of the stay you had to drag him from the river. No, he never managed to catch another salmon, in fact only two were caught in the Deanich water all season, but he caught his fair share of trout.

His father, too, thoroughly enjoyed re-discovering the fly fishing skills he had learned as a youngster and he successfully caught a fair number of trout.

We had taken with us the Brno .22 rifle and the .450 Purdey Black Powder Express rifle restored by Derek Fearn. The boys had great fun shooting the .22 under our supervision in that vast landscape but the highlight was when Marcus Munro of Alladale and Ronnie Ross of Braelangwell spent a day with us.

Marcus brought the .400 Holland and Holland Black Powder Express he has on loan together with his space-age high velocity .22 rifles with huge telescopic sights and silencers. He instructed the boys on how to handle rifles safely and correctly and it was an object lesson to us, too.

Marcus had infinite patience and never said to the boys "Do you understand?" Having explained a point he would say: "Does this sound right?" I am sure that they will never forget being instructed by Marcus Munro.

We shot the Expresses at the target, about seventy yards out, which was great fun with their huge cloud of black powder smoke. The recoil of a black powder rifle is more of a push than a jolt so Adam managed very well. Poor Clive was miffed at being left out but we felt that at only nine years old the recoil could have put him off. Next year, perhaps! Sir Charles Ross would have tried his Black Powder Expresses at the same spot well over a century before.

More luck for Clive, however, with Marcus' high powered .22 Max. Clive hit the bull at 114 yards and was absolutely delighted!

So a memorable day in glorious weather.

Marcus instructs Adam on the .400 Holland and Holland, then Adam fires it.

Marcus instructs Clive on the .22 Max.
Marcus congratulates Clive on hitting the bull at 114 yards with the .22 Max.

The actual stag killed by Louie Bierman's ramrod.

Chapter Forty Two
Louie Bierman's Remarkable MacNab

Rogart is a close-knit crofting community near Golspie, Sutherland and has produced many "remarkable" characters. None more so than Louie Bierman.

Louie was of German extraction who worked at a number of jobs, including shepherd and groom. During the Second World War Louie would gloomily predict: "The Germans will be here any day now!" Private Fraser of Dad's Army would have nodded in lugubrious agreement!

He thoroughly enjoyed a dish of brose, oatmeal with water or milk and kept three bags of meal in the kitchen near the door.

The top bag was Louie's, the next for the dog and the far from fresh bag at the bottom was for the hens. The postie would always look in on Louie and if a fresh bag of meal had arrived he would always give the postie a pinch. "What do you think of that, mate? Bloody good!" Louie would always say.

Those bags of meal, however, were a great attraction for rats and mice, despite Louie's cats. One day, however, when the postie called Louie was enjoying his meal, as usual, at the always overcrowded table, In the middle of the table was a huge rat, dead in a trap. "Ho, ho, mate. Got the bugger!" was Louie's triumphant greeting.

Every sportsman would love to achieve a "MacNab", a stag, grouse and salmon in one day. This from John Buchan's novel *John MacNab* in which three bored but wealthy young men wrote to estate owners under the nom-de-plume of John MacNab stating that they would poach a stag and salmon on a given day. Great fun! Nowadays a grouse is included to complete a MacNab.

Louie loved to tell all sorts of tall tales and one of his favourites was this: One day he saw a stag on the far side of the river Leadach. He raced home, loaded his old muzzle loader, but in his haste forgot to extract the ramrod. He fired at the stag but at that moment a salmon jumped in the river. The ramrod went through the salmon then continued on to fatally wound the stag.

The stag fell onto a covey of grouse, killing one of them and when Louie got up to the stag and grabbed its horns prior to bleeding it, the stag in its final death throes hurled Louis down the hill onto a covey of partridges, killing one. So Louie not only achieved a "MacNab", a stag, a grouse and a salmon in one day but with the additional bonus of a partridge, and all with one shot!

But was it true? Well, use your imagination. After all, Louie did!

Private Fraser of Dad's Army who would gloomily have agreed with Louie's pessimistic predictions.

Clive and Peter try Marcus Munro's space-age rifles for size.

Post Script

Half a century of gun collecting has added an important dimension to my life and opened up a huge range of fascinating vistas:

The thrill of the chase, appreciation of the skill, artistry and craftsmanship in the world of guns. Researching the development of the guns and the craftsmen who made them. Looking into their life and times and wondering at the huge changes in the nineteenth century.

Finding, rescuing, restoring and preserving fine guns and rifles to the benefit of future generations. Shooting the muzzle loading guns and rifles and, of course, the Black Powder Expresses.

Many memorable moments: First air rifle, first muzzle loader, first twelve bore, first .22, first stalking rifle.

Wonderful Scottish Highland days in the kingdom of the deer. Those marvellous un-modernised Highland lodges where the autumn gales struck like thunderclaps.

Most important of all the enormous pleasure of meeting so many "remarkable" people in the very best sense of the word. Collectors, restorers, gunsmiths, dealers all with so much knowledge that they were delighted to share with a fellow enthusiast.

"Every man I meet is in some way my master." So said Doctor Johnson and how true this is. No matter how talented you may be, there are so many people with skills, abilities and knowledge that you cannot match. Never more so than in the world of guns and rifles.

Although none of the guns and rifles are in my ownership now they have provided a kaleidoscope of memories and I have enjoyed every minute of it.

So my thanks to everyone I met during my gun quest.

Sources

The National Rifle Association. **Bisley**. A focus on the rifleman's Mecca.

AKEHURST, Richard. **Game, guns and rifles**. (Bell 1869.) A short history. Well worth reading.

BLACKMORE, Howard.L. **British Military Firearms 1560-1850**. (Herbert Jenkins, 1961.) Scholarly work on this specialised subject.

BOOTHROYD, Geoffrey. **Boothroyd's Revised Directory of British Gunmakers**. (The Sportsman's Press, London 1997.) Superlative A to Z look at the gun trade with many descriptions of the gunmakers.

BUCHAN, John. **John MacNab**. (Hodder and Stoughton. 1925.) Stalking adventure in the Highlands. A story that never fades.

DALTON, Lawrence. **Those Elegant Rolls-Royce**. (Dalton Watson Ltd 1967.) A galaxy of automobile excellence.

DE WITT BAILEY and NIE, Douglas A. **English Gunmakers**. (Arms and Armour Press 1978.) In depth list of the Birmingham and Provincial gunmakers of the 18th and 19th century.

DURDIK, MUDRA and SADA. **Firearms a Collector's Guide: 1326 – 1900**. A comprehensive survey of guns from the earliest days.

GARNIER RUFFER, Jonathon. **The Big Shots**. (Debretts Peerage, 1977.) Light-hearted look at the big shoots and the big shots in the hey-day of game shooting.

GREENER, W.W. **The Gun**. (Cassal 1881.) Massive tome, comprehensively covering the history and development of the gun.

HORN, Pamela. **Pleasures and Pastimes in Victorian Britain**. (Sutton Publishing, 1999.) Extremely informative and readable account of the development of leisure in Victorian times.

McMANUS, Peter. **One Man's Motorcycles 1939-1949** and **One Man's Scotland**. (M.E.P. Publishing 2000 and 2002.) Both provided the inspiration for this book and **One Man's Scotland** is very much a companion volume.

NEAL, W. KEITH and BACK, D. H. L. **The Mantons**. (Herbert Jenkins, 1966) and **The Manton Supplement**. (The Compton Press, 1978.) These books cover the work of Joseph and John Manton in great depth. Also by the same authors, **Forsyth and Co., Patent Gunmakers**. (G. Bell and Sons, 1969.) The definitive work on Forsyth.

PILKINGTON, Stephen. **With a Gun to the Hill**. (Herbet Jenkins 1948.) This is the book that decided me to start deer stalking.

POPE, Dudley. **Guns**. (Weidenfeld and Nicholson 1965.) This really is a "massive tome" covering the history of guns from the discovery of gunpowder to the Second World War. Featured are some superlative cut-away drawings by the incomparable Max Millar. Get hold of a copy if you can!

PRIESTLEY.J.B. **Victoria's Heyday**. (Heinman 1972.) A spotlight on one of the most momentous decades of the Victorian era, the 1850's. One of my favourite books. Amusing, informative, superbly written.

STONEHENGE. **The Shot-gun and Sporting Rifle**. (Routledge, Warne and Routledge 1859.) A comprehensive work covering all aspects of guns, rifles, keepering, dogs, game etc..

WILSON, A N. **The Victorians**. (Hutchinson 2002.) Wonderful stuff. An amazing survey of the Victorian era. Essential reading for anyone interested in the 19th Century.

WINANS, Walter. **The Sporting Rifle**. (Putnam 1908.) Memoirs by the American millionaire who stalked on the grand scale and was a brilliant shot at running deer.

WINANT, Lewis. **Early Percussion Firearms**. (William Morrow and Company 1959.) One of the most comprehensive books on early percussion systems.

Other books by the author.

Yes, a motorcycle theme but there is much more than that:

Starting in the motorcycle business after the War, buying, selling, restoring and racing motorcycles of the 1920's, 30's and 40's.

This book tells the story of the motorcycles and the characters who rode them against the backdrop of those times.

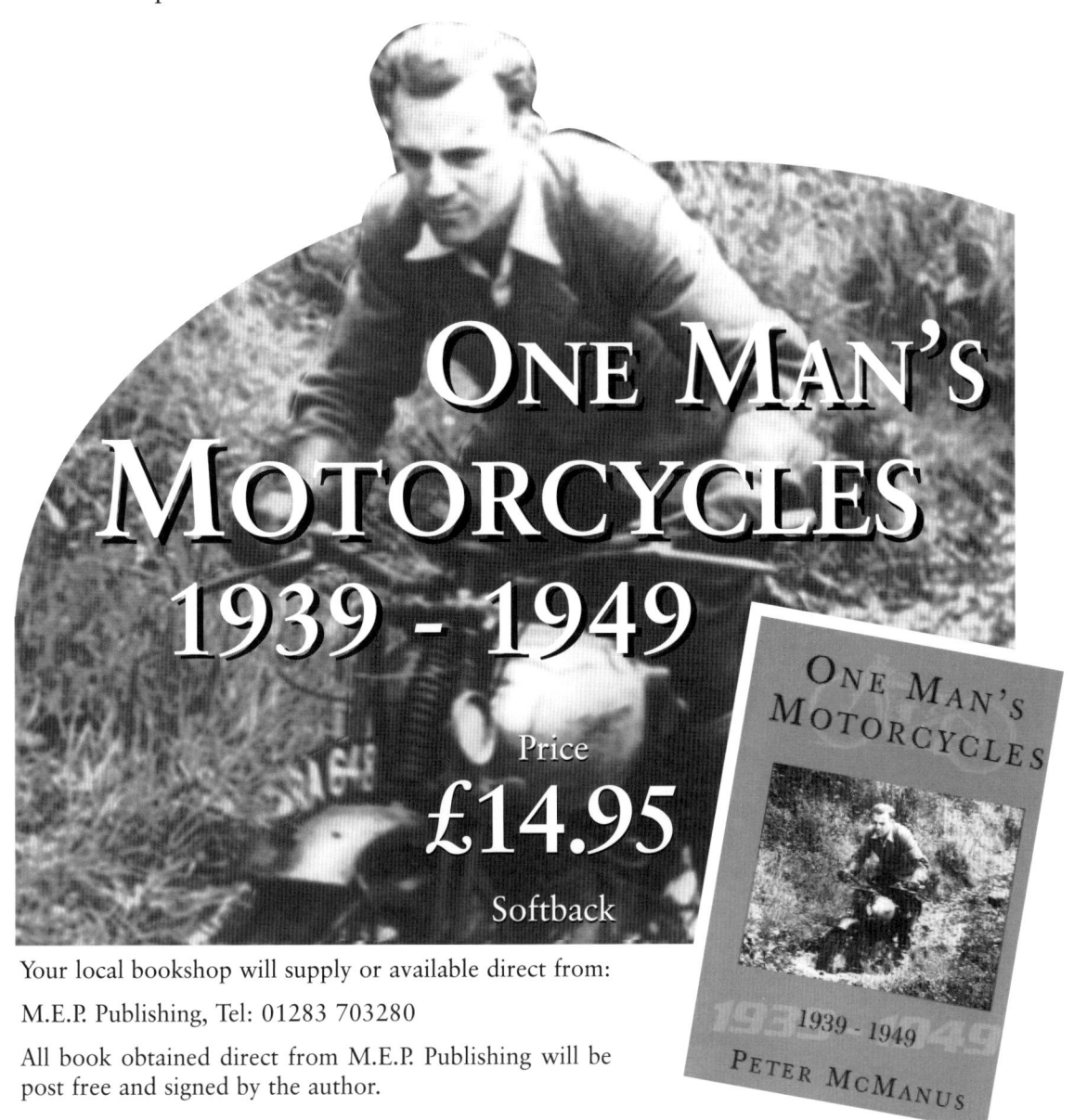

One Man's Motorcycles 1939 - 1949

Price **£14.95** Softback

Your local bookshop will supply or available direct from:

M.E.P. Publishing, Tel: 01283 703280

All book obtained direct from M.E.P. Publishing will be post free and signed by the author.

PETER McMANUS

Peter McManus' fascination with the Highlands started on his first visit in 1954 and has never waned. Since then he has stalked from Perthshire in the south to Caithness in the north. Along the way he has met many remarkable characters and enjoyed many memorable moments.

Scotland is steeped in history and this book is a mixture of personal experiences and the historical; particularly of the deerstalking era from its start in the early 19th Century to the present day.

ONE MAN'S SCOTLAND

Price
£16.95
Softback

Your local bookshop will supply or available direct from:

M.E.P. Publishing, Tel: 01283 703280

All book obtained direct from M.E.P. Publishing will be post free and signed by the author.

August 2003, Deanich Lodge by Ardgay, Sutherland. Grandson Clive, then aged 9, proudly displays his salmon and trout. It was not only his first salmon but the first fish he had ever caught. L to R: Grandson Adam, almost 12, Edna, daughter Caroline, her husband Iain, son Ross, Iain's mother Vera, Clive in front.

All the world's a stage.
And all the men and women merely players:
They have their exits and their entrances
And one man in his time plays many parts.

William Shakespeare